CHOOSING DEATH

The Improbable History of Death Metal & Grindcore

By Albert Mudrian

FERAL HOUSE

Choosing Death:
The Improbable History of Death Metal & Grindcore ©2004 by Albert Mudrian & Feral House

ISBN: 1-932595-04-X

Feral House
PO Box 39910
Los Angeles, CA 90039

www.feralhouse.com

info@feralhouse.com

10 9 8 7 6 5 4 3

Edited by Eóin Ennis

Copy Editing by Amy Gallick and Patty Moran

Book Design by Rick Mariani

Front and Back Cover Design and Concept by
Orion Landau and Jonathan Canady

Front Cover Photo Credits:
Obituary photo: Tim Hubbard
Carcass photo: Ingrid Martin
Napalm Death author unknown
Morbid Angel photo: Frank White

Back Cover Photo Credits:
Nile photo: Scott Kinkade
Repulsion author unknown
Cannibal Corpse photo: Frank White
Napalm Death photo: Nick Royles
Nihilist author unknown
Death photo: Alex McKnight

www.feralhouse.com
www.choosingdeath.com

Contents

Thanks a Lot:

Mikael Åkerfeldt, Simon Alper, Mike Amott, Matt Anker, Ann at Moonfog Productions, Irving Azoff, Trey Azagthoth, Chris Barnes, Jeff Becerra, Jo Bench, Jonas Bjorler, Justin Broadrick, Mike Browning, Richard Brunelle, Nick Bullen, Terry Butler, Scott Carlson, Mitch Carpenter, Paul Carty, Max Cavalera, Uffe Cerderlund, Steve Charlesworth, Monte Conner, Daniel Coston, Steve Disrupter, Ross Dolan, Lee Dorrian, Kristen Driscoll, Johan Edlund, Mike Faley, Benjamin Falgoust, Jill Farthing, Andy Farrow, Fenriz, Maria Ferrero, King Fowley, Tim Fraser, Anders Fridén, Oscar Garcia, Joaquim Ghirotti, Lou Giordano, Ian Glasper, Angela Gossow, David Gray, Nick Green, Barney Greenway, Matt Harvey, Johnny Hedlund, Scott Helland, Dave Hewson, Rich Hoak, Paula Hogan, Sean Hogan, Nick Holmes, Scott Hull, Tim Hubbard, Pete Hurley, Anders Jakobson, Andy Johnson, Joey Jordison, David Kahne, Robert Kampf, Matti Kärki, Erich Keller, Scott Kinkade, Patrick Klopf, Christopher Krabathor, Borivoj Krgin, Vicky Langham, Kam Lee, Danny Lilker, Tomas Lindberg, Lisa the Wolf, Patrick Lowe, Gregor Mackintosh, Mad Mex of Philadelphia, Kelli Malella, J Mascis, John McEntee, Jason Mendonca, Flo Mounier, James Murphy, Jennifer Murray, Naki, Alex Newport, Eva Nue, Hilary Okun, Matt Olivo, Ken Owen, Aaron Pepelis, Trevor Peres, Jesse Pintado, Riki Rachtman, Jack Rabid, Chris Radok, Will Rahmer, Chris Reifert, Curran Reynolds, Colin Richarson, Lora Richarson, Tony "Bones" Roberts, Calvin Robertshaw, Julia Robinson, Michelle Roche, the inspiration of Henry Rollins, Nick Royles, Daz Russell, Erik Rutan, Samoth, Karl Sanders, Jörgen Sandström, Richard Santos, Josh Sarubin, Jane Schuldiner, Dan Seagrave, Kevin Sharp, Tomas Skogsberg, Brian Slagel, Mike Smith, Paul Speckmann, Markus Staiger, Bill Steer, Peter Tägtgren, John Tardy, Steve Tucker, Alex Wank, Alex Webster, Heather West, Frank White, Jim Whiteley, Robert Williams, Peter Wiwczarek, Brian Woody, Doug Wright, Loana dP Valencia, George Vallee, David Vincent

Very Special Thanks:

Mom, Dad, James Zack Wesser, Adam Parfrey and Feral House, John Peel, Sheila Ravenscroft, Steven Blush, Jarrod Tranguch, Günter Ford, Nicke Andersson, Mitch Dickinson, Mr. Pants, Martin Nesbitt, Ben Morgan, Maria Gonzales, Brian Baker, Hammy, Mark Adams, Jamie Leary, Scott Hungarter, Robert Roberts-Jolly, and all at Red Flag Media, Scott Burns, Greg Wineman, Chris Sleboda, Brian Stillman, Jonathan Selzer, Philip Anselmo, Dieter Szczypiniski, Dan Tobin, Michael Mazur, Debbie Sellnow, and all at Mazur PR, Orion Landau, Jon Canady, Carl Schultz, Natalie Rauch, Matt Jacobson and all at Relapse Records

Couldn't-Have-Done-It-Without-You Thanks (those who suffered the most):

Alex Mulcahy, Eóin Ennis, Patty Moran, Scott Koerber, Brent DeFranco, Rick Mariani, Gordon Conrad, Jeff Walker, Shane Embury, Mick Harris, Jim Welch, Digby Pearson, Nick Terry

A Very Extra Special Thank You:

To my extraordinarily patient and encouraging girl Amy Gallick

This book is dedicated to the lasting memory of Richard Mudrian (1949—2003).

Cast of Characters

Mikael Åkerfeldt: Opeth bassist 1990—1992, Opeth guitarist/vocalist 1992 to present

Mike Amott: Carnage guitarist 1988—1990, Carcass guitarist 1990—1994, Arch Enemy guitarist 1996 to present

Nicke Andersson: Nihilist drummer 1987—1989, Entombed drummer 1989—1997

Irving Azoff: Giant Records founder; CEO 1989—1999

Trey Azagthoth: Morbid Angel guitarist 1983 to present

Chris Barnes: Cannibal Corpse vocalist 1988—1996, Six Feet Under vocalist 1994 to present

Jeff Becerra: Possessed guitarist/vocalist 1983—1987

Jo Bench: Bolt Thrower bassist 1987 to present

Glen Benton: Amon bassist/vocalist 1987—1990, Deicide bassist/vocalist 1990 to present

Justin Broadrick: Napalm Death guitarist 1985—1986, Head of David drummer 1986—1988, Godflesh guitarist/vocalist 1988—2002

Mike Browning: Morbid Angel drummer 1983—1986 drummer/vocalist 1985—1986, Nocturnus drummer/vocalist 1987—1991, drummer 1992

Richard Brunelle: Morbid Angel guitarist 1985—1992

Karl Buechner: Earth Crisis vocalist 1991—2001

Nick Bullen: Napalm Death frontman 1981—1986

Scott Burns: American death metal producer

Terry Butler: Massacre bassist 1986—1987, 1990—1992, Death bassist 1987—1990, Six Feet Under bassist 1994 to present

Scott Carlson: Tempter bassist/vocalist 1983—1984, Ultraviolence bassist/vocalist 1984, Genocide bassist/vocalist 1984—1986, Repulsion bassist/vocalist 1986—1989, 1990, 1991

Max Cavalera: Sepultura guitarist/vocalist 1984—1996

Steve Charlesworth: Heresy drummer 1985—1988

Monte Conner: Roadrunner Records A&R

Mitch Dickinson: Unseen Terror guitarist 1985—1987, Heresy guitarist 1986—1988

Ross Dolan: Immolation bassist/vocalist 1988 to present

Lee Dorrian: Napalm Death vocalist 1987—1989, Cathedral vocalist 1989 to present

Shane Embury: Napalm Death bassist 1987 to present

Mike Faley: Metal Blade President

Fenriz: Darkthrone drummer 1987 to present

Johan Edlund: Tiamat guitarist/vocalist 1988 to present

Ben Falgoust: Soilent Green vocalist 1993 to present

Günter Ford: World Management

King Fowley: Deceased drummer/vocalist 1985—2002, Deceased vocalist 2002 to present

Anders Fridén: Dark Tranquillity vocalist 1989—1994, In Flames vocalist 1994 to present

Oscar Garcia: Terrorizer guitarist/vocalist 1986—1988, 1989

Lou Giordano: American hardcore producer

Angela Gossow: Arch Enemy vocalist 2001 to present

David Gray: Akercocke drummer 1996 to present

Barney Greenway: Benediction vocalist 1988—1989, Napalm Death vocalist 1989 to present

Hammy: Peaceville Records founder

Mick Harris: Napalm Death drummer 1986—1991, Extreme Noise Terror drummer 1987—1988

Johnny Hedlund: Nihilist bassist 1988—1989, Unleashed frontman 1989 to present

Dave Hewson: Slaughter (Canada) guitarist 1984—1990

Terrance Hobbs: Suffocation guitarist 1989—1998, 2002 to present

Nick Holmes: Paradise Lost vocalist 1988 to present

Scott Hull: Agoraphobic Nosebleed guitarist 1994 to present, Pig Destroyer guitarist 1997 to present

Pete Hurley: Extreme Noise Terror guitarist 1985—1995

Matt Jacobson: Relapse Records founder

Anders Jakobson: Nasum drummer 1994 to present

Joey Jordison: Slipknot drummer 1995 to present

David Kahne: Head of Columbia A&R 1991—1995

Robert Kampf: Century Media Records founder

Matti Kärki: Carnage vocalist 1990, Dismember vocalist 1990 to present

Erich Keller: Fear of God vocalist 1987—1988

Patrick Klopf: Disharmonic Orchestra guitarist/vocalist 1987 to present

Christopher Krabathor: Krabathor guitarist/vocalist 1984 to present

Borivoj Krgin: Extreme music journalist, Godly Records co-founder

Kam Lee: Mantas drummer/vocalist 1983—1984, Death drummer/vocalist, 1984—1985, Massacre vocalist 1985—1994

Danny Lilker: Brutal Truth bassist 1990—1998

Tomas Lindberg: Grotesque vocalist 1987—1990, At the Gates vocalist 1990—1996

Gregor Mackintosh: Paradise Lost guitarist 1988 to present

J Mascis: Deep Wound drummer 1981—1984

John McEntee: Incantation guitarist 1989—2003, guitarist/vocalist 2003 to present

Flo Mounier: Cryptopsy drummer 1992 to present

James Murphy: Death guitarist 1989—1990, Obituary guitarist 1990—1991, Disincarnate guitarist 1991—1994

Martin Nesbitt: Earache Records 1988—1991, Carcass Manager 1991—1996

Eva Nue: US *Headbanger's Ball* associate producer 1989—1994

Matt Olivo: Tempter guitarist 1983—1984, Ultraviolence guitarist 1984, Genocide guitarist 1984—1986, Repulsion guitarist 1986—1989, 1990, 1991

Ken Owen: Carcass drummer 1985—1996

Digby Pearson: Earache Records founder

Justin Pearson: The Locust bassist/vocalist 1995 to present

John Peel: BBC Radio 1 DJ

Trevor Peres: Xecutioner guitarist 1984—1989, Obituary guitarist 1989—1998

Jesse Pintado: Terrorizer guitarist 1986—1988, 1989, Napalm Death guitarist 1989 to present

Riki Rachtman: *Headbanger's Ball* host 1990—1994

Will Rahmer: Mortician bassist/vocalist 1989 to present

Chris Reifert: Death drummer 1986—1987, Autopsy drummer/vocalist 1987—1995, Abscess drummer/vocalist 1994 to present

Tony "Bones" Roberts: Discharge guitarist 1977—1982

Calvin Robertshaw: My Dying Bride guitarist 1990—1999

Colin Richardson: English death metal and grindcore producer

Daz Russell: English hardcore promoter

Erik Rutan: Morbid Angel guitarist 1993—1997, 1999—2003, Hate Eternal guitarist/ vocalist 1997 to present

Samoth: Emperor guitarist 1991—2001, Zyklon guitarist 1998 to present

Karl Sanders: Nile guitarist 1993 to present

Jörgen Sandström: Corpse guitarist/vocalist 1986, Grave guitarist/vocalist 1987—1995, Entombed bassist 1996 to present

Josh Sarubin: Columbia Records A&R 1992—1999

Chuck Schuldiner: Mantas guitarist/vocalist 1983—1984, Death guitarist/vocalist, 1984—2001

Jane Schuldiner: Mother of Chuck Schuldiner

Dan Seagrave: Album cover artist

Kevin Sharp: Extreme music journalist, Brutal Truth vocalist 1990—1998

Tomas Skogsberg: Swedish death metal producer

Brian Slagel: Metal Blade CEO

Paul Speckmann: Master guitarist/vocalist 1983 to present, Deathstrike guitarist/vocalist in early 1980s.

Markus Staiger: Nuclear Blast Records founder

Bill Steer: Napalm Death guitarist 1987—1989, Carcass guitarist/vocalist 1985—1996

John Tardy: Xecutioner vocalist 1984—1989, Obituary vocalist 1989—1998

Nick Terry: *Terrorizer* Magazine editor 1996—2000

Dan Tobin: Earache Records A&R

Steve Tucker: Morbid Angel bassist/vocalist 1997—2002, 2003 to present

Jeff Walker: Carcass bassist/vocalist 1987—1996

Alex Wank: Pungent Stench drummer 1988 to present

Alex Webster: Cannibal Corpse bassist 1988 to present

Jim Welch: Relativity 1989—1991, Earache US 1991—1993, Columbia Records A&R 1993—1996.

Jim Whiteley: Napalm Death bassist 1987

Robert Williams: Siege drummer 1983—1986, 1990

Peter Wiwczarek: Vader guitarist/vocalist 1983 to present

David Vincent: Morbid Angel bassist/vocalist 1986—1996

Introduction by John Peel

ON AIR

The sun shines. Trees bud. If I opened the window, I'm sure I would hear birds singing. And this morning, when I took the dogs for a walk, I found a fully-grown deer dead in the stream that gurgles past our house, half its head blown away by a hunter. This, I thought, as I watched the dogs evacuating their bowels at the roadside, is an omen from God—or if not from God, from Vashti, Handmaiden of Baal or someone like her—to warn me that I'd better sit down and get that book introduction written.

But where to start?

Well, I could whirl you back in time to the mid-'50s and try to explain yet again the impact that hearing Elvis for the first time had on my young and bourgeois life, or I could tell you about the gig I did at Southampton University with Hendrix, but it might make more sense to return to a riverside pub in Putney, London, at the end of 1986.

I don't recall whose idea it was, but I'd trekked to Putney to see the Stupids. Punk, let me remind you, had happened nine years earlier and had evolved into art rock subgenres every bit as beastly as the muck that it had, in theory, swept aside. What was needed, my BBC Radio 1 producer, John Walters, and I felt, was a return to rousing vulgarity. What we were looking for was a band that, metaphorically at least, lit their farts on stage. The Stupids, bless them, were that band. Was that band? Who cares?

The Stupids were funny, fast, loud, clever/stupid and they took the piss out of Walters and myself. They also came from East Anglia, the part of the country in which I still live and in which the deer discussed above died. They were shit hot and local. How could you not love them? They also told me—warned might be a better word—of another local phenomenon, Extreme Noise Terror. ENT, with Mick Harris on drums and with charismatic, blue-haired Dean Jones on vocals, played from time to time at the Caribbean Centre in nearby Ipswich, so I took Sheila, my wife, and our son, William, to see them play. That's the way to bring up your kids. Trust me, I know. ENT were amazing. So were their fans. Any track more than 20 seconds long was greeted with derisive cries of "too long, too slow" or "fucking prog-rockers" from the Caribbean Centre faithful, most of whom looked as though they had but recently risen from shallow graves alongside the A12, the arterial road that runs from London to Ipswich. The only disappointment for Sheila, William and me was that the band, constrained, no doubt, by economic factors, wasn't loud enough. We wanted to leave the Centre with blood trickling from our ears.

Well, one thing led to another. At one of those Ipswich gigs, ENT were joined by the even faster Napalm Death, at another by the short-lived but murderous Intense Degree. All three bands recorded sessions for my radio programmes and most of the tracks they recorded ended up on the *Hardcore Holocaust* compilations. Almost everyone I knew who heard these compilations, or tracks from them, thought they were all crap. A result, I thought. Then along came Carcass. Who could have failed to be appalled by titles such as "Exhume to Consume" or even the essentially meaningless "Empathological Necroticism," both recorded and broadcast repeatedly by the BBC?

Then, early in the 1990s, something went wrong, for me at least. The willfulness, the wild-eyed exuberance went out of the music, to be replaced with… with what? Well, I suppose it was, to a degree, heavy metal. I'd really had enough of that in the '70s to last me several lifetimes, so Slayer, Metallica, those bands never meant a thing to me, I'm afraid. There was also the breaking down of the music into subgenre after subgenre, to the point at which it became somehow incomprehensible. The same thing happens, to be honest, in dance music. Take happy hardcore, for example. Ludicrously fast, basic to a fault, oafish and wonderful, dance purists hated it. Now it is called hard trance—or was last week anyway—and they still hate it. They're missing the point.

So it's 2004, and I'm still wandering the record shops, still standing amongst the boys searching the racks marked "metal," boys who probably assume that this old feller is there to touch their pert, young bottoms, and I'm still hoping to hear something that will thrill me and make me laugh out loud as Carcass, Napalm Death and Extreme Noise Terror did. Current favourites include several of the Relapse bands and Teen Cthulu—great name, great band—and only last night, in a programme I was recording for Radio Eins in Potsdam, Germany, I played a couple of raging tracks from the cover-mounted CD with issue 108 of *Terrorizer* magazine.

I don't know why *Terrorizer* is called *Terrorizer* rather than, in the British spelling, *Terroriser*, but it is right that it is. That Z just looks better than a mere S. The tracks I played were "Clotted Cryptic Writings" (what can that possibly mean?) lifted from the LP *Three on a Meathook* by the Ravenous and "Flesh for the Twelfth Omnipotent" (who's He? Or She?) by Japan's Intestinal Baalism. I mean, how could you not play them? Of course, people will warn me, as they have warned me about so many other things, from Little Richard to Run-DMC ("You shouldn't play that. That's the music of black criminals," a colleague told me), stuff like that can be damaging to impressionable young minds. What, more damaging than the diet of war, rape, pestilence and unearned celebrity they're fed daily by the media? I don't think so.

"Swarming Vulgar Mass of Infected Virulency" anyone? Come on in. The blood's fine…

Foreword by Nick Terry

EXHUMED / AUTOPSY / TERRORIZER / SUICIDE / DEICIDE / NAPALM DEATH / NAPALM DEATH / ENTOMBED

I could emulate Peelie's reminiscences and tell you a few stories by way of a foreword. Sure I have some fond memories of death metal and grind-core. Who wouldn't? Things like watching Carcass supporting Death at the London Astoria in '91, entranced by Mike Amott and Bill Steer hair-twirling in time to "Pedigree Butchery." Or picking up the latest issue of the *New Musical Express* in November '88 and wondering just who the hell these guys Napalm Death were, what this thing called "Britcore" was and whether I'd like it. Or, years later, meeting Glen Benton from Deicide in a basement in his record company offices that looked exactly like the legendary cellar in *Evil Dead II*...

But the reminiscences we have to tell about ourselves are rarely the whole picture, especially of something as complex and organic as the story of the rise, fall and resurrection of the musical forms known as death metal and grindcore. For starters, it's a story that spans both sides of the Atlantic and the Pacific, in America, Britain, Brazil, Japan, Poland and Sweden, to name just a few of the countries which have spawned bands who have contributed to these genres.

Ever since punk opened up the possibilities of do-it-yourself, cheap record-ing and independent labels in the mid-'70s and blew apart the dominance of the major record labels, underground music of any kind has scattered its seeds farther afield than ever before. Death metal and grindcore raised—or perhaps more appropriately, sunk—what it meant to be underground to another level altogether. Just as US hardcore and punk depended on a circuit of squat venues to bring their heroes to their audience, so death metal depended on tape trad-ing, letter writing and mutual acquaintanceship. If it hadn't been for the demo tape-trading underground, death metal and grindcore wouldn't have reached the attention of their audiences, of the record companies who signed the bands, or of the musicians themselves. Time and time again in this book, you'll read about how musician X finally got a hold of the demo tape by musician Y and suddenly saw new possibilities for his music open up before his very eyes. The mutual influence of one death metal band on the next can only be described as "scenius."

Also, with just as much aptness as "genius," if you think in terms of "gen-eration." For the story described in this book so eloquently by Albert Mudrian is largely the tale of a very specific generation of musicians, who grew up on traditional heavy metal, thrash and speed metal, punk, industrial and hardcore, imbibing freely from all these wells, who went on to devastate the world be-tween approximately 1988 and 1993. Many a band from before this time can rightly claim to have influenced death metal in some primeval fashion, whether it's the deathgrunt vocals of Tom G. Warrior of Swiss cuckoos Celtic Frost, or the brutality and speed of Slayer's thrash metal. But this book isn't about them, nor should it be. Possessed may have come up with the very term "death metal" and delivered the hugely influential *Seven Churches* album in 1985, but this isn't a Possessed biography; they're in here, but so are other undoubted godfathers of death metal and grindcore such as UK punks Discharge. Nor is this book an encyclopaedia of all things death metal and grindcore. If you're flicking through looking for an honourable mention in dispatches for your favourite underground band, or for your own band even, who ruled the roost in the back of half of a dozen fanzines for a brief moment in 1994, you shouldn't expect to find it here. Such a way of telling the story might have the virtue of comprehensiveness, but what it would gain in pseudo democracy, it would lose in clarity and focus.

That focus is on the musicians who made up the ever-changing ranks of bands like Napalm Death, Death, Morbid Angel, Carcass, Obituary, Deicide, Entombed and Cannibal Corpse. They've all been described as the heavyweights of their genre a thousand times in 'zines all over the world, and that's exactly right: they are and were the bands who kick-started the mass appeal madness of death metal. But this book also goes deeper, and tells the hitherto unheard stories of the largely unsung progenitors—Siege, Repulsion, Terrorizer—as well as the tales of the producers, record company bosses and A&Rs who helped sign, shape and sell the music. If you're a death metal obsessive who has been following the genre for a decade or more, you'll still find out things inside this book about people you've read interviews with a dozen times that you never knew before; you'll also meet a few characters who you probably never even heard of, learn about previously unknown friendships and feuds, not to mention a few surprise connections. Who'd have thought that singer/songwriter Aimee Mann, formerly of '80s popsters 'Til Tuesday, could have had anything to do with grindcore? But she does, even if it isn't what you might think.

Since its heyday in the early '90s, death metal has returned to the native soil of the birthplace that nurtured it—the underground. And just in case you thought that should read "grave," then this book will also tell you about the remarkable comeback made by the genre in the late '90s and through to the present day. The mid '90s explosion of black metal in Scandinavia might have grabbed the headlines at the time, but without the death metal and grindcore scenes, black metal would most probably never have existed. By the end of the decade, parts of the two styles practically converged into one common genre of extreme metal. Bands like Emperor, Vader or Akercocke owe as much to death metal as they do to black metal. But that's not all that death metal has had to offer in recent years. Not only has the genre thrown up bands—such as Nile—every bit as good as the classic forefathers, death metal has also infiltrated just about every other style of underground and mainstream rock and heavy metal. You can find gothic, melodic, atmospheric and hardcore-style death metal; you can find grindcore in abundance in every nook and cranny of the hardcore and noisecore scenes; you can even find nü death metal behind the masks of megastars Slipknot.

The enduring influence and continued vitality of death metal and grindcore owes its causes above all to the power of the music. Long before "shock and awe" became a Pentagon slogan for bombing a city back to the stone age, death metal and grindcore bands were engaged in an arms race to produce the fastest, heaviest, most brutal music on the planet. The nicknames of drummers like Mick "Human Tornado" Harris of Napalm Death and Pete "Commando" Sandoval of Morbid Angel speak volumes about the dedication and ability of the players. It's this musical ferocity that marks out death metal and grindcore, not the lyrics, attitude or imagery. The extremism of death metal and grindcore comes down to inhuman vocals, grinding guitars and vicious blast beats, not to any political or religious ideology. And in contrast to black metal or hip-hop, no death metal musician ever murdered another, or their record company boss, much as some of them might have liked to at one point or another.

The story of death metal and grindcore, then, is a human one. Even if you never heard these musics before, I guarantee you that you'll be intrigued by their secret histories. Those tales took well over 100 interviews and two years of obsessive research by the author to tease out, but that's the kind of hard work it takes to get to the bottom of the story. After reading this book, you'll agree with me that it's also hard work that ultimately pays off in terms of a truly fascinating read.

Nick Terry
Editor, *Terrorizer* magazine (1996—2000)

Punk is a Rotting Corpse

HOME TO NEARLY ONE MILLION PEOPLE, Birmingham, England is second only in population to the country's capital city of London. Located in the country's West Midlands region, Birmingham is surrounded by a ring of industrial towns within a 50-mile radius where approximately six million more people reside.

A considerable percentage of those residents work in the car industry, as both Jaguar and Land Rover have based automobile assembly plants in the city for decades. As a result, Birmingham is very much a working-class town, which is why the rule of Margaret Thatcher's conservative government in the late 1970s had such an acute impact on the city's populace. The lack of workers' rights and continual cutting of public services were some of the concerns that were helping birth the punk rock explosion throughout the rest of the United Kingdom in 1977. But beyond Johnny Rotten's snarl of "I wanna be—anarchy," noisier sounds became the vehicle for social and political protest of truly disgruntled English youth. Soon a faster and more confrontational second wave of UK punk in the form of anarchist bands such as Crass, the Exploited and Discharge

Meriden Center

were unleashing their filth and fury in the city's small club circuit.

Musical proficiency was generally an afterthought to the bands; velocity and urgency colored with a righteous anger were what mattered. Ultimately, this form of aggressive music was the only manner in which these adolescents could properly express themselves.

Those reverberations traveled about eight miles outside the Birmingham city limits to a place called Meriden. Surrounded by evergreen woodlands on two sides, the small village of about 600 people is reputed to be the "Center of England," marked by a stone monument in the exact geographic middle of the country. It's also where a young Nicholas Bullen was raised.

(top left) Discharge live. Photo: Steve Disrupter. (top right) Napalm Death circa 1982. Photo courtesy of Miles Ratledge and Joaquim C. Ghirotti

"We lived in a caravan for a few years while my mom and dad built a house out of this old cottage," recalls Bullen. "So there was lots of time to get into things. By 1978 I was 10, and punk music was on the TV and the radio. That's when I bought my first singles. To that point, I really liked pop music—my mother's '50s and '60s pop singles. We had a great all-in-one mono record player portable that had every speed. I used to play my mom's old movie theme records and classical records. I used to tape them and loop them, the parts I liked. I'm still not a big fan of key changes and bridges. I've never been a great believer in counterpoint in music. I think it destroys the mood. I didn't know that then. I just taped the bits I liked."

By late 1979, Bullen and a friend named Miles Ratledge—affectionately known as "Rat"—formed their first band, which, according to Bullen, was nothing more than "just acoustic guitar and some tubs." Over the next year, the duo was joined by a revolving door of young fellow musicians (Simon Oppenhiemer, Finbar Quinn, Gram "Robo" Robertson and Daryl "Sid" Fideski among them) and began playing sporadic gigs in the Birmingham area under various monikers such as The Mess, Undead Hatred and Civil Defence.

"I suppose that we had a kinda stable lineup at the end of '81/early '82 when we started calling ourselves Napalm Death," says Bullen, who began playing guitar and singing while Rat manned the drums. "I think it was probably Rat that came up with it. We both really liked films like *Apocalypse Now* and *The Ninth Configuration*, which is probably why Napalm Death eventually stuck."

Their musical inspiration was equally contemporary, closely mirroring the atavistic sounds of the first wave of anarcho (short for anarchist) punk bands.

"We were more influenced by hardcore punk and especially Crass—that was our main focus. At the time, the music was rudimentary and also more melodic, but I just wanted to move the band more towards Discharge."

For Bullen and many others, Discharge was the ultimate crossover act, marrying the passion and intensity of punk with the speed and extremity of heavy metal.

"There are a lot of angry people over here," says Discharge guitarist and co-founder Tony "Bones" Roberts. "For them, the Sex Pistols and the Clash just didn't cut it. It was the same for us. When we first started we sounded like the Sex Pistols. But we just started rehearsing more and came up with something different, something heavier and faster. I've talked to a lot of people that were playing in bands that just sounded like Clash and the Sex Pistols at the time but when they heard us they started playing more hardcore, like the Discharge stuff.

"Nobody said to us, 'You've gotta go faster and faster!,'" Roberts continues. "Because there was nobody doing that stuff then anyway. There was nobody to copy it and say, 'We've gotta go as fast as this.' There was no competition. We just did what we wanted to do."

Despite their developing Discharge-isms, Napalm Death's first hint of recognition came with a little help from the band's earliest influence, Crass. Released on Crass' own Crass Records, the *Bullshit Detector #3* compilation gave Napalm their first bit of exposure with the track "The Crucifixion of Possessions." Before long the group's earliest demo and rehearsal recordings began circulating not only at local gigs but also via pen pals and underground fanzine editors whom they were making contact with throughout Europe and North America.

"We had done about three or four demos before that, just recorded on four-tracks," says Bullen, who along with Rat also edited their own fanzines. "It wasn't really for record companies—you just made a tape. We'd write six letters a night and get together and do tape-trading with people. Me and Rat had been trading tapes for two or three years by '82 with people from all around the world. So we had a lot of things like Swedish thrash and American thrash stuff and old American punk, and had a lot of friends in the tape-trading scene."

One of those people who heard some of the early recordings was a young English hardcore promoter named Digby Pearson. In 1982, Pearson began booking shows throughout his hometown of Nottingham, simply as a fan of underground music. Soon Pearson was intimately familiar with the anarcho punk scene.

"I promoted shows by my favorite bands—political UK hardcore bands like Flux of Pink Indians, Antisect, Subhumans, and like-minded US bands like Millions of Dead Cops, Crucifux and Toxic Reasons when they toured the UK," recalls Pearson, who, at only 22 years old, was one of the elder statesmen of the scene. "None of the regular clubs in town would let an outsider book a show, so I had to seek out alternative venues, usually hiring out community centers in Nottingham, like Queens Walk, Sherwood and Beeston."

In April of 1983, Pearson tapped Napalm Death to play its first show outside of the immediate Birmingham area at the Nottingham Boat Club, a rowing club next to the banks of the river Trent that held only 150 people.

"The lineup," remembers Pearson, "was a who's-who of the scene at the time—Chaos UK, Subhumans, Amebix, Antisect, Disorder. And opening the show, I booked one of my favorite new bands, Napalm Death. At the time, they were all like 14 or 15 years old."

"This gig is also notable because it was the first time I used the word 'Earache' anywhere," Pearson adds. "It proudly says 'Earache Presents' at the top of the flyer."

Over the next few months, however, Napalm began fading from the scene, playing only a handful of gigs before nearly taking a sabbatical through all of 1984, save one gig. "We all had girlfriends and stuff. We were going to gigs with them and taking drugs and things like that," explains Bullen, who, in true punk

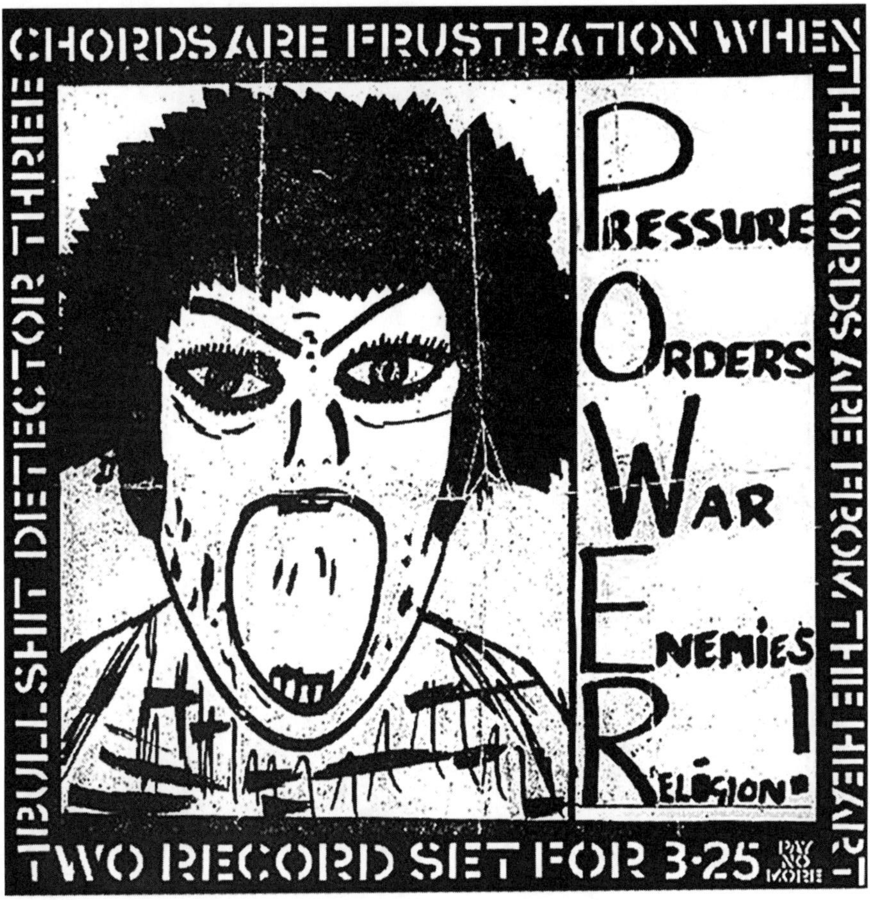

CHORDS ARE FRUSTRATION WHEN

BULLSHIT DETECTOR THREE

PRESSURE
ORDERS
WAR
ENEMIES
RELIGION

THE WORDS ARE FROM THE HEART

TWO RECORD SET FOR 3·25 PAY NO MORE

Bullshit Detector #3

fashion had recently eliminated the letter *c* from his first name. "We never had an American ethos of practicing five or six days a week."

During Napalm's hiatus, another British punk band began making noise of its own in the city of Nottingham. Initially dubbed Plasmid in late 1984, the band was rechristened Heresy the next year after enlisting local Kalv Piper to play bass. Before long the group of youths was garnering sterling reviews for their rapid hardcore in the underground punk digest *Maximum Rock n' Roll*.

"At first it was like a more sped-up Discharge pace, but then I wanted to pick it up a bit more," recalls Heresy drummer Steve Charlesworth, just 15 years old at the time of the band's formation. "Kalv and I were definitely interested in getting faster like a lot of the US bands we were just listening to at that time, like Siege and Deep Wound."

"Heresy were friends of mine," says Digby Pearson, "and I would always give them the fastest hardcore band tape that I would trade at the time, and Steve would try to play faster than that."

Another ridiculously fast band rose from the scene in 1985. Based in Ipswich—approximately four hours' drive from Birmingham—vocalist Phil Vane and guitarist Pete Hurley cut their teeth in a variety of Discharge-style punk bands such as Victims of War and Freestate before regrouping as the fiercely political Extreme Noise Terror.

"The [band] name was taken from a small picture on an insert to an album from the Dutch band Larm," says ENT guitarist Hurley. "It featured a bandanna-ed hardcore kid with 'Extreme Noise Terror' surrounding him. Those three words summed up *exactly* what we were aiming at. The scene in the UK at that point

(bottom) Heresy live. Photo: Alex Wank. (top) Nik Bullen of Napalm Death live. Photo: Jeff Walker

was saturated with bands that wanted to just play mindlessly—as fast as was humanly possible. We never really came from that stable. As a band, we really favored the Discharge way of doing things. We were primarily a hardcore punk band."

It was clear, however, by possessing ear-shredding dual vocalists in Vane and Dean Jones and the rapid beats of drummer Pig Killer, ENT were far more extreme than the typical anarcho punk outfit. In fact, after performing just a single gig opening for Chaos UK, Extreme Noise Terror signed a record contract with the tiny UK-based indie label Manic Ears. "After that night," says Hurley, "things seemed to go mental."

While Heresy and Extreme Noise Terror were busy abusing British ears, Napalm Death slowly began regrouping. In the spring of 1985, Nik Bullen recruited Napalm's newest member, guitarist and Birmingham native Justin Broadrick, whom he had first met two years earlier.

"There was a place in Birmingham called the 'Rag Market,'" Broadrick explains, "which was this real shithole—a great big indoor market that sold secondhand clothes and stuff. And in there were a couple of guys who ran a bootleg tape store. I was down there one day browsing through the Throbbing Gristle tapes and saw a kid next to me that was doing the same thing. You'd literally talk to anyone that was looking at a similar thing and if they were a similar age you'd feel like, 'Shit, I've got a potential friend!' And it was Nik Bullen that turned around and said, 'Are you into this Throbbing Gristle?' And I was like, 'Yeah, it's awesome.' And we just started talking and he mentioned that he had a band called Napalm Death."

"Then we kept in touch and lost touch for a little, and then in '85 we met up again," says Bullen. "We did a gig with his band that was grinding to a halt so we said, 'Do you wanna come and join us?'"

"At first, I was awful," says Broadrick, who was only 14 years old when he became a member of the band. "I couldn't even play fast riffs. I remember playing one of our first shows when I was in the band and people were openly laughing at my guitar playing—it was fucking terrible. But anyway, the big turning point for Nik Bullen and I was when we heard Siege from Boston and we heard DRI, and we were just like, 'Holy fucking shit, man. This is faster than anything we'd been listening to for years.' We thought Discharge was lightning speed, and we were just like, 'This is what we wanna do.'"

At the same time, metal—particularly thrash—was no longer considered a dirty word within the punk community. Early American thrashers like Slayer and Metallica balanced their high-velocity attack with a technically sound approach to performing, while European thrash acts like Kreator, Destruction and Celtic Frost tuned down their instruments, stripped down their sound and delivered a simpler—and altogether sloppier—approach with which most punks could easily identify.

"When it came to Celtic Frost, for some reason, we were just utterly blown away," says Broadrick. "And that was when me and Nik Bullen came up with the idea of the whole style we wanted to purvey. We wanted to put together a mixture of Siege and Celtic Frost. We wanted that hardcore energy meeting slowed-down, primitive metal riffs, and to basically marry that to a political message.

"By now, we were like 15, and it wasn't even that focused," he continues. "It sounds like we had some grand master plan and that we were gonna take over the world with this new style, but it couldn't be further from the truth."

With Bullen, Broadrick, Rat and a new bassist simply referred to as Peanut aboard, Napalm Death recorded a new demo, *Hatred Surge*, in September of 1985. The tape marked a much faster and more aggressive direction for the band, which was now regularly playing shows in Coventry and Nottingham, but still concentrating on gigs in their hometown of Birmingham. Moreover, October 1985 marked the first time that Napalm Death played the infamous Mermaid Pub, a bar located in the low-income Sparkhill area of Birmingham.

"It was a dive," offers Pearson. "Downstairs was the pub. Upstairs it was just basically a function room of the pub that you could hire out because it would affect the downstairs and the bar. The pub was friendly enough to have punks and crusty kind of people frequenting the bar and the upstairs room. You could ram maybe between 200 and 250 people in there."

"It was the roughest, dirtiest shithole you could imagine," Broadrick concurs.

Dean Jones of Extreme Noise Terror. Photo: Alex Wank

Extreme Noise Terror live. Photo: Nick Royles

"It was really just a shitty pub in a really shitty area, which just meant that you could get away with a lot more. Any commercial venue at the time would just not have any of the music that we were involved with. There was no way on earth that anyone would accommodate it for commercial reasons, and for the fact that we were all just a bunch of little kids, as far as everyone was concerned, playing stupid, sped-up punk rock. So it was just like a laugh for a lot of people. Even for us at the time, we tried to be serious, but because of our ages it wasn't so focused. It was all purely accidental. But by the time the Mermaid was [regularly having gigs] anyone could set up a show there. The landlords of the pub didn't give two shits. You could just literally go in there and say, 'I wanna put a show on in here in two weeks time.' And they'd just say, 'Yeah, what day?'"

While there were sporadic gigs hosted at the venue for years prior, it was local promoter Daz Russell who was booking nearly all of the punk and hardcore shows at the club for the autumn of 1985, often adding locals like Heresy, Concrete Sox and Napalm Death to bills already featuring international touring bands like DRI, Antisect and MDC.

"Daz Russell was good in some ways because he would try and get bands on," recalls Bullen, "but he wouldn't always pay them."

"True enough there was often no money to pay everyone or anyone sometimes," says Russell. "But don't think I was some rich promoter with a big car and house. I was 18 and worked in a carpet warehouse at the time earning £50 a week. These gigs were cheap—like £1.50 for nine bands. I didn't do it for the money. I just enjoyed it and wanted to see bands play in Birmingham. I did make money sometimes, but I also lost it sometimes."

One of the newest paying Mermaid patrons was a young Birmingham punker by the name of Mick Harris.

"I discovered the Mermaid and Napalm Death at the same time, and it was an instant magnetic attraction," recalls Harris. "I don't know what I heard in Napalm—there was just something there that attracted me to them. I used to go watch them every fucking weekend and I just got heavily, heavily into it. I would go to dance to them, to the faster songs. There were particular tracks I was waiting for every time. I was living for it. I was loving it."

"He just came up to us at the Mermaid and he had this psychobilly haircut, which is like a flattop, this little guy who was covered in tattoos, and he just said, 'I fucking love this stuff that Napalm Death do,'" says Broadrick. "And we were like, 'Oh, right, yeah, great.' Like any kid that would come up, you'd just be like, 'Thanks.' And we were still talking about a handful of people. We were legends in our own backyard and that was it."

Harris' enthusiasm, however, clearly set him apart from other fans of the band. Though he already played drums in a punk band of his own called Anorexia, which also featured future Head of David bass player Dave Cochran, Harris actually first offered Bullen and Broadick his musical services as a vocalist and then as a drummer during that initial conversation with the pair.

"We didn't want to use him as a singer, but he also said, 'I drum as well and I drum fast,'" Broadrick relates. "So I went down to a rehearsal to see Anorexia, and basically they were pretty backwards punk shit, but I noticed this psychobilly guy that had come up to us, Mick Harris, was playing very, very fast. And at the end of the rehearsal, he was like, 'Check this out.' And he just played really fucking fast."

"At the time, Peanut was already gone and Rat wasn't *that* interested in playing fast, really," Bullen recalls. "He was interested in a certain velocity and no more."

Further intrigued with Harris' abilities, Bullen and Broadrick put the young drummer through some informal exams.

"We played him tapes of Siege and DRI, and he didn't know this stuff," says Broadrick.

"But after we played him it and he could play it within about two days, then we were like, 'We're unfortunately gonna have to get rid of Rat. This is what we wanna go for. This is definitely it.'"

After only one rehearsal in November of 1985, Harris was officially the new drummer of Napalm Death.

"I started rehearsing with Justin in my bedroom in December of '85," Harris explains. "By then he'd turned me on to a few things like Sodom and Destruction. I didn't know that side of things. I had heard some stuff, but I had never owned any rock records in my youth. I just didn't grow up with it. So that was my first turn on to metal. It wasn't really what I knew of metal. This was punk. This was aggressive."

A handful of practices later, Napalm were ready for their first Rat-free performance on January 17th at the Mermaid. Harris made an immediate impact on fans of the band.

"I remember listening to the slow parts in the Napalm Death songs out on the dancefloor, and then Mick would start the beat and we would all look at each other because, the floorboards would literally vibrate from the kick drum," recalls Pearson, who would regularly make the 50-mile journey from Nottingham to the Birmingham club.

"I can still remember how it hit me. It was just phenomenal. You could just feel the floor move to the pace of the bass drum. You could feel the speed. You knew it wasn't just hitting on the snare. There's a big difference. The power comes from the kick drum when they play so fast. It was new to the scene."

So original, in fact, that Harris even developed the idiom "blast beat" for the wickedly fast 64th notes he played on the snare drum. Additionally, the drummer coined the term "grindcore" to properly represent this rapidly developing new genre of music.

"Grindcore came from 'grind,' which was the only word I could use to describe Swans after buying their first record in '84," Harris explains. "Then with this new hardcore movement that started to really bloom in '85, I thought 'grind' really fit because of the speed so I started to call it grindcore."

Moreover, Harris' initial show with Napalm Death also marked the first time the band played on the same Mermaid bill with breakneck contemporaries Heresy, whose drummer Steve Charlesworth would enter into a friendly rivalry with Harris.

"I suppose there might have been a bit of competition, but I think it wasn't anything that boiled up," says Charlesworth. "It wasn't necessarily just playing fast for me. Micky just went for the full-on, just as fast as possible, whereas we wanted to get it as intense as possible with fills, as well. The speed was foremost, but it had it be with something else more—I won't say technical—but more controlled, at least."

"Heresy would play, and then Mick Harris would try to play faster than Steve," contends Pearson. "It was kind of a little competition. Then the next time Heresy played the Mermaid, Steve would drum for Heresy as fast as he could, then Mick Harris would get up on the stage with Napalm Death and be faster. Watching that was half the appeal of going to the club—just to see the drum war going on. That was kinda how grindcore started in that little club, those two guys egging each other on because there was no one else around playing so fast—not

Napalm Death live. Photo: Nick Royles

Jim Whiteley. Photo: Nick Royles

that we knew anyway."

"At first, most people weren't that interested," says Bullen of the band's first few Mermaid gigs. "We were vaguely a laughingstock in some respects. To most people, it was kinda like, 'That's just racket.'"

"We'd be like, 'How fast can we play this?'" says Broadrick. "About half of the songs that were written before Mick Harris joined were slower, then we just sped them all up. We simply sped everything up, apart from the slow breaks. Literally, we were laughing in rehearsal—we were on the floor. That's how we wrote 'You Suffer.' We would play at gigs in front of maybe 70 people at the Mermaid and we'd play 'You Suffer,' since it was just over a second long, like, 50 times. People would just be yelling, 'Again, again, again!' It was pure comedy. Obviously, we had a serious political message and everything, but we were still just kids."

Over the next few months, however, Napalm Death began drawing larger crowds and, thanks in significant part to Daz Russell, playing the Mermaid up to four times a week.

"By about March of '86 it sorta dawned on us that loads and loads of people

Justin Broadrick at the Mermaid circa May 1986. Photo: Mitch Dickinson

were coming to see us play," says Bullen. "And they were actually people we didn't know."

Among those new attendees was the pair of Mitch Dickinson and Shane Embury from the small town of Broseley, located 40 miles from Birmingham.

"Completely by accident I met Justin Broadrick and Nik Bullen in a Virgin Records in Birmingham, and they were impressed with the fact that I had Celtic Frost and Siege written on the same jacket," recalls Dickinson. "So they said, 'We're in a band called Napalm Death and we're kinda like a mixture of those bands.' And they gave me a flyer, and Shane and I were off a week later on March 22nd of 1986—I still remember the exact date—to see them. We walked in and it was just a room full of guys with mohawks and dreadlocks and green hair, and there was us metal guys in leather jackets with our own paintings on them. We stood out like sore thumbs, but because of our enthusiasm and genuine interest in that scene we quickly got accepted."

Ultimately, Embury and Dickinson's warm reception was symbolic of the metal and hardcore scenes' developing bond, which was further strengthened by tape-trading between the genres.

"It was good because we were tape-trading with lots of Americans at the time," says Embury, "and all of a sudden we found our own scene that we would trade in, so we were trading English demos for American bands."

In fact, to most people involved in the scene, Embury was the most active tape trader in all of England.

"There was a magazine called *Metal Forces* back in '85," he explains. "It was the only magazine then that used to feature bands like Slayer and Mercyful Fate. There was a section in the back of the magazine called 'Pen Bangers,' and it was little ads for pen pals where kids would list the bands they were into such as Slayer and Possessed and Venom. And Mitch and I picked out a couple guys and we wrote to them and they wrote back, and we started swapping tapes of loads of things that I'd never heard. After a little while we amassed a little of our own, which was like 30 or 40 demo tapes. And then we put our little ads in the back of *Metal Forces,* and kids started writing to us, and it snowballed from there.

"At the time I wasn't working," Embury continues. "I had a couple of jobs that hadn't lasted very long because I always was getting fired for going to see bands play in London. So during the day, I was literally living in front of the tape deck, sometimes up to eight hours a day. I know at one point, from about January of '86 to about August of '86, I must have sent out between 30 and 40 cassettes under the door per week."

"I remember Shane giving me these tape lists, and I was like, 'Wow, look at all this stuff.' I had heard of this stuff—Genocide and Death—but I could never get my hands on it. It was heavier and more underground than what Sodom is

A young Justin Broadrick. Photo: Nick Royles

and what Destruction is and what Slayer is. This seems to be what I need to get into. I was turning Shane on to hardcore, Japanese hardcore and other extreme hardcore and the D.C. stuff that he liked, like the faster end. So we really fucking hit it off."

Soon Embury and Dickinson were inviting metal friends of their own to experience the noisy sounds of the club, two of whom were the young Bill Steer and Ken Owen, natives of a group of small towns just outside of Liverpool known as the Wirral.

"At the Mermaid, there were loads of bands and people, and, in a way, everybody knew each other," recalls Steer. "So there was a load of people just a bit sluggish from drinking too much, and these bands aren't necessarily supposed to try that hard. Generally, it all blends into one thing and nobody stands out. But that first day I saw Napalm Death, I thought Mick *did*. There was just so much power. I was just blown away by what the guy was doing. Steve from Heresy was a great drummer that had an incredible amount of respect from everybody. But

Mick Harris rocks the Mermaid circa May 1986. Photo: Mitch Dickinson

with Mick, the guy was just a force of nature. It wasn't just like watching a great drummer—it was kinda terrifying how much intensity was there."

With a growing demand for new recorded material featuring Harris in the lineup, the band scraped together £120—largely financed by promoter Daz Russell—and booked two days worth of time at Rich Bitch studios in Birmingham in August of 1986. The group didn't know it at the time, but that 12-track recording would one day become the A-side of Napalm Death's debut album *Scum*.

"This was for no reason other than it being a demo," Broadrick insists. "There was no label then, obviously. But we played it to a number of people, including Digby, who hadn't even released one album, I think. But he still couldn't decide what he could do with it and didn't get back to us. Everything was still so small and selling such small amounts of records. It was a big risk and a lot of money, even to press a thousand."

Shortly after the recording, the band recruited Birmingham local and fellow Mermaid frequenter Jim Whiteley on bass. For much of the year, Whiteley's apartment served as a makeshift hotel for the numerous out-of-town teenagers attending weekend gigs at the Mermaid.

"I lived in a multi-story, 92-apartment tower block on a large '60s council housing project in Kings Norton, about nine miles out of the center, and the

Napalm Death live at the Mermaid circa 1986. Photos: Jeff Walker

Napalm Death downstairs at the Mermaid Pub. Photo: Andy Fish

Mermaid was located nearer to the city center, about two miles out on the junction of the Stratford and Warwick roads," says Whiteley. "The most [people] I had stay was between 20 and 30. I lost count. There were bodies everywhere, even on the external balcony. And if Shane and Mitch ended up crashing that usually meant Mick Harris would tag along, also, so no one got any sleep whether there was music blaring or not."

"Jimmy started to play the bass because my enthusiasm was waning," says Bullen. "I said, 'Oh, let someone else play the bass. I'll just sing.'"

Shortly after the addition of Whiteley, Broadrick was offered the drummer position in Birmingham rock band Head of David, who had recently released a record on Blast First, then the UK home to acts like Sonic Youth and Big Black. He accepted, partially because of his desire to join a band he perceived as successful—Head of David recently entered the UK independent charts—but also because of the rapidly declining internal state of Napalm Death.

"Literally, within the space of a couple of months, the band really turned to shit with loads of infighting," says Broadrick. "This was just the product of being young. I mean, even in rehearsals, there were many times that I would literally stand there and watch Nik Bullen and Mick Harris rolling on the floor fighting. It was quite mad, to be honest. It was a lot of very volatile personalities. Almost inevitably, it would come to blows."

"Sorry, but being the one who has done the least drugs and booze, I have no recollection of any fights whatsoever," offers Harris. "Both Nik and Justin got bored from where I was standing. Justin always wanted to go places, and with the offer of joining Head of David on drums—a band that was ready to sign a big deal and tour—that was his break, his way out. Nik seemed less and less interested as time went by. Each rehearsal he would turn up more and more drunk, and I remember having to ask him if he was bothered [to rehearse] anymore, and he never came to rehearsal again."

Harris did his best to keep Napalm moving forward, but with Broadrick's departure and Bullen's lack of commitment, a split of the band seemed unavoidable.

"I got a bit bored with it," says Bullen of his Napalm Death experience. "I liked hip-hop and things like Joy Division and power electronic and '60s drug music, and I got a bit bored, because at that point as people were in the audience just shouting, 'Faster, faster!' I was thinking, 'Well, if everybody just wants us to play faster and faster, it is a bit like a novelty act,' and they're not really understanding on some level why we wanted to play it fast in the first place, which was just to mirror their kinds of emotions and to bludgeon, really. And when Justin left, I had a lot of respect for him and I got on better with him, and I just thought,

Napalm Death live in Leeds circa 1986. Photo: Nick Royles

NAPALM DEATH

Napalm Death are a band who've been doing their thing for almost a year now. The line up is Nick (of 'black cross' fanzine) (of 'twisted nerve' fanzine) - drums,-vocals,Miles and Robbo-bass.Before their present name they were called Civil Defence but the bassist they had then wasn't really interested in the band and sold his bass for a C.B. radio.They only played one gig under that moniker and it was seemingly a shambles.Influences include The Snipers,The Sinyx, Crass and The Ex,who Miles tells me are the only group they sound remotley like but since I haven't heard them I can't comment on that. At the moment they have 10 songs which are all on the tape I was sent Most are slow and plodding with jangly guitar and militant drumming but in my view are spoilt by the whining vocals.Lyrics deal with such subjects as the dumping of nuclear waste (in 'pollution') ,tribalism (in 'rival factions') and punk (in 'punk is a rotting corpse') .A state-ment that sparked of a postal argument (all cleared up now) betw-een me and Miles.The bands views are they are opposed to bloodsports,war, vivisection and tribalism.If you want to contact the band see addres-ses on the A to Z of punk 'zines.

PUNK IS A ROTTING CORPSE
OH NO,IT'S FUCKING NOT!

'Well, it's gonna change now.' And it did change, and so I just sorta stopped going to rehearsals."

"To be honest," says Broadrick, "no one in the band cared at all about anything. And I was left with the master tape, and I was gonna give—literally, just give it—to this other label Manic Ears. It was gonna be a split album with another band. And this guy Shane Dabinett who ran the Manic Ears label actually turned it down in the end. He said that he just couldn't be bothered, and he might be able to release it in about six months. So I managed to get Digby's phone number and just said, 'Do you want this Napalm Death thing? I've left the band and nobody else seems to care.' And I sent it to him for no money and that was it. I joined Head of David and went on tour to Germany. And I thought, 'That's it. That's as far it goes. That's a piece of history.'"

Whirlwind Struggle

DESPITE THE SOCIOECONOMIC SIMILARITIES, the American underground music scene couldn't possibly develop in the concentrated manner its English counterpart did. Instead, such a sprawling territory gave birth to several select pockets of disenfranchised youth throughout the country. And in the early part of the '80s, America's extreme music strength was underground hardcore—an accelerated, altogether angrier take on traditional punk rock. Washington, D.C. birthed the hyperspeed formula of the Bad Brains and Minor Threat. New York City unleashed the metallics of Agnostic Front and the Cro-Mags, while Los Angeles spit forth bands like the Descendents, the Circle Jerks and the primal power of Black Flag. Though sometimes overlooked, Boston had a powerful scene of its own. To most, Boston hardcore is forever defined by SS (Society System) Decontrol and their confrontational brand of punk, which, along with Minor Threat, helped characterize the straight edge movement. But the

Deep Wound early '80s

Boston area, quite simply, had the fastest bands, several of which actually hailed from small suburban towns in western Massachusetts.

Amherst was such a place. A two-hour drive west of Boston, the picturesque college town was also home to a young local named Joseph Mascis. In 1982, the 15-year-old Mascis—simply known as J to friends—wasn't much different from the town's other few proud punk rockers, often spending his free time roaming the racks of local record store Main Street Records in North Hampton.

"I met this kid in that store that looked kinda like Dee Dee Ramone," Mascis recalls. "I talked to him a little bit and he seemed to be into some of the same hardcore stuff as me. The next week I saw a flyer up in the record store and I figured it had to be that kid because I didn't know anybody else that was into stuff like Discharge and Minor Threat."

That kid was Scott Helland, who, along with his friend Lou Barlow, sought a drummer to play "superfast beats"—as their flyer bluntly stated—for their fledgling hardcore band. The group was practicing for several months before the painfully shy Mascis answered the advertisement. After joining, Mascis insisted the band draft his friend Charlie Nakajima to sing. Days later, Mascis christened the group Deep Wound, and within a few short months they began playing sporadic gigs with local hardcore punk groups, such as Helland's other outfit The Outpatients.

"We just wanted to play as fast as possible, and, I think, sometimes it was to the detriment of our songs," says Mascis. "All we were concerned with, really, was playing faster and faster."

For that crown, Deep Wound would have some competition. In another small western Massachusetts suburb named Weymouth, local drummer Robert Williams and his 10th grade classmates, guitarist Kurt Habelt and bassist Henry McNamee, had been instigating a racket since 1981, shortly after their first exposure Minor Threat and Discharge. On the weekends, the trio frequently made the half-hour journey east to Boston's premier independent record store, Newbury Comics, to feed their appetites for scorching punk rock.

"It was such a special time to be discovering music," recalls Williams. "I can remember coming home from Newbury Comics—which was just a closet, with cardboard boxes of comic books and 7-inches on wooden shelves—and my hands were shaking I was so excited to play these records. I remember the look of absolute snobbery and disgust on the face of the cashier—a young pre-'Til Tuesday Aimee Mann—when I came up to the register with an original pressing of the Meatmen's 'Blood Sausage' 7-inch, which had a used condom with pubic hair on the cover. I had a rating system—the faster my mom would run upstairs to get me to shut it off, the better it was. I couldn't get through a side of Black Flag's *Damaged.* Flipper, [I] couldn't even get through a song."

Further inspired by their trips into the city to see Black Flag and NYC punkers the Misfits, Williams devoted more time to his musical project, which had recently been dubbed Siege.

"The three of us were jamming together in Hank's garage and then later in a church, making absolutely hellish dissonance that resounded through the neighborhood," Williams remembers. "Locals still come up to me, now grown, and talk about how they used to drink beers in the woods with their friends and listen."

Soon the quartet recruited singer Kevin Mahoney, from yet another western Mass. suburb, Braintree—a town rich in hardcore heritage and home of the original Gang Green and Jerry's Kids. By 1983, Siege began playing shows in this rapidly developing western Mass. community.

"It was a healthy, awesome, real DIY scene out there in western Mass.—a clique of very excited groups," Williams explains. "It was one of the places that you played when you made the rounds, another being Stamford, Connecticut. They were very positive scenes, but very few of them made the ride to Boston to play shows. They were younger, artsy types and they weren't the most driven, savvy entertainers in the world. These were just punk kids and they happened to live in a very remote place. More often, Boston would go out to western Mass. to play." That community had already accepted the speedy Deep Wound, but withstanding the sheer velocity, violent lyrics and developing metallic leanings of Siege would be an even greater test. After all, this was a band both faster and heavier than the crossover thrash punk of Cryptic Slaughter and Septic Death, which was then regarded as the pinnacle of aural intensity in the US.

Siege Maximum Rock n' Roll feature

"There was a time when we made a deliberate decision to set out to be the absolute fastest band," says Williams, whose speed training included playing AC/DC's *Highway to Hell* LP at 45 RPM and duplicating the drum beats while wearing headphones. "The track 'Beating Around the Bush' becomes galloping Brit punk when played on 45," he notes. "I loved metal, too—Venom, Priest, Motörhead's 'Iron Fist.' In fact, we covered Venom's 'Warhead' at our first show, which was at our high school's battle of the bands—we got disqualified for obscenity, plus our bassist Hank smashed his bass. But it was about speed. We would listen to the fastest punk and hardcore bands we could find and say, 'Okay, we're gonna deliberately write something that is faster than them, because we are going to be the fastest.' We took it very seriously."

Williams and the rest of Siege, however, didn't hold Boston's straight edge movement in similar regard.

"I was a heavy pot smoker," says Williams, whose drug use was in direct contrast to the prevailing sentiment within the hardcore scene at the time. "And we were younger guys, newcomers, certainly not straight edge, and didn't fit in with the original Boston crew, who were bullies. Their thing kind of grew into the jock-infested macho one-dimensional shit that half of hardcore is now—the baseball cap-wearing, smack a kid up shit. The other half being the *Maximum Rock n'*

Siege drummer Robert Williams

GREENFIELD GUIDING STAR GRANGE

401 CHAPMAN ST

sat. feb. 18

all ages

siege

cancerous growth

outpatients

the freeze

Siege live circa 1984

Roll peace-punk, crust leftist, reverse conformism—but this was before all those terms and before things were so clichéd."

By the time Siege was making its own way in early 1984, however, their kindred spirits in Deep Wound were simply going away.

"The hardcore scene was kinda dead to us," says Mascis. "I was more into the Birthday Party and the noisier types of bands after that. Scott, the bass player, was really busy with the his other band Outpatients, too, so basically he went in the Outpatients full-time and the rest of us formed Dinosaur, but we were called Mogo then and we still had the same singer from Deep Wound, Charlie, but then after one gig we decided that Charlie was a no go and then we officially started Dinosaur [which later became Dinosaur Jr]. We had a totally different concept. We went for being a kinda really loud country [band] or something, because hardcore had just died out for us."

Before Deep Wound officially disbanded, however, the group managed to record a self-titled 7-inch EP and a few tracks for the *Bands That Could Be God* compilation with local producer Lou Giordano at Boston's Radio Beat Studios. Giordano recorded Boston's top punk and hardcore acts, such as SS Decontrol, Negative FX, the FU's, Jerry's Kids and Proletariat in the tiny reconstructed AM radio station in the heart of Kenmore Square.

"There was a small staff there." Giordano explains. "There was the owner, Jimmy Dufour, and then I joined up in late '82, and that was right about the time that the Boston scene was really exploding. Black Flag had come through town and basically just freaked everybody out, and it was never the same after that. And the Boston bands were kinda racing to catch up with the rest of the country ,and all these bands sprung up overnight with a completely different sound than anywhere else—it was like they passed them all."

Unsurprisingly, Siege elected to make their first recordings there as well, entering the studio with Giordano in February of 1984.

"The way our studio operated was that anything that comes in—there's no value judgments made about the music," Giordano recalls. "We just record it. Still, one of the things that I guess was cool about being a staff engineer is that I wouldn't have sought out a band like that. I wasn't philosophically into anything that they were doing, but that they were all good musicians—you would have to be to stay together at the speeds they were playing at. So there was that aspect of it, and just the whole pushing the envelope thing. It sounds like it's just gonna completely break apart going 700 miles through the sky and then all of a sudden everything just comes right together again.

"And they were some of the most unassuming, laid-back people to ever work with," he continues. "I mean, they had no attitude at all. They just came in and they were just really polite and very thankful, and then when they turned on the amps and made that noise, it was just unbelievable that it was coming from them."

"He had seen a lot of that kind of thing, but we were serious about equipment, and that may have been one thing that set us apart," Williams remembers. "But it was nothing new to him. He was really adept."

Siege would return to the studio in October of that same year, recording three more tracks—"Walls," "Cold War" and "Sad But True"—for a compilation assembled by artist and *Maximum Rock n' Roll* scribe Pushead called *Cleanse the Bacteria*. That session would be this lineup's last. A little over a year later, with internal tensions mounting, Siege imploded before what was to be their first ever New York City gig at the celebrated rock club CBGB's. "The vocalist was bickering with the guitarist," Williams explains. "The van was loaded for our show. We never played the show. Kev never showed up, and I really can't blame him. After that, we stopped playing."

There were several false starts over the next few years, the last of which occurred in 1990, when Williams and guitarist Kurt Habelt were joined by local Boston vocalist Seth Putnam.

"We were recording and writing, and I had written a bunch of revolutionary stuff, like violent lyrics, and that same guitarist changed some of my lyrics with weak rhyme, making them pacifist rather than revolutionary, and really changing their context," says Williams. "He delivered that to Seth in the studio behind our backs. And he went so far as to erase one line of Seth's singing and put in his own voice. I still have genocidal resentment about that. We never planned on compromising our extremity."

Some 750 miles west, in the midsized industrial town of Flint, Michigan (population: 450,000), locals Matt Olivo and Scott Carlson shared a similar idealism. Although the pair initially met when "we didn't even have front teeth," according to Olivo, they didn't become good friends until junior high school, years later. By then, the two had cultivated a healthy love of traditional heavy metal bands like Judas Priest and Iron Maiden.

"In the early '80s we started getting into stuff like Motörhead," Olivo recalls. "We'd find out that Lemmy would wear a Discharge shirt and we'd go buy a Discharge record, and then suddenly we were listening to a pretty wide variety of hardcore punk and heavy metal."

"Discharge especially had a profound impact on my musical direction just because they were so doom," says Carlson. "Everything was about the end of the world. Some metal bands said similar things, but Discharge was describing it in gory detail, sort of like putting it right in front of your face, and I think that's what I liked about them so much, that they were kind of scary."

In late 1983, however, the pair's primary focus was still very much heavy met-

(left) Flyer from Ultraviolence show. (lower right) Genocide

al. Olivo, in fact, was busy playing guitar in his own heavy metal band—an outfit that strictly adhered to Maiden and Priest covers—when Carlson introduced him to the speedy thrash of the first Slayer LP *Show No Mercy*.

"Matt came back to me with this song that would later be titled 'Armies of the Dead,'" says Carlson. "It was Matt playing this extreme Slayer riff—except for the fact that we were playing in a garage and our equipment was a lot crappier than theirs. We were down-tuned too, and, it just sounded sludgier. But we knew we wanted to play something that fast."

The discovery led the pair to form their first band, a proto-thrash metal act dubbed Tempter, with locals Sean McDonald handling bass, James Auten behind the drums, and Carlson supplying the vocals.

"The first Tempter gig we played was at a punk show," Olivo recalls, "and we were a little worried because we had on Metallica t-shirts. Back then the punkers were still kinda like, 'I don't know about these metal dudes,' and metallers were like, 'I don't know about these punk dudes.' But in that first gig in our little hometown of Flint, after the first song people just went nuts. It was like this huge reception that we got, and from that point on, we just had a home."

Yet unlike most hardcore and punk outfits, whose message was often both personal and political, this quartet drew lyrical inspiration from the goriest horror and slasher films they could find.

"If you knew us back then, we just had fun," says Olivo. "We got into horror movies. We got into going to punk shows and stage diving and all of that stuff. But we weren't into real autopsies and stuff. Really, we just wanted to get more hardcore than the guys that we were with. They weren't quite with us [in the band], so we just started all over again."

Those revisions consisted of a brief name change to Ultraviolence—when the band actually opened for Slayer in Flint in 1984—before altering the moniker again to Genocide only a few months later. After drummer Phil Hiles replaced Auten, the band recorded their first rehearsal demo in Hiles' basement in November of '84. While the group still didn't exceed the archetypal thrash metal velocity, the recording was Genocide's introduction to the extreme metal underground. Soon Carlson and Olivo were tape-trading with national contacts they made via underground zines like *Brain Damage* and, of course, *Maximum Rock n' Roll*.

By early 1985, the pair was regularly corresponding with a young Floridian named Chuck Schuldiner, who fronted his own extreme metal project simply called Death.

"I wrote Chuck a letter because Death sounded like they were sorta kindred spirits," says Carlson. "Chuck sent me a tape with all of their material on it and I played it for Matt, and I was like, 'This is pretty similar to what we're doing.'"

"Chuck was sending horribly misspelled letters as correspondence because he was into Genocide and we were into Death," says Olivo. "He would send us pictures of, like, dead rats and shit and we would

Genocide's/Repulsion's Scott Carlson

talk about how we wanted our bands to be the sickest bands in the world."

The two groups often commiserated as well. Over the next few weeks, Genocide's lineup quickly disintegrated, leaving only Carlson and Olivo as members, while Schuldiner expelled Rick Rozz, the guitarist with whom he had continually butted heads, from Death.

Repulsion live in 1986

"In the spring of 1985, Chuck and Scott were brainstorming," says Olivo. "They were like, 'Let's just merge the two groups.'"

18-year-old Carlson graduated high school, and Olivo, a year his junior, quit school before the pair packed their belongings and journeyed 1,200 miles south-east to Schuldiner's parents' house in Altamont Springs, Florida.

"We just drove down there straight through, it was like a 24-hour drive, and knocked on Chuck's door," Carlson explains. "And the next day we were set up in the garage rehearsing. Matt and I held a bunch of crappy jobs while we were there. Chuck was working at Del Taco, which is like Taco Bell in the South. All we wanted to do was rock, then act like idiots."

Only two weeks into the new union, however, Death drummer Kam Lee left the group. "It was such a bummer," says Olivo. "So we hung around and tried a few different drummers, but nothing really seemed to work."

"Since Kam wasn't around, we just started writing," says Carlson. "It became evident really fast that Chuck wanted to be more technical and do a lot more gui-tar stuff and, we just wanted to completely thrash out. We didn't have a drummer, there was nothing going on, and we still really wanted to do something extreme. After just a couple of months there we just went back home."

Upon their Flint homecoming, Olivo returned to school before he and Carl-son resurrected the Genocide name and began their search for a drummer.

"The only guy that anyone knew that was available was Dave Hollingshead, who had been in some collegiate-type punk rock band, just kind of college rock," remembers Carlson. "And he had recently made headlines in the local newspapers for getting arrested for grave-robbing, and I thought, 'Perfect, that's our man.'"

Rechristened Dave Grave for such behavior, the drummer had a difficult time initially adjusting to the band's rapid tempos.

"To just keep the sort of thrashy Slayer drumbeat, Dave would struggle," Carl-son admits. "So he would do this thing where he was hitting the hi-hat every other time that he wasn't hitting the snare, like a country drummer or a polka drummer would."

The band showcased their newfound velocity on an October 1985 rehearsal demo titled *Violent Death*, leading to regular live performances at punk and hardcore shows in the band's hometown of Flint. Thanks in part to the increased gigging, within a few short months, Hollingshead's drumming skills improved dramatically.

"After a while Dave just became so proficient at what we called the cheating drum beat," Carlson says. "It became ridiculously fast, and we realized that the beats per minute on the snare drum were so much faster than any other band, that we just tried to keep pushing that element forward. The reason that a lot of the initial songs sound so manic is that they were written to be played at about the speed of a Slayer song, and they ended up so fast that the lyrics are just garbled on songs like 'The Lurking Fear,' 'Six Feet Under,' 'The Stench of Burning Death'— those songs were written to be played at a much slower speed, and they just sort of mutated into what they were. I give Dave a lot of credit for that, because at the time he wasn't good enough to play it. By the time it was over, he was one of the gods, one of the guys that people measured themselves up to as far as speed. It was very accidental."

By the time the group entered the studio of local public radio station WFBE to record their first proper demo in late January 1986, Genocide was the fastest band in the world. The band implored their friend Aaron Freeman to also play guitar on the recording engineered by studio employee Ken Roberts.

"They were normally recording classical symphony stuff in that studio," remembers Carlson. "It was a big huge room with a bunch of music stands and chairs, and we went in there and he set up microphones, and we went straight to two-track recording. So the whole thing was just done as a live recording—there were no overdubs whatsoever. And [we did] one or two takes of each song, and we were like, 'We've got a real demo, guys.' And before the thing had even cooled off I was already addressing envelopes and sending it to every key person I could think

(left) Scott Carlson. (right) Dave "Grave" Hollingshead

Repulsion at the bar

of; whether they were a musician or a record label or a magazine, I was sending it to everybody. I probably sent out 25 copies of it the day after we recorded it, and then I just kept sending it to people unsolicited."

This time, Carlson and Olivo's efforts created an international impact in the extreme music underground. Most notably, copies of *The Stench of Burning Death* tape made their way to England, where members of the UK's rapidly developing hardcore scene were exposed to Genocide's heart-racing speed. But just as Genocide was beginning to make a name for themselves, they changed theirs. In May of '86, with several other bands operating under the same moniker of Genocide, the group was rechristened Repulsion. This alteration, however, wasn't enough to garner interest in the group from any record labels. Undeterred, the band decided to self-finance their own full-length LP, with Freeman now officially entrenched as the band's second guitarist. Local record store owner and ardent supporter Doug Earp funded the $300 recording session in June of 1986. Although the resultant 18-track *Slaughter of the Innocent* was yet another step forward from their previous record in terms of speed, the label interest in the band remained much the same.

"We started sending that around, and I thought someone would pick it up and put that out, but it didn't happen and we were just confused," states Carlson. "I thought it was so great, I believed in it so much and I just couldn't understand why nobody else was interested in it."

"We were really hoping at one point to start a career of some kind, even if it was a little career," says Olivo. "I remember thinking, 'I know that a career would probably only last two or three albums, but I would just love to do it and then move on with my life.' But it wasn't happening. Hope was just dwindling."

Soon the band's members began drifting their separate ways. First, Hollings head departed for the army in July of '86. "Dave totally lost interest because Matt and I just ruled things with such an iron fist," Carlson admits. "We were constantly just pushing him to get better, and I think after a while he just got sick of it."

Following a brief unsuccessful stint with replacement drummer Tom Puro, the band went on an unofficial hiatus in September of '86. After one reunion show featuring Hollingshead back behind the drums in November 1987, Repulsion officially folded.

"It was just such an intense and very short period, like six or eight months, when we wrote those songs," says Carlson. "Then it was just over. That was the statement. To me, all that Repulsion ever had to say was on that record. It was over, and I don't think we could have done it any more extreme."

The extremity threshold Repulsion attained was about to be tested in Los Angeles, California. Although his hometown's music scene was currently besieged by the era's glam metal insurgence, south central L.A. native Oscar Garcia was enraptured by the aggressive sounds of Slayer and Celtic Frost. After causing a brief clamor in the company of friends Eric Castro and Carlos Reveles with the atavistic rumble of an exclusively demo project called Majesty, Garcia sought a serious group he could front as a vocalist/guitarist. In fact, he began recruiting his band members right off the street, starting with 15-year-old local Jesse Pintado.

"I remembered Jesse from seeing him around because he would be wearing Iron Maiden shirts," Garcia recalls. "One day I was walking down the street and saw him and told him that I was trying to get a band together and I asked him if he knew how to play. He said, 'No, not really.' So I just taught him a few chords myself, because I wasn't that great of a guitar player either. We just basically learned from each other."

Soon after Pintado and Garcia realized their fundamentals, the pair dubbed the new thrash metal union Terrorizer, after a song from an underground Chicago metal act called Master.

"It's common knowledge that the Terrrorizer name came from the first Master demo," agrees Master guitarist/vocalist Paul Speckmann. "If you ask any real metal band if they have heard of Master, the response is more than likely, 'Yes'" Thanks to the international tape-trading network, Master, as well as recordings from Speckmann's other project Deathstrike, was a cult favorite throughout the underground for their extreme take on traditional thrash metal.

"Actually," says Speckmann, "I received many letters from the original Napalm Death patch [at the time]. It's a really small world."

The newly minted Terrorizer drafted a local friend named Alfredo—a baseball fanatic, who they nicknamed Garvey after his favorite player, Steve Garvey—to play bass. Following a revolving cast of drummers the group settled on an L.A.

local simply known as Fish. "I don't know why," says Garcia, "but everybody called him Fish. He was a cool guy, but he wasn't that great of a drummer. Basically, he couldn't play much faster than a Slayer kind of beat."

The band spent the next year attempting to secure an adequate practice space, playing at Fish's parents' house and Garcia's garage before moving their equipment into a mutual friend's garage near the end of 1986. By then, Pintado and Garcia's tastes grew more extreme as they became deeply immersed in the international tape-trading underground.

"After your Metallicas and Slayers came around, trading more obscure music just made it more extreme," says Pintado. "Because the obscure stuff was more extreme than stuff you could get in vinyl. Bands like Death and Master, at the time, you couldn't get the records because they didn't *have* records—it was just flyers and demos. The curiosity of seeking out more crazy stuff drew out our influences."

"Jesse ended up getting the Napalm Death demo that would become the A-side of *Scum*," Garcia explains. "I remember one day he said, 'Check this out.' And when I listened to it the first time, I called him and I said, 'That's it—that's the way I wanna play.' There were other bands that I heard that were supposedly trying to

Master live circa early '80s

play as fast as they could, but it was nothing like Napalm Death."

Napalm's velocity wasn't on the menu for Fish, however. And soon it was clear the drummer's commitment to Terrorizer was, at the very least, floundering.

"I remember one afternoon we were waiting for Fish, and he never showed up because he went to the beach," Garcia recalls. "He knew that were gonna practice at this time, and he just blew us off. And me, Garvey and Jesse would all wanna practice, so we would just stand around and try to make up stuff without a drummer. So that day this guy we knew walked in and he told us that he knew a drummer. I said, 'Is he any good?' And he said, 'Yeah, he's good.' So we said, 'Bring him.' We naturally thought that he would bring him a week later or something, but about 30 minutes later he walked in with Pete."

Pete was L.A. local Pete Sandoval. After a brief introduction, his first rehearsal came behind Fish's drum kit, which was fastened together with a generous amount of duct tape.

"The first beat that he played was a superfast beat," says Garcia, "and when we heard that, Jesse and I looked at each other and we looked at Pete, and we were like, 'Hey, man, you wanna join this band?' And he said, 'You guys haven't seen me play.' And I said, 'We've heard enough.'"

Sandoval immediately accepted and hurried home. Shortly after his return with his personal drum kit a half-hour later, Terrorizer were moving at top speed. "When Pete started playing our older songs with his style of drumming," Garcia explains, "everything just started to click."

With the lineup finally stabilized, the band recorded several rehearsal demos over the next year and began searching for shows in the L.A. area.

"We weren't doing any clubs or anything in L.A.," Pintado explains. "We were doing backyard parties, and we refused to do the 'Pay to Play'

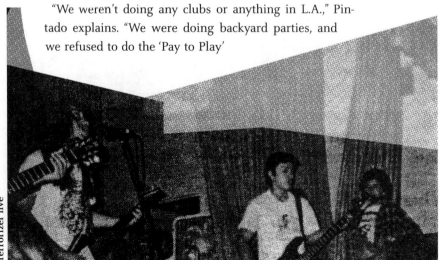

Terrorizer live

Terrorizer live

Hollywood scene, so we had trouble really finding a home. Terrorizer was too fast for the metallers and not hardcore enough for the punks. You show up with long hair and they were like, 'Get the fuck out of here.'"

"We played with metal bands, we played with hardcore bands—we played with everybody," says Garcia. "At a lot of shows people, didn't like us, but we just kept doing it. Basically, we were our own thing out there."

Just a year later, however, the band was rehearsing and gigging with less frequency. When bassist Garvey became mixed up with L.A.'s gang culture and was sentenced to jail time in early 1988, the group turned to Garcia's old friend Carlos Reveles, who filled in admirably on bass. But to Pintado, it was clear that Terrorizer was faltering. "We were just barely rehearsing and doing not that much." he says. "Nothing was going on."

In the summer of '88, Pintado received a call from David Vincent, a pen pal from North Carolina. At the time, Vincent's band Morbid Angel was in search of a drummer capable of breakneck speed.

Recalls Pintado, "David said, 'We're looking for someone to play fast. Can we get Pete's address and phone number?' And I said, 'Here you go. Call him up.'"

"At the time I thought we were just about ready to do an album," says Garcia. "Then one day out of the blue at a practice, Pete just busted out saying that he was leaving the band and that he was moving out of state. And that was pretty much it for us then. It was like we never had a chance."

Death By Metal

WITH A LITTLE IMAGINATION, one could argue that Iron Maiden's ubiquitous skeletal mascot Eddie is actually the catalyst of Florida's entire death metal scene.

In 1983 at Lake Brantley High School, the only public school in the quiet Orlando suburb of Altamonte Springs (then with a population of just over 20,000), students like Barney Lee scribbled on notebook covers as a welcome distraction to pass time. Your average scraggly-haired high school pariah, Lee also sought solace in the music and garish logos of punk bands such as the Misfits and Samhain as well as the politically minded Dead Kennedys and the Exploited.

"One day I was sitting by myself, of course, and I was doodling," Lee recalls of that day in 1983. "I was drawing these little skeleton people, and this guy just happened to be looking over my shoulder, and he said, 'Can you draw Eddie from Iron Maiden?' And I was like, 'Yeah, that's no problem.' And then we got to talking."

That guy was a young metalhead named Frederick DeLillo, who immediately struck up a friendship with Lee and began foisting European heavy metal acts, such as Accept, Raven and Mercyful Fate upon him. Lee, however, remained relatively skeptical of the music.

"I would listen to the stuff and I would appreciate it, but it really wasn't my kind of thing," he explains. "I liked the Fate, but I never liked the high-pitched vocal stuff. But one day Rick came to me and said, 'I got this band you've gotta listen to. It's like Motörhead, but even more extreme.' And he happened to bring in *Black Metal* from Venom, and that sealed it for me. I was like, 'Yes, we can do music like this.'"

Venom's musical interpretation of the New Wave of British Heavy Metal may have been crude and their lyrical interpretation utterly juvenile, but it was all the inspiration DeLillo and Lee needed. Soon the pair decided to form a band of their own. Lee would handle the drums and vocals, while DeLillo could provide the guitar—but the band still required more like-minded members. Within weeks, DeLillo contacted a fellow Altamonte Springs resident—the Long Island-born, 15-year-old guitarist Chuck Schuldiner, whom DeLillo had recently met through a mutual metal friend. When DeLillo introduced Lee to Schuldiner at a party in late 1983, Mantas was officially born.

Lifting their nomenclature from the stage moniker of Venom guitarist Jeff Dunn, the youngsters similarly altered their own names—DeLillo becoming Rick Rozz, Lee shifting to Kam Lee and Schuldiner adopting Evil Chuck—well before becoming proficient musicians.

"When I first started the band," Schuldiner told *Guitar School* nearly a decade later, "I'd only been playing guitar for six or seven months—I couldn't even play a lead."

The group compensated for their musical deficiencies by developing an aggressive theatrical element to Mantas, covering themselves in fake blood for their first and only official live performance. But their true objective remained clear to Schuldiner.

"My main goal was to bash out the most brutal riffs ever," he said in that same interview, "with the most brutal guitar sound ever."

That search helped foster Schuldiner's growing obsession with tape-trading. Armed with dubbed copies of both Mantas' debut rehearsal demo *Death by Metal* (recorded in his parents' garage during the summer of 1984) and the band's October '84 "proper" demo *Reign of Terror*, Schuldiner set out to uncover the fastest,

Mantas/Death circa 1984

heaviest band in the world. Soon he discovered the demo of a California band called Possessed.

Formed by San Pablo native Jeff Beccera, along with junior high school friends Mike Torreo and Mike Sus in 1982, Possessed began gigging almost immediately, perplexing audiences throughout their area with a blistering take on thrash metal and overtly Satanic image.

"At first people didn't know what to think, because there really weren't any other bands doing the kind of thing we were doing," says Beccera, just 15 years old at the start of the band. "After a while people started to catch on, especially by the time we had a record out to sell them."

In 1984, Possessed signed a recording contract with the tiny Combat Records label, and a year later set out to Prairie Sun Studios in Cotati, California, to record their debut LP *Seven Churches*.

"To this day I still refer to that album as 'Seven Chickens,'" Beccera explains. "It was on a chicken ranch. Most of them were in chicken coops. And I remember they were running around, and when you'd actually start playing they'd go to the other side of the yard. Horses will do that, too, when you play death metal—it's completely unnatural to them. Death metal scares the fuck out of people, too, and 99.9% will hate you, animals included."

The result was an overtly dark and violent thrash-paced album. Moreover, it was the first proper LP to feature what would become the standard growling death metal vocals for the genre.

"Mike [Torreo] said, 'Try to be like Cronos from Venom and try to be like [Slayer's] Tom Araya,'" recalls Beccera of his vocal coaching. "He said, 'Just go rr-

rooaarr!' So I pretty much just yelled my guts out. The first time I ever sang it sounded too heavy. I'm yelling on *Seven Churches,* but it was really much heavier than that, it was just too much. So *Seven Churches* is really a calmed-down version of the earlier stuff."

"To me, Possessed is still the first American death metal band," offers Lee, who discovered the band shortly after Schuldiner. "When we were in Mantas we still had a more Venom/Motörhead sound kinda going on. And then I remember Chuck getting the Possessed demo, and I just remember hearing it and just freaking out like, 'Man, this is the way we gotta be.'"

It was Possessed's Beccera, in fact, who is widely credited with actually coining the term death metal, writing *Seven Churches'* closing song, simply titled "Death Metal."

"I came up with that during an English class in high school," the bassist/vocalist explains. "I figured speed metal and black metal were already taken, so what the fuck? So I said death metal, because that word wasn't associated with Venom or anybody else. It wasn't even about redefining it. We were playing this music and we were trying to be the heaviest thing on the face of the planet. We wanted just to piss people off and send everybody home. And that can't be, like, flower metal."

Fearing their obvious Slayer and Venom influences were no longer extreme enough to be considered death metal, the Mantas members reevaluated their approach just before that Christmas.

"I remember it was just after the movie *Evil Dead* had come out to the theaters, and we were going constantly," says Lee. "First *Evil Dead* premiered at the theater, and then they started playing it as a midnight movie every weekend, and we were going every weekend. And I remember we were standing in line all talking, and Chuck said, 'Why don't we just change the name of the band from Mantas to Death?' And we were like, 'That's perfect.'"

Now more specifically categorized, according to Lee, under the blood-soaked banner of "Corpse-Grinding Death Metal," the band played their first gig as Death opening for Florida thrashers Nasty Savage at Ruby's Pub in Brandon on New Year's Eve 1984, a show which was recorded and circulated throughout the tape-trading underground. Only a few weeks after that initial triumph, however, it was clear that the band's relationship with guitarist Rick Rozz was deteriorating beyond repair, leading to his dismissal.

It was then, in the spring of '85, that Schuldiner hatched his ill-fated plan to merge forces with Scott Carlson and Matt Olivo of Michigan metallers Genocide. Within only two weeks of uniting under the Death moniker, Lee exited the new group.

"A lot of people think Chuck kicked me out, but the truth is I quit because me and Chuck started being a little bit different," Lee contends. "Chuck wanted to step in more and sing more songs because, at the time, Chuck was only singing about a third of the songs and I was doing the vocals, and he said he wanted me to concentrate more on drums. And the fact is, at that time I wanted to step down from drumming. I was talking to Scott and Matt about maybe getting their [old] drummer to move down and Chuck didn't wanna do that. You hear it all the time, but 'creative differences' is exactly what it was. And pretty much the basis of the whole thing was, I no longer wanted to play drums. I wanted to become a front-man vocalist, and Chuck wanted to also be a vocalist, and that wasn't gonna work. And it turned into a heated argument, and basically I ended up quitting."

The remaining band members spent the next few months trying to find a proper drummer before Carlson and Olivo returned home to Michigan. Before they left, however, the pair became enamored with the *Surrender or Die* demo recording from underground Canadian metal band Slaughter.

"We took a little of everything we loved and grinded out some of the heaviest shit around," offers former Slaughter guitarist Dave Hewson. "Not just speed for the sake of speed, but our fast parts worked well off of our slower, heavier parts. But, I must say that when we played fast, we played *fast*. [It was] some of the

(left) Nasty Savage flyer. (right) "Evil" Chuck Schuldiner

fastest metal, with no blast beats. We just went right for the throat and in for the kill—fast and painful."

"Chuck had the Slaughter demo at his house, and I put it on, and I immediately wanted to stop playing with Death and just change my musical direction, and go faster and harder," recalls Carlson. "When I played it for Matt, he too was like, 'Oh, my God, these guys are amazing.' It was total Celtic Frost, but much, much faster and they had this wicked sense of humor that Matt and I were both totally into. And we just said that we wanted to do something more like this."

In terms of extremity, Slaughter may have been only a very fast thrash metal band, but Schuldiner was equally captivated with the group, and set out to start a band of his own that was even faster and heavier than the speedy Toronto-based outfit. Requiring a rapidfire drummer, Schuldiner moved to San Francisco in September, teaming up with ex-D.R.I. drummer Eric Brecht. After recording only a single rehearsal demo with Brecht, Schuldiner quickly grew weary of the union's

Genocide's Scott Carlson

unadulterated brutality and returned to Florida by December of '85 in hopes of developing a more dynamic outfit.

Only a month after his Florida homecoming, however, Schuldiner made contact with Slaughter guitarist Dave Hewson, who convinced the young frontman to relocate yet again and join his band as rhythm guitarist.

"Chuck flew up and we rented him some gear and we rehearsed for about ten days," recalls Hewson. "Some of the tapes we made were fucking heavy. The living arrangements were not working out, though, as Chuck was living in Terry's parents' basement—not to their liking. We also felt Chuck was not ready to retire Death, nor were we totally comfortable being a four-piece. With the recording of [our album] *Strappado* only a few weeks away, it was decided to part ways."

"When [Chuck] called after two weeks to tell us of his change in plans, we wired the money to him to fly home," recalls Schuldiner's mother Jane. "His father and I respected his decisions and gave him financial freedom to go wherever his search led him for his career."

By the time the nearly nomadic Schuldiner returned home to Altamonte Springs, his former bandmate Lee had departed 95 miles southwest to Tampa, where the thrash tandem of Savatage and Nasty Savage led the city's burgeoning underground metal scene.

"I was there about three months, just going to shows, and I got word that there was this death metal band looking for a vocalist," Lee explains. "It happened to be this band called Massacre, and it was just horrible. The vocalist that they had was more or less kinda like [former Anthrax frontman] Joey Belladonna. When I'd gone to the rehearsal, they pretty much had no originals at all. They were playing Anthrax covers and a couple Overkill songs and some S.O.D. songs. And the first thing I said—I guess I came off kinda cocky—was, 'Look, if you guys want me to sing, this stuff that you're playing now has gotta go. You just gotta completely start over from scratch.'"

The band, rounded out by Bill Andrews, Alan West and Mike Borders, generally agreed with Lee's blunt appraisal.

"These guys had come to that show when Death had played with Nasty Savage, so they knew what I could do," Lee continues. "So they said, 'Try it out and see what you think of us.' So when it came to Massacre, I said, 'I wanna step away from what I was doing in Death, I wanna go even deeper with my voice.' And when that came out, a lot of people said, 'God, that sounds like you're vomiting.' And it got nicknamed 'death vomit vocals,' but I never came up with that. Before that, I don't think anyone was growling that deep.

"But it was probably three weeks after that initial meeting that we were just practicing, and we had enough material to put out the first Massacre demo," Lee continues. "At the time, Alan and Mike both had some kind of hook where we

Chuck Schuldiner and Chris Reifert circa 1986

could go into a student project studio for free. So '85 was like, 'Boom!' I moved to Tampa, I was there three months, and I was already in a band. It happened really fast."

Chuck Schuldiner, however, was in a much different situation. Disillusioned with the dearth of like-minded musicians in his hometown, he decided again to relocate to San Francisco in early 1986. Within a few short weeks of his arrival, Schuldiner began actively courting local musicians to play with. In the small San Francisco suburb of Concord, a young drummer named Chris Reifert soon got the word.

"I was still in high school, and they had—and still do—a high school radio station. And they were about to place an ad for Death looking for a drummer, which was insane because I had been buying and trading Death demos for the past year or two, and thought, like, 'No way, it couldn't be the same Death,'" says Reifert, about to turn 17 at the time. "And I knew this girl who worked at the radio station, and she said, 'Hey, we're gonna run this ad, and I thought I'd tell you about it before I ran it.' So I called up—I think it was even before it was on the air—and I just said, 'Is this the same band?' And they said, 'Yep, we're just over here now.' I was one out of either one or two calls that he received, so it was pretty much a cinch."

The pair immediately recorded a two-song rehearsal tape late in March of '86 before quickly following it up with the band's most polished material in the form of the three-track *Mutilation* demo several months later.

"Something teased me from the very start," Schuldiner later told *Aardschok-Metal Hammer* in April of 1989. "All the time I kept one main goal: a record deal!"

Mutilation earned Schuldiner that elusive recording contract with the tiny New York indie Combat Records. That summer he convinced Reifert to relocate to Florida to record Death's debut album.

"We did all the rough tracks and they sounded so lame that Combat just decided to throw them away as a mistake and just start all over again," says Reifert of the ill-fated session. "So we had to basically start from scratch."

This time Schuldiner and Reifert packed up and headed to Los Angeles' Music Grinder studios in November of 1986. There, with little incident, they laid down the tracks for *Scream Bloody Gore* with producer Randy Burns.

"I was totally happy with the way the record came out," Schuldiner told *Metal Forces* when *Scream Bloody Gore* was released in May of the next year.

Metal Forces agreed, describing *Scream Bloody Gore* as "death metal at its utmost extreme, brutal, raw, and offensive—the kind that separates the true death metallers from countless trend-following wimps. Just one listen will have you either thrashing around your room like a mindless maniac, or heading for the nearest toilet in total disgust. If anything, it should certainly establish the band as one of the heaviest acts on the face of the earth."

"Randy gave us a superheavy production, and he was very easy to work with in the studio," Schuldiner said in that same piece. "The only thing I kind of regret now is not hanging around for the final mixes."

Schuldiner, however, definitely wasn't interested in hanging around California. Again he tried to coerce Reifert into moving to Tampa, but

Chris Reifert in an early incarnation of Autopsy. Photo: Steve DiGiorgio

this time the drummer wasn't budging.

"Chuck said, 'This is where I belong, and you can come down and keep with it,'" recalls Reifert. "And I was like, 'I think I'll just stay here.' I didn't feel like—Florida is so fucking hot, man. It's like humid and just kinda redneck, so I wasn't into it, and I just wanted to stay here, so I just did that and started Autopsy from there. It was like, time to start a new band—there's nothing else to do. So it was out of necessity or desperation or both."

Arguably that same motivation guided another group of young locals. Like kindred Florida spirits Death, this outfit's initial stages developed in high school, where in 1982 both 11th grade guitarist George Emanuelle III and senior Mike Browning attended Tampa's H.B. Plant High School.

Bonding over their mutual appreciation of bands such as Black Sabbath and Iron Maiden, within months of their meeting the pair formed their own heavy metal cover band called Ice.

"Our first show was actually the school's talent show," laughs Browning, who handled the drums for the group. "We weren't Ice for very long."

Upon graduating from Plant in 1984, Emanuelle moved to Temple Terrace on the other side of town, effectively ending Browning's stint in Ice. Emanuelle replaced him with a local drummer and recruited friend Dallas Ward on bass and

Morbid Angel rehearsal circa 1984

continued to further develop the band by crafting his first set of original material.

"When I first started playing guitar, and writing songs I wanted to try to make something that had the feeling of the really fast, aggressive stuff with the more deep, trippy stuff," he says. "I wanted to have multiple styles together—maybe examples were like mixing Slayer, with, like Mercyful Fate and trying make a song that had those two worlds coming together."

Before long, however, Emmanuel found himself yet again without a drummer. Without hesitation, he asked Browning to rejoin the group, which was then operating under the name Heretic.

"We soon found out there already was a Heretic," says Browning, "and that's when we got the name Morbid Angel."

"I just came up with that, because I was looking for a great name to actually call the band," Emanuelle says. "We had all of these working titles, but I came up with that name in '84. Before that it was us playing funny parties and just doing goofy stuff, going to a park and just setting up and playing. But 1984's when Morbid Angel really got started."

"The first thing was that you wanna have a cool logo so people think it's cool, and t-shirts—you wanna get the imagery out there," he continues. "And you wanna have some kind of message, some kind of thing where as far as what the intended meaning is. I always wanted that to be about the real magic about life and the idea of spiritualism."

Additionally, Emanuelle, who always felt uncomfortable with his regal-sounding full name, embraced the nickname Trey, complementing his namesake stature as the third. He also chose the appellation Azagthoth—a blind, mad god of abomination often referred to as the "Lord of Chaos"—as his new surname.

Morbid Angel itself underwent several other renovations. The young guitarist devised a lyrical approach directly inspired from the Satanic tome the *Necronomicon*, while his music reflected that content, growing darker, faster and altogether heavier.

Despite such artistic strides, a proper vocalist continued to elude the band. Their first frontman selection was local Kenny Bamber.

"He was a lot older than we were at the time, and he looked like a big Ted Nugent kinda guy, but he tried to sing in a falsetto, like King Diamond, for some reason," recalls Browning. "So we tried it, and he was in the band for about a month. But the guy wanted to pay for a recording, so we went in and recorded a couple of songs."

With Bamber ousted shortly after the '85 recording, bassist Ward assumed the primary vocal duties. Only weeks later, another Florida native, Richard Brunelle, entered as the group's rhythm guitarist, joining Ward as a second vocalist.

(bottom left) Morbid Angel circa 1984. (top left) Morbid Angel's Mike Browning at rehearsal

"Dallas kept getting in a lot of trouble with the law, so he ended up getting arrested," Browning explains. "Richard wasn't really into doing the vocals because he had a problem singing and playing guitar at the same time. So we really didn't have anybody that could just sing, so I said, 'I'll try it.' And for some reason, it just kinda came out that way with me growling, and it worked."

With a suitable vocalist finally in place, and the additions of guitarist John Ortega and bassist Sterling Scarborough, who soon adopted "Von" as a faux middle name, Morbid Angel spent much of the next year writing new material. During that stage, Browning made acquaintances with a Charlotte, North Carolina musician named David Vincent.

"There was a guy singing for David's band, Metal Mike, who was a friend of mine that used to live in Brandon, Florida," says Browning. "Mike called me one day at my house from North Carolina and said, 'Hey, do you still have that Morbid Angel band going? I'm working for this guy that's got a record label, and he wants to hear you guys.'"

"I was going back and forth, working with hardcore punk-type stuff, and what was around at the time essentially a circuit of heavy metal cover bands," says Vincent. "There was a bar, like a rock club, that was attached to this porno shop I was working at, so I would just get off work and go immediately over there, have a beer and hang out and watch bands. And every time bands would come through, like some of the bigger bands from the circuit, I'd always push them to add more heaviness. They'd come in and I'd play a tape for them, like, 'Check this out. These guys are ridiculous.' And usually the drummer would be the first one to frown, because he'd be thinking, 'I don't want my guitar player talking to this guy anymore, because he's gonna ask me to play these hyperspeed beats.' In reality, they were not that fast. It was around like Slayer *Show No Mercy,* and that was before [Slayer drummer] Dave Lombardo really went sick with it. It was a new thing. It wasn't really accepted. Nobody really knew much about it, especially in backwards-ass North Carolina."

"We sent him a practice tape and that's how he signed us," Browning recalls. "He never saw us, and he got one practice tape and that was it."

With Vincent's financial backing, Morbid Angel traveled to a Charlotte studio in the spring of 1986 to record their debut album and debut release for Vincent's embryonic Goreque Records. While the resultant *Abominations of Desolation* LP was certainly the group's heaviest and most uncompromising output to date, some of the band members, including Azagthoth, who stayed an extra week in Charlotte to assist in mixing, weren't completely satisfied with the finished product.

"We all liked the recording at the time," says Browning. "I mean, it wasn't perfect, but it had a lot of feeling to it."

(bottom) Flyer for original *Abominations of Desolation* on Goreque Records. (top) old Morbid Angel show

"Because of their performances, I just didn't really feel the songs were really able to come to their potential," Azagthoth counters. "I thought that a lot of the stuff still needed to be worked on. I didn't really feel that the drumming was fitting in, and it was kinda hard to tell at practice because the practice space was kinda noisy. But once we recorded it, it seemed like it was missing stuff. I felt that the songs could have been a lot better, so I just really wanted to scrap that whole thing. So I deny it as far as being a record."

In fact, Azagthoth was so displeased with the result, he elected to dissolve Morbid Angel's lineup, booting Scarborough, Ortega and Browning from the band.

"When we came up there, I guess David was pretty amazed at the way that Trey played guitar, and he was just like, 'I gotta have this guy in my band,'" Browning says. "So that's basically what he told Trey when me and Richard and Johnny went back. First of all, he said that Johnny was a horrible bass player. I mean, I thought he was all right. And he said, 'Get rid of Johnny and get Sterling.' So when [that version of] Morbid Angel broke up, it was in late 1986."

"Trey called me and said, 'Not to worry you or anything, but I just parted ways with the drummer and bass player,'" says Vincent. "So it was just he and Richard at the time, and I thought, that's funny—I was working with a drummer who was into basically the same stuff that I was—and I said, 'Why don't we get together and see what happens?'"

After agreeing to shelve the *Abominations of Desolation* recording indefinitely, Azgathoth and Brunell traveled 600 miles north to Charlotte, joining forces with drummer Wayne Hartzel and Vincent, who would handle the bassist/vocalist duties in yet another rendering of Morbid Angel.

"Well, David saw what I was doing, and basically copied that and improved it," claims Browning of his vocal delivery. "He got those guys and he brought them down there and, they fucking worked 24 hours a day."

"They came up and hung out," says Vincent. "We started jamming, and it sounded really good to the point that we sounded, in our opinion, tighter and better and heavier than the record."

The entire group moved into a six-bedroom house on Charlotte's south side (what Vincent succinctly characterizes as "a kinda shitty part of town") where they rehearsed and—invariably partied—nightly.

"At the time we were all young—I was only 19—and me and Trey were heavily into reading the occult and gore movies, and just doing everything on the dark side and trying to shock people," says Morbid Angel guitarist Richard Brunelle. "It was pretty crazy. We used to stir up some attention. We used to go out of our way just to shock people. It was more than just music. Music was a big part of it, but it was a whole lifestyle."

That lifestyle often carried over into the band's live performances, where Brunelle and Azgathoth would regularly engage in the act of self-mutilation, slicing their arms open with razor blades on stage.

"Back then the big thing in metal was all about poofy hair and makeup, and we wanted to show that we were real," Brunelle explains. "We cut ourselves to show people that we're not fake and that we live the lifestyle and that we're really into what we do. So doing that was to kinda prove the fact that we live what we do.

"Trey went further than I did," he continues. "He used to eat live worms and spit them out onstage. I did the cutting and all the stuff, but that dude was overboard. He was just into it so hard. He'd literally go out and dig them out of the ground and save them and get them all ready for a show. It didn't last too long, though. I don't think it tasted too good."

Unsurprisingly, Morbid Angel gained attention. And over the next several months, the group and their monstrous home became familiar fixtures to local metal hopefuls such as South Carolina teenager Karl Sanders.

"I stayed there for about a month once, because I was doing a classical gig with one of David's friends and it was in Charlotte, so I needed a place to stay," says Sanders, who also played guitar in a thrash metal outfit at the time. "I stayed in the spare bedroom. It was in between Trey's room and Richard's room, and it

(left) Trey Azagthoth practices self-mutilation on stage. Photo: Frank White

(top right) Morbid Angel's Charlotte house as it stands today. Photo: Daniel Coston.

was in the middle of a stereo war. Each one of these guys had like 500-watt stereos that had speakers four feet tall, capable of massive levels of destruction. And each one of them would crank up and start blasting away with their little pet things that they liked. The drummer was really funny. He couldn't afford to buy death metal records so he took his Iron Maiden records and spun them at 45, and swore that it was every bit as meaningful as that death metal stuff that everyone was listening to."

Other amenities included a huge pit bull, which Sanders alleges band members "fed live cats," and an old Buick stripped of paint and covered in death metal graffiti. In order to offset such costs, all four members of Morbid Angel took jobs at a car wash called the Auto Bell. "Back then if you lived in Charlotte," says Sanders, "you could get your car washed by Morbid Angel."

"We would just walk to work up the street, work our hours and come back and just like literally play all night, like six, seven hours a night practicing," says Vincent. "And we just came up with a lot of really fucked-up shit. At that point, this is like when tape-trading was not passé, but we didn't really focus in on it that much. We just focused mainly on staying at home, playing, writing a lot, working out new things, just melding, just making this beast."

Still, the group was discovering some new music—particularly the high-velocity sounds of bands like Napalm Death, who were currently enrapturing underground ears throughout Europe.

"I remember I was at the Morbid house," recalls Sanders, "and Trey came running out of his bedroom, holding up one of the very first Napalm records—it might have been *Scum*—running out going, 'Oh, my God, I cannot believe this. Listen to how fast this is. They call this a blast beat.'

"But ultimately," Sanders continues, "I saw Morbid Angel in its infancy rehearsing these things. You would just go to practice and sit there, and it was this incredible unheard-of thing at that point. They were just taking things to this incredible new level. I was quite stunned. Just the guitar work, the drumming, the song structures—it was just amazing stuff, like music on warp 10."

Indeed, over the next several months, the band developed as virtuosos at their respective instruments—Azagthoth's contorted rhythms and demented soloing, in particular, bordering on the unfathomable. Some of the resulting compositions, according to Azagthoth, were even drawn from classical music arrangements.

After spending over a year and a half further defining their sound in Charlotte, where the band recorded 1987's three-track *Thy Kingdom Come* demo in parts throughout three different studios and their rehearsal space, by 1988, Morbid Angel were ready to return to Florida.

"The cost of living was a big factor," says Azagthoth. "It's probably one of the least expensive places to live without it being out in the middle of nowhere. And

Karl Sanders performs with local metal band circa 1987. Trey Azagthoth pictured headbanging at front of stage

there are places to play and, for me, it was more or less home."

That summer the band relocated to the Daytona Beach area, where only after a few weeks, Hartzel mysteriously exited the group.

"I don't know what his deal was, but he just flaked," says Vincent. "One day he was up and was like, 'I'm gonna go do something,' and, like, in the middle of the night he packed up all of his stuff and bailed."

The band was determined not to allow Hartzel's departure to slow them down. In many ways, in fact, the drummer's exodus accelerated Morbid Angel's pace. The group's first choice for a replacement, however—Terrorizer drummer Pete Sandoval—was located on the opposite coast of the United States, in Los Angeles, California.

"Trey had gotten this Terrorizer demo through tape-trading," Vincent remembers. "And we were talking about it, and he was like, 'Man, I really want this guy in the band.' So I said, 'Why don't we find out about it?'"

Vincent immediately approached Sandoval's Terrorizer bandmate Jesse Pintado, with whom he recently corresponded via tape-trading.

"I called up Jesse and said, 'Are you guys doing anything? What's up with your drummer?'" Vincent explains. "And he said, 'It's really relaxed. We practice every now and then, play a show at some high school.' It wasn't an on-the-front-burner kinda thing. So I said, 'Why don't you give me Pete's number? Maybe he knows some drummers that play kinda like he does.' So he gave me his number, and I said, 'Maybe I could just take Pete.' And Jesse goes, 'Yeah, go for it.' So we're like, 'Well, fuck it.'

"So I call, and I finally get Pete on the phone," Vincent continues, "and as

Former Morbid Angel drummer Wayne Hartzel

I start talking to him, Trey grabs the phone out of my hands and just started blowing up on the phone, 'Hey dude, look, you're gonna come down here! You're gonna join our band!' And the guy was probably just sitting down eating some dinner and watching some TV or something and there's Trey going off on the phone."

"I guess I was just really excited," offers Azagthoth. "I felt that we had a lot of stuff going on and I believed that the band was really gonna do something, and I guess I just expressed a lot of excitement to him. I just said, 'We've got this position and we love your drumming, it's phenomenal, and I think we'll make a great team. If you wanna come and take a chance with it, then let's do it.' Of course, we sent him a couple tapes of material that we had, like the *Thy Kingdom Come* demo and some rehearsal tapes, just so he could hear what it was about. But he really didn't know much about our band at the time."

On the strength of essentially only a few telephone calls, Sandoval sold his van, packed his belongings, bought a bus ticket and relocated some 2,500 miles to Daytona Beach, Florida.

"He came in and got right to work," says Vincent. "The guy is literally the hardest-working person I have ever been in a band with. When he came to us he could not play double bass. Trey and I are good coaches, we showed him the math of what he needed to do, and he went down into our practice place and taught himself how to do it, just went on and on. We'd go to work, we'd come home from work, we wouldn't hear any noise, all the lights would be off, and we'd go down to the space—it was like a basement underneath the house—and there would be Pete passed out on the floor in a puddle of his own sweat. We'd say, 'Dude, are you all right?'

(left) Morbid Angel upon returning to Florida.

(right) Pete Sandoval at rehearsal

And he'd say, 'Oh, gotta get back to work. Gotta get back to work.' And he'd just sit up there going dit-da-dit-da-dit-da-dit-da for hours and hours at a time. And within two months he was going sick."

By then, in the autumn of 1988, the band was ready to embark on their first US tour. The only problem was they didn't have a record, let alone a label to support them. Quickly Vincent and Azgathoth began phoning their East Coast friends in other death metal and thrash bands, hoping they could organize enough shows in their areas where Morbid Angel could perform a sustained tour.

"Basically, they called us up from Florida," explains Ross Dolan, frontman of fledgling New York City-based death metallers Immolation. "This is when Pete was just in the band—and I remember talking to them on the phone and I was like, 'What's that in the background? It sounds like you're jamming.' And they were like, 'Oh, that's just Pete working on his double kicks.'

"They were like, 'Listen, we wanna come up and do some shows. Can you guys maybe book a show for us?' So we booked them three shows, a show right here in New York at a really good place called Streets, which was Morbid Angel's first New York appearance ever. And then we booked a show out in Sundance, which was in Long Island, and we booked a show for them at a place called Escapades in New Jersey. And this was all in October of '88."

"They were small shows, sometimes just 50 people," says Vincent. "But we managed to get out there and make our way around. We had an old school bus that we had converted into our tour bus. We just did everything ourselves—we were hands-on guys. We had a tool kit, and when something broke we got out on the side of the road and fixed the shit. We were just so driven that there wasn't anything that was gonna get in the way. We ate, drank and slept Morbid Angel, and whatever it took to do what we needed to do, we found a way to do it. We made it happen. We forced it to happen. And that really showed its way into the music. The music was really brutal—everything that we did, the approach to everything that we did in life was with that same brutality."

Upon returning from the mini tour, the band relocated yet again, this time to its original birthplace of Tampa, where a pair of vile new bands was helping to further define Florida death metal.

While Morbid Angel and Death may have cut their collective teeth in high school, brothers John and Donald Tardy actually assembled the skeleton of their first metal band in elementary school a year later after their family moved from Miami to the Tampa suburb of Brandon in 1980.

"At the time we did not have any instruments of our own," recalls the elder Tardy, John. "We started going over a friend's house who had a drum set that we all started to play."

Over the next few years, the Tardys found inspiration in the area's small but supportive underground metal community.

"Living in Brandon, Savatage and Nasty Savage were really getting popular at that time, and we started hanging out with those people, and I thought they were the greatest," recalls Tardy. "So, even though I don't really think our music was influenced by them, those were some of the early bands that we just kinda looked at as motivation and support to start something out on our own."

For the troubled young Glen Benton, however, encouragement of most kind was in short supply. "I grew up with the understanding that I was evil and that everyone else was good," says Benton, "so I went with it."

Growing up in the predominately Catholic town of Niagara Falls, New York before his family relocated to Clearwater, Florida when he was 6 years old, Benton was the son of a Quality Control Inspector for ITT Industries and a Lutheran Sunday schoolteacher.

"My mother kicked me out of her Sunday school class," he recalls with a laugh. "I was just there to scarf on the fucking cookies and Kool-aid. The rest of the time I was there, I was picking on other kids."

Instead, Benton sought direction from an aunt on his father's side of the family, who was a practicing witch. "She was a very powerful, very brave person who used her mind to manipulate situations," says Benton. "I learned a lot from her. It helped me consider myself a Satanist as a little kid. I was coined that early on by my relatives. My old man still thinks I need to be exorcised. He used to tell me that I was possessed by the devil when I was a kid. But, hey, he also told me to be a plumber."

His father's job eventually led Benton back to Niagara Falls before the family was forced to relocate yet again to Georgia for nearly two years.

"That's where I finished school—well, I didn't actually finish," says Benton. "I was more or less brought home in handcuffs, so my school days ended there. And I came back out here to Florida and just pursued my music."

The Tardy boys already had a head start on Benton. Dubbing their family duo Executioner in 1984, the brothers began practicing in their parents' garage, with Donald behind the drums and John filling in with whatever instruments he could find. That, of course, was before they discovered their first bandmate in Donald's classmate and metal comrade, Trevor Peres.

"It was in the fall of 10th grade that Donald and I were in the hallway, and we were like, 'Dude, we should start jamming,'" recalls the Jacksonville-born Peres. "He had a drum set and I had a guitar, and we barely knew how to play either one of them. John got recruited to sing by virtue of the fact that we needed a singer so we were like, 'Why don't you just fill in for now?'"

"Trevor would start to come over, and we just started jamming every day after school," says John. "We got right into the garage, and we pretty much started writ-

Amon's Glen Benton. Photo: Tim Hubbard

ing our own stuff right from the get-go. We really did not play a lot of cover stuff at all, even though we were listening to a lot of Venom at the time."

"In '84, we did a demo tape, which was totally fucking cheesy, but it was cool," says Peres of the recording, which featured songs such as "Metal Up Your Ass" and "Psychopathic Mind." "We were the rock stars of our high school for a little bit."

Clearly, Executioner's influences were rooted in contemporary thrash metal, such as earlier Slayer and Metallica, but the youngsters continually sought out more aggressive sounds.

"When I got Celtic Frost's *Morbid Tales* album, we literally threw handfuls of songs away and started all over from scratch," says Peres. "So I wrote what was our heaviest song at the time called 'I'm in Pain,' and that was the first time that John actually sung heavy for us. Before that, we had all of this thrash stuff and it was kinda thrashy singing, but then with 'I'm in Pain' I kept begging him to do something heavier. I had him listen to *Morbid Tales,* and finally one day he went 'Rrroooaaaar!'"

"Venom was probably about the earliest band that I can remember sitting there singing along with their songs with more of a growl," says Tardy, whose own gravel-gargling howl stripped paint off any wall within earshot. "Keep in mind that I grew up with my older brother Greg, and he was all into Lynyrd Skynyrd kind of southern rock, which is what I grew up listening to, so when we started jamming I was like, 'Well, I don't wanna sing all that heavy,' but ultimately it did not take that long before it started coming out that way. It kinda turned us into a real band."

Conversely, Benton was still unable to locate suitable musicians in Clearwater to assemble a proper band of his own.

"I put an ad in one of the local music magazines, and I was just at my wits' end," he recalls. "I was looking for people to hook up with after I dealt with every fucking poseur in the state. It just got to the point where it was like there's just nobody here that's into the same shit that I'm into, so I was like, 'I'll put one more ad in, and after that I'll go to California and put something together out there.' So I put the ad in the paper and I got a call one afternoon—it was July 21st, 1987, I can't forget that date—and it was Brian Hoffman, and he said, 'Me and my brother play guitar and we've got a drummer.' So I said, 'I'll come over and check it out.' I went over there and I really liked what I heard. But they were rehearsing in this house which was completely fucking riddled with cat shit everywhere, and I couldn't stand the smell in there, so I was like, 'Listen, I got a nice clean garage over at my house, get your stuff together and bring it over.' So the next day we brought all of that shit over and started writing songs, and within the first week or two we had like four or five songs."

Within days, Benton christened his new group Amon, after an ancient Egyptian god, and recorded the crude *Feasting the Beast* demo in his garage less than a month later. Though certainly musically and creatively feral, Amon wasn't deterred from playing the occasional gig in the Tampa area.

"We'd do shows and there would be like 25 people there, but the 25 people would leave covered in blood from just totally bashing away," says Benton. "I used to take mannequins and fill them up with pig guts and blood, and then during the show we used to have a few of our roadies disassemble them. And then it just turned into one big fucking food fight."

Sans the mess, Executioner was developing equally as fast. With their sound further cultivated by John Tardy's malevolent vocal delivery, the band filled out its first proper lineup in 1986, recruiting former Massacre guitarist Allen West and bassist Daniel Tucker. After Peres left the band for a brief six-month hiatus that year ("My parents were being dicks, stifling me," he says. "They wouldn't let me play music for a summer, and then I rebelled and said, 'I'm outta here.'"), the group recorded a demo in early '87, just prior to the guitarist's return.

The recording quickly traveled through the tape-trading channels, landing in the grasp of *Violent Noise* zine editor and underground enthusiast Borivoj Krgin.

(left) A very young (E)xecutioner. (right) *Raging Death* compilation cover

"I just immediately fell in love with John Tardy's voice," Krgin recalls. "When I first heard it, I thought it was the most brutal death metal voice I had ever heard in my entire life, and I just wanted people to hear it."

He wasn't kidding. Along with tape-trading Californian correspondent Marty Eger, the pair conceived a compilation LP featuring their favorite demo recordings of unsigned metal bands from the tape-trading underground.

"We didn't really have any serious plans or long-term goals," Krgin admits. "It was just an idea, and we would press up a bunch of copies and talk to some of these bands that we were in contact with directly and get their permission to do it without even really having any kind of written agreement; just get their okay and try and sell it with the understanding that they wouldn't get paid. And of course, we didn't have permission to do anything else with these recordings, and as soon as they got signed, if they wanted to re-record some of these songs or even use the exact same recordings, they had the option to do that. It was just something that we wanted to do to get the name of these bands out, and it seemed like a fun thing to do."

Showcasing the track "Find the Arise" in the pole position from the new rechristened Xecutioner (the augmentation a direct result of a Boston hardcore band called Executioner who had recently released a record through the New Renaissance label), as well as songs from fellow Floridians R.A.V.A.G.E. (Raging Atheists Vowing A Gory End) and thrashers Sadus, the resulting *Raging Death* compilation was released in the summer of 1987. The LP was under Krgin's own Godly Records and was sold almost exclusively via mail order.

"There were only 2,000 or so of them pressed," says Krgin. "I think over time the legend grew much larger than the album itself."

Krgin, however, saw bigger things for Xecutioner.

"After that, we were ready to record, and Borivoj said he would try to shop us

Xecutioner live in Tampa, Florida. Courtesy Mick Harris

around," recalls Peres. "He literally told us that if he couldn't find a record label to sign us he'd put the record out himself under Godly Records."

"The band asked me if we would put it out if they gave us a finished album," says Krgin. "They wanted to know if we would press it up and basically release it for them. I even gave them some money towards the recording session—very little, though, it was like a few hundred dollars—because they didn't have the money to pay the balance of the recording costs."

Taking place at the end of 1987 at Morrisound Studios in Tampa, those eight-track recording sessions became the first metal production credits for a young studio engineer named Scott Burns.

"They were just kids, so I thought they were pretty cool," says Burns of Xe-cutioner. "And at the time, I thought these guys were pretty heavy—it was pretty extreme. I didn't know if I was totally into it, but I thought it was a bit different. So they asked me to do live sound for them, and I went out to the local shows and was helping them out. So then a few months later, Rick—the engineer that was doing their recording at Morrisound—he got sick and had to take some time off, so I just kinda finished it up midway."

"Once I got a copy of the tape," recalls Krgin, "I thought that it would be to everyone's benefit if I perhaps tried to shop the tape around and see if I could get them a proper record deal, rather than insist on us putting it out."

Before the cassette had even cooled, Krgin played the recording for his good friend Monte Conner, the director of A&R at Roadrunner Records.

"I knew him well enough that I could just go to him directly and play him the tape and explain to him where everything stood," Krgin states. "In the event that Roadrunner decided to pick up the band we would, at the very least, be able to be reimbursed for costs and make a little money on top of that."

"Roadrunner picked us up and paid back Borivoj the money he invested," says Peres. "They gave us more money to record four more songs, which is weird, because we went back in as a whole separate studio session. If you listen closely, you can hear songs that the production is a little different. But we didn't care, we were happy we were gonna have a record, even though, before long, so would just about everyone else in the state of Florida."

Across the Open Sea

W HILE THE UNITED STATES AND THE UNITED KINGDOM clearly had running starts in the death metal and grindcore sweepstakes, the rest of Europe, particularly Sweden, wasn't far behind. Of course, Sweden's socialist government didn't trigger the same repressive rebellion that US and UK youth experienced, but young fans of hardcore and punk still gathered in the country's capital city of Stockholm—where Nicke Andersson was raised on that same steady musical diet.

"When I was 7 years old I saw a picture of Kiss, and that was it for me," recalls Andersson. "I thought that they were the best band in the world; you know how it is when you're a kid. But then we got into punk rock, and the link for me was quite easy. We didn't know any other people that liked punk rock music, so we went into the stores and looked at the band pictures on records. So we ended up buying the records of the guys with the freakiest hair, like GBH and Discharge, and got really into the fast stuff. I didn't grow up listening to Slayer. I spent years before hearing that."

Inspired by such aggressive sounds, the youngster proceeded to make a racket in his home, taking up both drums and guitar. Andersson's parents' only reprieve came during the summer, when they dispatched him to *Smedsbo* summer camp.

"I thought summer camp was always more fun than school," says Andersson, who started attending the camp at the age of 8. "There were more people there listening to what I had to say."

Two of them were fellow campgoers Alex Hellid and Leif "Leffe" Cuzner, whom Andersson met in the summer of 1985 when he was only 13 years old. Over the three-week stay the trio developed a friendship that was initially based on a common appreciation for aggressive music.

Nihilist circa 1987 (left to right: Leif, Nicke, Buffla, Alex)

"It was probably because of those guys and summer camp that I got into metal," says Andersson. "That's where we formed our first band, Sons of Satan, because they had equipment at the summer camp."

Although Sons of Satan never emerged from a campsite tent, Hellid, Cuzner and Andersson remained good friends over the next two years, eventually forming a new hardcore band called Brainwarp in early 1987.

"We were into Jerry's Kids, DRI, Suicidal Tendencies, Bad Brains, and that kind of stuff," Andersson recalls. "It was a crossover period."

This was certainly accurate for Andersson, who had also been playing in a thrash metal-inclined act since the 8th grade with local friends Lars-Goran "L G" Petrov and Uffe Cederlund under a moniker, which, according to the drummer, "changed names every Thursday."

"For me," he says, "it didn't matter if it was metal or punk, it just had to be super fucking fast. I remember going into the [Stockholm] record store Heavy Sounds, that carried all the speed metal, death metal, and punk records, and you would listen to a record on the headphones, and after two seconds if it wasn't fast enough you took it off and had to hear another record."

In direct response to his need for speed, the drummer elected to combine the lineups of Brainwarp and his unnamed metal project into a wickedly fast new death metal band called Nihilist in mid-1987. "Well, we put in those blast beats," says Andersson. "The only other bands doing that would be hardcore bands at the time. But the influences definitely came from Napalm Death and Repulsion."

Guitarist Cederlund and vocalist Petrov, however, were only considered "session musicians" by the time Nihilist recorded their first demo, the three-track *Premature Autopsy*, just a few months later in March of 1988.

"We were looking for a vocalist, and L-G, I don't think he was an actual member," says Andersson. "But it just turned out that we were onto something good."

Well, kind of. Shortly before the recording, the band recruited vocalist Matthias Boström, crediting him as Nihilist's new frontman in the *Premature Autopsy* liner notes, even through he was unable to perform on the recording. Just a few months later, however, Boström departed, and Petrov was installed as Nihilist's full-time vocalist. But when Cuzner expressed his wish to move to guitar, the group was again in need of a bassist. Fortunately, the band's members knew everyone within the city limits who might be interested in filling the position.

The first candidate was lifelong Stockholm resident Johnny Hedlund. 18 years old at the time, he may have been a little more mature than the rest of the group, but he wasn't exactly exuding responsibility.

"He was four years older than us, so he was the one who went to the government liquor store," says Andersson. "He was really cool about it. He was like an older brother, sorta. He took care of us and made sure that we didn't drink too much."

Socializing with a group of underground metalheads affectionately dubbed *Bajsligan* (Swedish for "the shit league"), the collective actually partied underground nightly in the city's subway tunnels after service ended for the day.

"Some of the stations in Sweden, they don't have any guards, so we figured, 'Let's take the biggest station where we knew the guards would be farthest away from the actual platform where people step on and off on the trains,'" Hedlund recalls. "So we would meet at 8:00 at night. After the first 15 or 20 people that showed up, that would be okay. But then when we started to be 50 or 60 or 70 people with tape recorders and beer bottles, that was just a terrible noise. And people had no idea what that was all about—all those people headbanging, it must have looked crazy. They would play very terrifying music to normal people. We played the first Morbid Angel demo or bands like R.A.V.A.G.E. at full volume, and it kinda disturbed a lot of people. We really had to find places where we didn't disturb people and where they would not call the police on us.

"Back then, all the people that were into death metal hung out at those parties." Hedlund continues. "In Stockholm, you could say that it was about 60 or 70 people in total that were really into this type of music—then maybe another 100 or 150 in the rest of the country. So it was really, really small back then in the mid-'80s. There were also really few extremely talented musicians. I mean, everybody was playing more for the heck of it and for the fact that we were definitely not poseurs. We wanted to start our own little world, which was pretty much what we did. And very few people that did not like extreme music would socialize with us. And then it grew. More and more people got into this music because they saw that we had a really good time. It was more or less like a family of people. As I remember it, I was probably just at a party where I was asked to join Nihilist because they knew I played the bass and they had a spot for me. But it was a natural thing to do as well. If I didn't join Nihilist in '88, it is very likely that I would have joined somebody else or formed my own band probably the same year."

With the addition of Hedlund on bass, Nihilist began writing new material and rehearsing with increased regularity.

"I was so fucking into the music," says Andersson of the period. "I hadn't even got laid by that time. That was really the wrong kind of music for that. There was no girl in that scene for at least five years."

In early December, the band recorded another three-song demo, *Only Shreds Remain*. It was also their first session at Sunlight Studio with engineer Tomas Skogsberg.

"I worked with some speed metal and stuff like that, but I think the death metal started for real in '87 and '88," recalls Skogsberg who founded the studio as a means to record his own punk rock bands in the mid-'80s. "The first band I did was Morbid, who were another Swedish band, but then it was Nihilist."

Often recognized for helping cultivate Nihilist's unique buzzing guitar sound, Skogsberg is actually quick to defer the credit to a small piece of electronic equipment.

"Some of the guys call me the king of midrange," the producer laughs. "I love midrange, that's my frequency. We used the distortion pedal DS1, the orange one.

(bottom) Nihilist early 1988 (left to right: Nicke, Alex, Johnny, Leif, L-G). (top) *Premature Autopsy* demo cover

Nihilist 1988: (left to right: Nicke, Uffe, Johnny, L-G, Alex)

I think I used it for everything in the beginning; for the vocal, for the hi-hat—everything."

"It was our guitarist, Leffe, who actually came up with that sound from the Boss Heavy Metal pedal," offers Andersson. "You have the midrange on full. I think you have everything on full. He bought the pedal and just cranked it. He's the one to blame."

Shortly after the recording, however, Cuzner's family moved back to his native Canada in early 1989, forcing the band to fill yet another personnel gap. The logical choice was former session guitarist Uffe Cederlund, who at the time was playing guitar for Swedish extreme metalists Morbid. Within months, the reconfigured Nihilist recorded their third demo, the two-song *Drowned*, and concentrated more on playing shows almost exclusively at Stockholm youth clubs.

"Nobody wanted to touch us, really," says Hedlund of the band's gigging reputation. "We were still the black dogs of hell. The media here in Sweden, they would spit at us. There would be no way in hell that they would accept our form of music or lyrics. We did this one show in '89, and it was at this place where they said, 'You guys are not gonna pull more than 100 people, so you can't demand money for this show or even food.' So we said, 'Look, there will be more than 100 people. We have friends that are 150 people.' And the amount of people that paid to see the show was about 350. There was another 200 that were outside that were about to tear the place apart since they could not get in. So at that time we realized, 'This is so big now that we could actually be able to do a record.'"

Hedlund, however, would never get that opportunity as a member of Nihilist. In fact, it was terminal creative differences between the bassist and Andersson that eventually led to the band's sudden breakup in late 1989.

"It was Nicke's band, really," Hedlund explains. "I was just the bass player. But we didn't agree on certain things. I think it was the right decision, still. I think that if we had been in the same band, I doubt that it would have been a good band, because we had very different ideas on how to play music and what the vocals should be like and what the live show should look like. Then, all of a sudden, professional aspects came into it all, because we were growing and we had to make decisions that we never had to make before, and everything just turned into a totally different situation."

"You're kids and you do stupid things," concedes Andersson. "And I think, to be quite honest, we didn't wanna play with Johnny anymore, so we broke up and formed again like four days later, which is fucking nasty. It's really brutal. I could have been like, 'Hey, it's not working,' because we had different ideas. It's cowardice, that's what it was."

Entombed, the new group formed by Andersson, was essentially Nihilist sans Hedlund. The music, lyrics and personnel all remained unchanged—even the band's logo was ultimately the same font as Nihilist's old logo with a new set of letters. Hedlund, meanwhile, recruited fellow musicians from the *Bajsligan* to form his new outfit Unleashed.

"I liked the music we played in Nihilist; I really enjoyed it," says Hedlund. "There were just small things here and there that I would want the band to stand for, and Nicke wanted his band to take a different direction. I also knew for a fact that if you're gonna start a band that's gonna last for some time, not only is there a business aspect of it that you have to consider, but you have to find the right person for the job. So you will have to get along, and not only get along, but get along very, very well. There was no doubt in my mind that I would find the right people, and the first lineup was

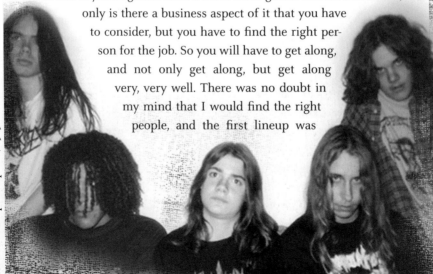

First Entombed promo photo, 1989

complete in November of 1989."

By then, the late Nihilist had inspired numerous Swedish youth to form new high-velocity, brutally heavy metal acts throughout the country. The earliest of these was fellow Stockholm band Carnage, which was founded by guitarist Michael Amott in early 1988.

"Before that, I was in a more hardcore band called Disaccord—kind of a mixture between thrash and hardcore," says Amott. "The band had come from the hardcore scene, but I had brought in a metal edge with more heavy metal guitar-type stuff. But when I wanted to go for the more death metal approach, they weren't happy with that, so the next day I formed Carnage.

"And I just couldn't find any people that were into it," Amott continues. "There were just problems all around finding like-minded musicians, because either people were into the punk hardcore scene or they were into the more traditional thrash scene; by that time I hated thrash because I was totally death metal, so I turned my back on thrash and I just hated everybody who listened to Metallica. At that time, Metallica had just released *...And Justice for All,* and seeing little kids in *...And Justice for All* t-shirts just made me angry. When you're a teenager, music is really important for your identity. So I was making my own Master t-shirts and Repulsion badges and stuff like that."

Before long, Amott recruited fellow guitarists Johnny Dordevic and Johan Liiva Axelsson, and drummer Jeppe Larsson, and recorded their first demo, the grinding *The Day Man Lost* in early 1989. Unsatisfied with the results, Amott actively courted more proficient musicians. His first choice was Fred Estby, drum-

Unleashed. Courtesy Century Media

mer of fellow Stockholm natives Dismember, who also began in 1988. Over a period of only 18 months, the group recorded a pair of demos, *Dismembered* and *Last Blasphemies*, both showcasing the buzzing guitar swarm established by Nihilist. But when Estby left Dismember in October 1989 to join Carnage, the original lineup of the band soon fell apart.

Carnage, however, quickly returned to the studio in mid-'89 to record their second demo, the far more intricate *Infestation of Evil*, which, like the early work of Dismember and Nihilist, featured a subtle sense of melody that much of the grindcore and death metal scenes had yet to explore.

"To me, that was kinda the natural thing to do, because as much as I was into the American death metal stuff like Repulsion and Master, it was really mono-tonic sounding with a lot of pretty simplistic riffs," says Amott. "I always liked the way Metallica and Megadeth took more melody into their music, and I first got into extreme metal through thrash, so I guess I brought that with me. With Nihilist and Carnage, I think a lot of the melody came from trying to incorporate horror film music, basically ripping off melodies from *The Exorcist* and *The Omen* soundtracks and stuff like that. We'd buy those horror movie soundtracks and basically try to play the melodies on the guitar. Usually, you'd get the melodies a little bit wrong. It's hard to create the big string arrangements with just a rhythm guitar behind a little melody—usually it would come out a lot more simplistic and fucked-up sounding. There's probably money due to some composer some-where."

Though Carnage's primary form of promotion remained tape trading within Sweden and abroad, the group performed the occasional show whenever possible.

"We didn't really play that many shows because we really didn't have that

(left) Carnage circa 1988

(right) Original Dismember lineup, early 1988

many opportunities," says Amott. "What people don't appreciate is, back then, that kind of music wasn't accepted. People just thought it was noise. All the metal people hated it and the punk kids didn't like the long hair. So we couldn't play the hardcore punk venues and we couldn't play the heavy metal venues. So when we got some gigs, we'd support thrash bands, because they were the most accepting.

"When Nihilist would invite us over to Stockholm to play, and we'd go up there and there would only be two other bands that were playing with us," the guitarist continues. "We'd play and we would just watch each other's set ,wondering why we weren't selling any of our t-shirts. Basically, you'd know everyone in the crowd. But it was so fresh then, and the cool thing is that I never thought of this as a career, really. I just wanted to play, because all of these American underground death metal bands that I was into, they didn't have any record deals, so I didn't think that was an option. We were playing so extreme that I thought we were just gonna keep on making demos. I didn't really think that there was any market for it. I couldn't even imagine looking at a vinyl album with a band like Testament—they just seemed like a totally different scene, just having an album out."

Carnage circa 1988

The scene seemed like an alternate universe to another another extreme metal act in the small suburb called Taby, just north of Stockholm. In early 1988, frontman Johan Edlund got the group off to a regrettable start, initially naming the band Treblinka after the Nazi concentration camp in Poland where approximately 870,000 Jews were murdered during World War II.

"We're not very proud of taking that name, and I'm very happy that we changed it," admits Edlund. "I know why we took the name. It had nothing to do with our music, so that was a stupid idea."

Soon Edlund sensibly renamed the band Tiamat and began developing a sound initially derived from other Swedish death metal bands, namely Nihilist.

"I think if someone should have credit for starting this whole thing it must be Nicke from Nihilist," says Edlund. "I remember he was the one that was really getting into it and ordering tapes from American bands. And I remember he had a Morbid Angel demo very early, and he just convinced us all that this was the new thing, and we believed him."

Still, after only a single 1988 demo, Tiamat evolved into something atypical of the Swedish scene.

"We were quite outside the Stockholm scene," says Edlund. "Although we were in the scene, because we knew all the guys and partied together and shared the same musical tastes, we sounded a little bit different. After the first demo, what we wanted to do was more go black metal, and we decided quite early to be

(left) Grave. Courtesy Century Media. (right) Tiamat's Johan Edlund as Hellslaughter

a black metal band. I guess we realized that we couldn't really compete with Nihilist. We thought that what they are doing is very good and they played a lot better than us. So we tried to find something that would fit us better."

As black metal was simultaneously gaining momentum in Sweden's neighboring country of Norway, Edlund adopted the stage moniker of Hellslaughter, donned spiked armlets and black-and-white corpsepaint, and incorporated more atmospheric elements, such as keyboards and acoustic guitars, into the band's approach.

"For me, black metal had a lot to do with the lyrics and the image of the band more than the sound," Edlund explains. "That's why I'd consider early bands, like early Venom and Mercyful Fate, black metal. But I remember we were always arguing over this with the Nihilist guys. I mean, they would never sing about Satan, for example, where we didn't want to sing about gore and zombies, so I guess that was the difference."

To one band located about 300 miles southeast of Stockholm, on the Swedish island of Gotland—the largest of the Baltic islands—gore and zombies held a greater appeal. Simply christened Corpse by guitarist/vocalist Jörgen Sandström, the teenage group lived far from the capital's death metal nirvana.

"We were quite isolated down there," admits Sandström, who co-founded the group in 1986 with guitarist Ola Lindgren and drummer Jensa Paulsson. "There was only us. There were a few heavy metal bands, but none of them were into death metal. We did maybe three shows or something over the years, and they all thought we sucked and laughed at us. Nobody understood what the hell we were doing."

And like nearly every other death metal band their age, Corpse found it difficult to keep a steady lineup intact.

"We decided to kick out our bass player [who was also named Jörgen] and it was in '87," he says. "We got to play a show, but we never told our bassist about the gig. Instead we just changed the name of the band to Grave and put it on the flyers and posters."

As Grave, the band grew heavier and more sonically accomplished, but still remained secluded in Gotland, save the six-hour ferry ride to Stockholm for the sole purpose of record shopping.

"In the beginning we hardly knew about anything beyond the underground scene in Gotland," says Sandström. "But later on we discovered a record store in Stockholm called Heavy Sounds, and they sold demo tapes. If you were in a band you could leave your tapes with them and they sold them for you. So we decided to make five copies of the Corpse demo, and ten of the first Grave demo and handed them over. So I think Nicke and Uffe from Nihilist bought a copy each. Then we ran into them at a gig somewhere and we bought their demos, and then they introduced us to the underground scene by sending us shitloads of tapes with bands we never had heard of."

Those tapes certainly left an impression with the band. Eschewing the buzzing approach of most Swedish death metallers, Grave soon developed a style more in line with groups from the international death metal underground.

"We didn't really look up to them," says Sandström, regarding the influence of his death metal countrymen. "We liked them and we became good friends with them, and we all supported each other spreading the demos and all that. And I don't think they looked at us any different either. I mean, we were all only like 16 when we all started to play death metal, and you really don't look up to someone your own age. We never tried to copy the other Swedish bands. We did like all of them, but our influences came from other bands. We all fucking worshiped Morbid Angel, Napalm Death and Repulsion."

Elsewhere, young Tomas Lindberg was nearly as secluded from Stockholm, but had the distinct advantage of living in Gothenburg, Sweden's second largest city. Located 500 miles west of Stockholm, on the coast of the country, Lindberg also had the benefit of regular access to the record collections of his older sister's boyfriends.

"Basically, the Stooges, the Ramones, MC5 all came from them," says Lindberg. "And after I found that out, I went a step further, to Discharge, Black Flag, and stuff like that. Then I got into Venom and Sodom and Slayer, and that's when it got worse. I think that the first music that I really found for myself without someone else helping me was death metal. You could easily find all the thrash records and all that, but finding death metal in '86, I was like, 'Wow, this is it! This is what I wanna do.'"

Only 15 years old, Lindberg adopted the moniker Goatspell and joined his first "serious" death metal band, Grotesque, with help from friend guitarist Kristian Wahlin—simply known as Necrolord—nearly two years later.

"It was mainly playing covers of Bathory and stuff like that the first year," Lindberg explains. "You tried to set up shows yourself with your friends and a lot of friends that weren't even into death metal because it was so new. But when you discover the whole underground thing, it's a huge thing to grasp when you're 16 years old. You're corresponding with people in Japan and Brazil, but in your hometown there are only two people that are into it. That was an attraction when you got into it. It's really special, like, 'I like this, but no one else does.' So what it all meant was that in three or four years, Grotesque played like four or five shows. Really, it took us two years to get going."

Unfortunately for Grotesque, they weren't going for very long. In November of 1989, the band recorded five songs, which collectively would be called *In the Embrace of Evil*, before entering Sunlight Studio a few months later to record

Grotesque circa 1988

their lone EP, the three-song *Incantation* for Swedish indie Dolores Records. But the band would get no further, splitting within weeks of the recording due to "internal differences."

"It ended up in this big mess," Lindberg admits. "When you're so young, you don't know how to be democratic or even polite. It wasn't a surprising end."

Quite extraordinary, however, was the unlikely breeding ground for extreme music that was the European country of Switzerland. The birthplace of avant-garde thrashers Celtic Frost in the early 1980s, central Switzerland was home to a small but vocal punk scene by the decade's end, out of which the quartet Fear of God formed in early 1987.

"In 1987, Celtic Frost's short thrash period was already over and [the pre-Frost band] Hellhammer seemed almost forgotten, at least in Switzerland," recalls Fear of God vocalist Erich Keller, 19 years old at the band's inception. "Then there was the hardcore punk scene with which all of us were heavily involved, but which, in return, didn't get involved with Fear of God too much. We were just too extreme. People used to walk out of our gigs. We didn't really get along well with other people anyway—we were so fully dedicated to our noise and our numerous scene involvements that it left little space for others."

Although at their onset not much faster than the speed punk of Discharge, Fear of God gained velocity with the addition of drummer Osi in late summer 1987.

"When Fear of God started out, high-speed was still fresh," Keller explains. "There had been bands from all over playing faster and faster, and of course, this was a huge influence for us. I mean, speedy drumming and fast riffing really set the music apart from older punk and metal bands, so it was of importance. But I can't say we wanted to be the fastest band in the world. We wanted to be as fast and tight as we could. That's more appropriate."

That meant 20-to-30-second bursts of grinding noise, which was nearly as rapid and devastating as early Napalm Death—and twice as politically minded.

"To us, Fear of God was a political band," says Keller. "Political not in terms of getting practically involved with the political fights that were going on around us at the time. Being political to us meant more being straight in what you do in your daily life—becoming vegetarian, boycotting multinationals or companies that were dealing with the racist apartheid regime in South Africa, and also silly things like smashing a butcher shop's windows. But the main thing was trying to build up a network of friends; self-managing the scene, keeping those out who tried to cash in."

And like many of Sweden's death metal bands, performing live was rarely an option for Fear of God. Playing no more than 15 shows throughout their existence, the band relied heavily on the underground tape-trading network to promote itself.

"I remember in the beginning I didn't know how to directly connect one tape deck to another, so I just used the built-in microphone," recalls Keller. "In order to obtain the best possible result, my whole family had to keep quiet until I got finished copying." The band released several live tapes in 1987 before eventually releasing one self-titled 7-inch in 1988. Within months, however, Fear of God met a swift demise.

"Mainly it was due to the fast-growing acceptance of what we did and the decline of other contemporary bands who, practically overnight, sold out or turned out to be complete nutshells," says Keller. "We suddenly felt quite alone, and when we played with Henry Rollins in Switzerland, in October 1988, and firsthand experienced all that rock 'n' roll bullshit, like not giving us time to soundcheck

Fear of God live 1987—88

properly or turning the PA down when we played, we decided right on the stage, during the set, that we'd call it off. It was also a very strange feeling to see that anonymous mass of people in front of you, little of which had come to see us or gave a shit other than, 'Wow, this is extreme! I can shock my parents with that if I buy it.' In retrospect, I would say that the band was about to lose its naive innocence that night, and all of us still cared enough not to let it become a tragedy. At that point in time, it was the right decision. Now, 15 years later, I still feel good about it."

By the time Fear of God officially folded, another grinding act was rising in the equally surprising locale of Vienna, Austria.

"Here in the '80s, there was hardly any metal, let alone extreme metal," says Alex Wank, a lifelong resident of the city. "There was nothing—zero. There really weren't many people that were interested, so it was just a couple of guys and we knew each other."

Like so many other aspiring young musicians, Wank dug deep into the underground and began corresponding with people from across Europe.

"I got all these tapes and played them for my friends," says Wank, whose

(left) Disharmonic Orchestra circa 1988. (right) Pungent Stench circa 1988

friends included Patrick Klopf, the future founder of one of Austria's earliest death metal bands, Disharmonic Orchestra, who formed in August 1987.

"We were influenced by Extreme Noise Terror, Heresy and Napalm Death," says Klopf, a native of Klagenfurt, located about 500 miles from Vienna. "But I'd say [we were influenced] mainly by Repulsion, old Master, Slaughter, Massacre, and a lot of old Voivod."

"More and more friends got interested in these bands, and some other blokes started tape trading, and slowly, but somehow, a scene got under way," says Wank. "Back then we used to listen to all these English grindcore bands, like Heresy, Ripcord, Concrete Sox, Doom—even from the older punk bands, like Chaos UK, but then early Earache stuff, of course. I played before in a band from '86 to '87, and they already tried to sound like these bands, or at least use a couple of influences."

In early 1988, Wank elected to combine those earlier grindcore influences with the death metal sounds emanating from the States in a new outfit he dubbed Pungent Stench. Equally important to the drummer was the band's lyrical concept, which delved deep into taboos such as sadomasochism, albeit with a healthy dose of humor in the generally furrow-browed underground.

"If we write something with extreme content then it must be hilarious for ourselves," Wank states. "If I have a good laugh when I finish something, then I think it's perfect and we use it. I think it's always been more serious in the States than it was in Europe for fans of death metal. It's aggressive music and it makes people even more aggressive. People were very, very serious about the music in general, which is okay, but they shouldn't take everything so serious."

Not quite as seriously, however, as they took things in Communist Poland in the early 1980s, where a small but passionate underground was beginning to evolve. Finding money and personal liberties in the final years of Communist rule was difficult, but getting heavy metal records from behind the Iron Curtain was nearly impossible.

"The only source was friends who had families outside of Poland or the 'black market,' but it was very expensive," says Piotr "Peter" Wiwczarek, who grew up in the city of Olsztyn, about a two-hour drive from Warsaw. "I usually traveled to Warsaw or Bialystok to tape some demos or vinyls. That was the only source for me. We would travel hours just to watch three Slayer tracks played from a videotape."

Wiwczarek gravitated toward the aggressive metallic sounds of Slayer and Dark Angel, but identified equally with the political stance taken by English punk bands like The Exploited and Antisect. Such interest eventually led the guitarist to form his first band, Vader, in 1983.

"It was a metal band, but not death metal," says Wiwczarek of Vader. "There

Vader live in 1985

was nothing like this at that time. We were among those who started extreme metal in our country, I guess. Some people were in shock [over what we were doing]. We were wearing pretty heavy armor, like spikes, chains and leather. For many, it was just funny, but the newborn metal generation loved that. Then we called Vader 'thrash black,' and that was extreme."

Communist metal wasn't limited to Poland, of course. Still under the strict rule of the Soviet Union, aspiring musicians in the country that was then known as Czechoslovakia had little opportunity to assemble any kind of rock band, much less some form of extreme metal.

"Our kind of music was a little forbidden, because the government felt that this kind of music is something from the west side of Europe, and they didn't like that," says Christopher Krabathor, a native of the South Moravia section of the country. "Not so many bands from the past here still exist, and if they do they just play in [what's now the] Czech Republic and Slovakia. They rarely get to play their music in foreign countries."

Krabathor, who adopted his surname from the metal band he founded

Krabathor's Christopher live circa 1988

in 1984, had nearly as much difficulty finding suitable musicians for such metal bands.

"We got lucky," Krabathor explains. "We were three friends in the beginning that wanted to play the same kind of music—something hard. Of course, people started to get older and they developed some other hobbies, too. I'm the only one from the old lineup. We have had a lot of people in the band. I guess that from ex-members we would be able to do four or five bands."

Vader seemingly had the opposite problem. "About 20 to 25 guys tried to play in Vader, but not too many knew what 'metal' meant," says Wiwczarek. "We had to wait about two years to fill up the lineup, and we were a five-piece band then. By then, in '87, we were not the only band [in Poland] playing this kind of metal. The others were Imperator, Slashing Death—where we found our drummer Doc—Merciless Death and Dragon. But nobody else survived.

"That was a different world then," Wiwczarek continues. "Shows, record stores, metal magazines, this was in short supply in our home country. But the passion was great—handmade t-shirts, self-painted patches. I remember, when Doc and I were in Stockholm, Sweden, and we got a chance to see a show with bands like Entombed, Carcass, Dismember—that was a real shock for both of us—so great! We only had one big metal festival in Poland once a year—Metalmania—and very few underground meetings."

Krabathor circa 1988

In Czechoslovakia, however, actual recording studios wouldn't even accept the rapidly developing death metal sounds of Krabathor. The band managed to record a trio of demo tapes—*Breath of Death, Total Destruction* and *Brutal Death*—on a friend's homemade mixing board in a small rehearsal room, but only after Christopher was forced by the government to enlist in the Czech army for 10 months and 22 days in 1989.

"I was supposed to be there two years, but after the regime fell I signed a paper and went home," Krabathor states. "Instead, I had to go to the civil service for nine months. It was a bad break for the band—just wasted time. But we wouldn't let any of that stop us."

Success?

ESPITE THE DEPARTURES of both Justin Broadrick and Nick Bullen, Mick Harris was determined to keep Napalm Death alive. In search of a guitarist, Harris turned to another Mermaid regular, Shane Embury, who only a few months earlier had started his own high-velocity project with his friend Mitch Dickinson. From the remnants of thrash act Warhammer, the pair formed Unseen Terror with Embury not only playing drums but also writing a great deal of the music. After much deliberating, however, the young multi-instrumentalist turned down the invitation to join his favorite band.

"I totally chickened out," Embury admits. "At first, I said, 'Yeah, I'd like to do it.' But then I just sat back and I didn't say anything. It was approaching Christmas and I just went quiet on everybody. And they said, 'Do you wanna do it?' And I was like, 'Well, I don't think I'm quite good enough to play guitar yet.'"

Frank Healy was the next local musician drafted to be Napalm's guitarist, but the union was both short-lived and unproductive.

"We tried for like two or three months and he did two gigs with us—one at the Mermaid and one in

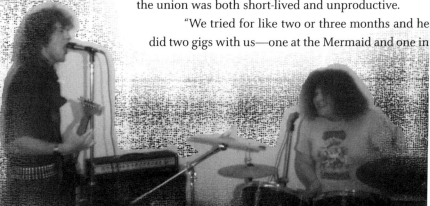

Unseen Terror at rehearsal. Photo: Lee Dorrian

Liverpool in front of Bill Steer and in front of Jeff Walker, who was singing with Electro Hippies at the time," Harris says. "It was disastrous, fucking disastrous."

"It was hysterical," recalls Steer, an eyewitness at the Liverpool club called Planet X. "They played this gig, and of course they didn't have a singer. A guy kept getting up and doing a little bit of vocal here and there, but it just wasn't coming through the PA. I think that was Rich Militia who would later join Sore Throat. But all I knew was there was a guy getting up on stage, lurching out with the microphone and there was no sound coming out. It was in shambles, but it was just fun because I got a kick out of watching people play that fast. I remember later that night I was talking to Mick and saying, 'Look, if you need a permanent guitarist, I'd be happy to do it.' So I think that's what started it off. He knew I was really into the band. I had met him before and he knew I was into the same kind of music. It was a big thing if you met somebody and they liked Death or Repulsion. You had a bond there straight away."

"Bill was about to start University, and he simply said to his parents, 'I wanna do this,'" Harris explains. "Basically the same as me. I had come out of a job and I didn't wanna continue with catering or go through the whole chef thing, so I think it was the same with Bill. So he asked his parents and they said, 'Well, look, the guy can come down here to practice.' So that's what we did. I taught myself—you're gonna love this—how to play guitar. I got myself a guitar, took all the strings off but the E and the A string, taught myself how to tune the A and the E to a bar chord, got myself a distortion pedal, plugged it through the stereo, and that was it. I still have my fucking notation to this day. It was a simple thing—Bill would come over and he had it down in one fucking rehearsal. He had the A-side of *Scum*—the demo—for so long. He knew the

Mick Harris rehearses with Extreme Noise Terror. Photo: Alex Wank

Lee Dorrian's first Napalm gig, Coventry. Photo: Gez McAteer songs back to front. I still have the rehearsal tape of me and Bill—a classic see-through TDK D-90. I still have got all of those from my tape-trading days. They were my preferred choice of tape. They were a good brand back then. And that was it—Bill was in."

With the addition of Steer, a vocalist was the only missing piece from Harris' ferocious puzzle. Coventry native Lee Dorrian was the next familiar face the drummer reached out to. Regularly promoting hardcore shows at a Coventry youth club called the Hand & Heart, Dorrian had booked Napalm Death several times over the previous year.

"Before I joined Napalm Death I must have seen them 50 or 60 times," says Dorrian. "Whenever they would go in a van to a gig somewhere outside of town, I would always jump in the van and go with them. I was just a fan of theirs, really. Mick and Jim just asked me if I wanted to join, and I was like, 'Well, yeah.' I had no intention of ever being in a band in my life. I just always loved the music and the scene.

"In fact, the first ever show I did with Napalm Death, I was promoting the show myself," he continues. "It was Antisect, Heresy, and Napalm Death opened. I remember one minute I was sitting at the door, the next minute I was on the stage, absolutely shitting myself, just staring at the ceiling and growling my head off."

With Napalm Death successfully resuscitated, Harris elected to do double-time in another band, accepting the drummer position for punk grinders Extreme Noise Terror.

"The addition of Mick came about as a result of original drummer Pig Killer turning a tad, shall we say, prima donna-ish, on us," says Extreme Noise Terror guitarist Pete Hurley. "He was seldom available to rehearse, let alone turn up to actually play gigs. He basically tried to hold us ransom, knowing that he would be hard to replace. Micky was a regular at the Mermaid and was a great drummer; unfortunately his personality was a different matter entirely."

Though Hurley sometimes clashed with Harris, the newly instated drummer soon became good friends with ENT vocalist Phil Vane, who nicknamed Harris the "Human Tornado" due to his hyperactive behavior. Such enthusiasm propelled Harris to make the four-and-a-half-hour trip by train from Birmingham to ENT's home base of Ipswich every other week.

"I used to wait for my unemployment check and buy my ticket," says Harris. "It started off that they'd pay my fare and then every other week it got less and less and less. But it was good fun, too. And whatever time wasn't spent with ENT at that point was spent with Napalm."

The newly assembled Napalm Death lineup, however, imposed certain limitations on the band. Above all, it effectively ended Napalm's days as the "house band" of the Mermaid.

Napalm Death live in Belgium 1987, featuring guitarist Mitch Dickinson filling in for Bill Steer.

"The way Mick put this band together, suddenly everybody was spread out," Steer explains. "He and Jimmy were living in Birmingham, Coventry was where Lee lived, and I was still up north. In fact, I'm certain we didn't do a gig together until we went to Europe."

Undeterred by geographic difficulties, the drummer continued to move Napalm—both figuratively and literally—at an accelerated pace. In May, the quartet returned to Rich Bitch Studios in Birmingham, where they had recorded just a few months prior, albeit with a much different lineup. Soon, however, their untried musical union faced another problem.

"Going into the studio, we hadn't rehearsed," says Harris. "Me and Bill had rehearsed. Jimmy knew the songs. Lee had only just finished writing some lyrics with Jimmy. So Lee brought all of these papers with him and wasn't quite sure where to sing."

"I had one rehearsal, and that was the night before we went in the studio, and I didn't know what I was doing, really," says Dorrian. "Mick had to cue me when it was time to come in and sing. I only kinda knew a few parts that I should have been doing on time and the rest was totally new to me."

"We just blasted the B-side out in a one-night session," states Harris. "Mitch [Dickinson] came along. Shane [Embury] came along and the Head of David guys came along. It was a confidence boost, because it was a few friends that had been into a studio—it certainly worked."

Although copies had been widely circulated throughout the underground tape-trading network, Digby Pearson still possessed the master tapes from Napalm Death's previous August recording session at Rich Bitch. When Justin Broadrick bequeathed him the recording in the fall of 1986, Pearson's bedroom distribution center/flexi-disc label Earache Records was still not a suitable means to properly distribute the music.

"I kinda spent the first year of the label in 1986 doing nothing, really, apart from research," says Pearson, who officially launched the Earache Records label at the age of 25. "Initially, it was a way to get off the dole in England. Back then, in the '80s, when you were unemployed in the UK, you had to go to visit the unemployment office every two weeks, and I didn't fancy doing that. If you start a company, you get the same amount of money and you don't have to visit the unemployment office every two weeks. You're not unemployed anymore, so it's a method for the government to reduce the jobless figures. It was called an 'Enterprise Allowance Scheme.' They didn't care what business you did, as long as you did something, and that meant that you were no longer unemployed. And it was an excuse to say, 'Wow, I'm a record company!' But the truth is I had no plans, nothing really."

By the time Napalm finished recording again, however, that had changed.

Pearson had already released a pair of legitimate records—an album from speedy California thrashers The Accused called *The Return of Martha Splatterhead,* and a split LP with British speedsters Concrete Sox and Heresy—under the Earache banner. Perhaps even more importantly, he secured distribution for the fledgling label throughout the United Kingdom.

"Living in the UK was quite important because of the strong independent music scene here and, even better, the strong independent distribution sector, which didn't exist until the punk explosion of the late '70s," says Pearson. "A company called Rough Trade came out of a record shop in West London and was very important in the whole scheme of things. Basically, they started Rough Trade Distribution, which was an independent distribution company, and for the first time ever it was like you didn't need to have major distribution in the UK to survive. So when I started my label there were people receptive to what you were doing. I mean, I was just some guy who wanted to put out an album by Napalm Death. Most people would be like, 'Get out of here.' But because of the history of the independent scene in the UK, it was actually no problem.

"I went to a company called Revolver," he continues. "They were part of the Rough Trade family and not afraid of left-field music. That was such an important moment, because they accepted my label. I had no track record or anything, and they were like, 'Yeah, sure, we'll distribute your records.' So I was like, 'Wow, I've got distribution. Great!'"

In light of this development, Pearson was now the clear choice to release Napalm Death's music. The band agreed to a deal with Earache to issue the August '86 Rich Bitch session featuring the Bullen/Broadrick/Harris lineup and the May '87 recording with the current incarnation of the band as one full-length LP. In June of 1987, Earache pressed and released 2,000 copies of Napalm Death's debut album *Scum* stickered with the words, "Debut album by the undisputed World's Fastest Band."

"I remember going down to the plant the day the record was pressed so I could get the first copy of *Scum* that came off the press," says Harris. "I was so excited and couldn't wait to just see it, so I took the first copy out of the first box and still have it to this day."

Almost immediately, Napalm embarked on their first genuine tour—a three-week European jaunt with Birmingham hardcore punkers Ripcord. By the time they returned to England in late July, bassist Jim Whiteley had grown disillusioned with what he believed was no longer a "level playing field" between the band's members. "I felt that the wholesale personality shift that had taken over Mick Harris during this period was irreconcilable with any reasons that I could find for wanting to contribute my time and effort any further," says Whiteley. "It felt like I was only there as a supplement to *his* band, even then only insomuch

Napalm Death in Holland, 1987. Photo: Steve

as I was capable of writing lyrics—though that didn't stop him from copywriting some of them as his own later. I've heard the one about bands being democracies led by dictators. I decided enough was enough."

"I can't say I took control," says Harris. "I felt some sort of responsibility that I just wanted to keep the whole thing together, but not as a leader, just keeping everything organized as far as rehearsals and shows and tours. Maybe that got to Jim, because he was a lot older and more educated."

A few weeks later, Napalm's outlook brightened. First, Whiteley was replaced by the once-reluctant guitarist Shane Embury on bass.

Perhaps even more importantly, the band was granted invaluable help from BBC Radio 1 DJ John Peel. A national treasure in England, Peel, who was hired by the BBC in 1965, continually sought out and championed new music, helping to usher in the punk and new wave eras of the '70s and early '80s. Every Tuesday, Wednesday and Thursday night, Peel willingly explored new directions and artists on his national radio program, helping break the careers of British pop luminaries like David Bowie and the Smiths in the process. A copy of *Scum* found its way onto Peel's desk and, like every other recording the DJ received, he spun it.

"I just thought that it was exciting and—obviously not a word the practitioners would like to see associated with this music—but I also thought it was fun," says Peel, who was 48 years old when he first played Napalm Death across national airwaves. "I started going to gigs and so on, and I liked the fact that people would do eight-second-long numbers and people would be shouting 'too long' or 'too slow!' A lot of various forms of popular music, people were becoming incredibly po-faced about it and wanted to see it as kinda exam subject material, so I quite liked the slightly tongue-in-cheek aspect of it."

One song in particular captivated the DJ—the one-and-a-half-second "You Suffer," which crammed the lyrics, "You suffer, but why?" into its brief eruption.

"I remember I was at Jimmy's on a Tuesday, and I was like, 'I wonder if [Peel's] gonna play it tonight?'" says Harris. "Then all of a sudden he put 'You Suffer' on and laughed, and he said, 'No, that can't be right?' And then he put it on again, and we were laughing, saying, 'He doesn't get it.' And then he played it a fucking third time. Then he plays 'The Kill,' and he played that twice, and I'll never forget, he said, 'I'll have to play some more of that tomorrow.' That was it. Obviously, students and other people who were listening to Peel as they did must have been assaulted and thought, 'What the hell was that?'"

"He played a couple of tracks and then he discovered 'You Suffer,'" recalls Dorrian. "That lasted just over a second, and he played it forwards, backwards, on 45, on 33, and he just couldn't believe the track."

Former Napalm Death guitarist Justin Broadrick was one of the many who heard Peel's initial Napalm Death broadcast.

"This is a day I'll never forget in my whole fucking life," he says. "I had just done a John Peel session—my first one ever—with Head of David, and we had come back home, and the following week it was on the radio. So I went to my friend's house, and we all sat around and listened to this Head of David session. He played the first Head of David song and then after that he played Napalm

Napalm Death circa 1987. Photo: Pat Evans

Death, and it was one of my songs, a song I actually wrote. It was 'The Kill.' We just sat there in absolute disbelief, like, 'Fucking John Peel is playing Napalm Death.' And as soon as we heard it we were like, 'What if Napalm Death becomes popular?'"

While their nation was still unsure what to make of Napalm Death, Peel clearly embraced them, inviting the foursome for their own Peel session on September 13th, 1987.

"It was fucking mental," says Harris. "We had no gear for the session. I still wasn't practicing. We just got together when it was time to do a record, because Shane and me were writing the material. Bill wasn't coming to Birmingham. I was going down there, and then finally Bill's parents were allowing him to come down. They used to drive him to Birmingham to my parents' house. He'd stop at my house, we'd have two rehearsals and then he'd go back home, and that was it. But we still managed to pull the session off."

The 12 tracks Napalm performed that day were, in fact, the most spectacularly fast things the band had recorded to that point. Within a matter of weeks of the broadcast, Earache was forced to re-press *Scum* to support the growing demand for the band's music. Out of morbid curiosity or genuine admiration, people were purchasing *Scum*, with sales even pushing the record as high as the eighth position on the UK independent charts. Just six months later, in March of 1988, Napalm Death were invited back to perform a second session on Peel's radio show.

"I was fucking stunned," says Broadrick of Napalm's growing countrywide reputation. "I really couldn't believe that this album that I just gave away one day without a due concern was now lauded as some fantastic novelty record. And for the first six months, regardless of how popular it was, it did appear that that would be it. You didn't think for a moment that this would grow into a big worldwide scene. Still, the network had gone past all of the early tape trading—this was serious now."

"It got to a stage where you'd have John Peel at night taking the band quite seriously, although it seemed a bit extreme and all that," says Dorrian. "But in the afternoon there was a guy called Steven Wright. He's a real prick DJ and he used to do a quiz, and if you got a question wrong you'd have to be subjected to hearing Napalm Death. So on the one side you kinda had people getting what it was about, and on the other side you had people that just thought it was a silly joke."

"Wright saw it is as a joke, which I always thought was deeply insulting," says Peel. "But there was nothing you could do about it apart from kill him, and that seemed to be rather extreme. But he now works on Radio 2, which is the kind of the middle-of-the-road station, which is almost comparable to death."

As the press discovered Napalm Death, the spotlight inevitably shined on the Earache record label as well. Pearson understood he needed to keep the re-leases coming. Fortunately, in his search for talent, he didn't need to look beyond Napalm. Pearson signed Shane Embury's pre-Napalm outfit, Unseen Terror, who entered Rich Bitch in September '87 and recorded their *Human Error* debut. The label chief was also keenly aware of guitarist Bill Steer's other band, the blister-ingly fast death metal act Carcass. In 1985, Steer, then 15 years old, started an em-bryonic version of the band with drummer and fellow Wirral native Ken Owen, also 15.

"There was the pair of us and a couple of school friends, and we decided to form a band," Steer explains. "We were really into Slayer, and stuff like that, so I think we maybe had two or three rehearsals, and that was it. The name of the band was Carcass, that was what I came up with and, then that band disappeared. And then a year or so later, I was playing with these other people, these sorta punk guys."

By then, it was early 1987, and Lancashire local Jeff Walker had just been dismissed from Liverpool Anarcho punks Electro Hippies.

"We did a gig up north in Lancashire, and we were driving back and they just dropped me off there in the middle of nowhere," recalls Walker of his former bandmates. "And even though it was the drummer's band, Bruno, the bass player was leaving and I think he was just put up to say, 'We don't want you in the band anymore.' The reasons were pretty wishy-washy—they didn't feel I was contribut-ing enough financially or whatever, but it turned out for the best. They did me a favor."

"Jeff then drifted into our band," says Steer. "Then I persuaded the rest of the group to change the name to Carcass. And then once Jeff was on board, I felt like there was a kindred spirit there, and he just said to me, 'C'mon, it's not gonna happen with these guys. If you're listening to Master or Repulsion, it's not gonna really sound like that because they don't play that way.' So then when we needed new members I thought about Ken again, because, by this point, Ken had a drum kit. The year before, he didn't."

In the summer of '87, with Owen in tow, the group enlisted the mysterious Liverpool native Sanjiv to provide vocals for the group's *Flesh Ripping Sonic Torment* demo.

"I doubt that anyone ever knew his last name," says Walker of Sanjiv. "He was a strange character. He was a bit older than everyone else. When we were turn-ing 20 he was like mid-to-late 20s and would walk around with Siege written on his hand in marker. He was an adult, and he'd get up in the morning and the first thing he would do was write Siege or Deep Wound on the back of his hand."

Sanjiv only performed a single show with the band before Walker and Steer assumed the vocals, adding them to their respective bass and guitar duties. Then based on their very first demo, Pearson handed Carcass a recording contract.

"Of course, at the time, Carcass really had nothing happening for us," says Steer. "The best thing we could do would be to play a Liverpool club called Planet X, so we'd do little bits and pieces there. So people didn't even know about the band until Dig offered us an album deal, and that happened really quickly; in retrospect, almost too quickly, because we just weren't ready, but we still got 22 songs together."

"Ken wrote some of the first songs and Bill started writing some, and I remember I was probably up my own ass at the time thinking we should have been singing something more serious, but I saw the lyric sheet and it suddenly clicked with me," says Walker. "On the surface, it was all these death metal lyrics and it was clichéd, but it was funny, and I suddenly just stopped being a miserable bastard and wised up to the fact that you don't have to be serious all time with the lyrics. So it was me that went overboard writing lyrics. I took out my sister's nurse's dictionary—she was just a student nurse at the time—and that's how the whole technical aspect came about. The whole medical thing was down to just that my sister had a medical dictionary in my parents' house, so I just applied that. I just tried to bring a whole new angle to the thing that Death and Repulsion were doing, just tried to make it more—intellectual is the wrong word—but more kind of professional? I don't know. More scientific, I guess, rather than just it being

Bill Steer at early Carcass rehearsal. Photo Aleister Steer

slasher/horror, I'm-gonna-kill-you stuff."

In December of '87, the band entered the increasingly occupied Rich Bitch to record their debut album with engineer Mike Ivory.

"The first album was really a three-way thing," Walker explains. "Ken wrote a lot of stuff, Bill did and I did. But I never wanted to be the singer, especially after being in the Electro Hippies. I remember we were on the train going up to Birmingham to do the vocals [for the first album], and we had just kind of kicked Sanjiv out. So we just sat on the train and ironed stuff out like, 'You do this. You do that. I'll do that.' And we all took a share of it."

Unhappy with the session's results, the trio remixed the album several times over the next few months before it was eventually released as *Reek of Putrefaction* in June of 1988.

"That record does sound kind of chaotic, but believe me, it could have been even worse," says Steer. "I think [Ivory] was even trying to persuade Ken to use Simmons drum pads or something bizarre at one point, because—you have to understand at that time, you'd go into the studio and the engineer wouldn't have any clue about what music you were playing. They had no reference point. Some of these people had never even recorded a standard heavy metal or punk band before."

"We did the album in a day, and the guy who was engineering it really messed it up," concurs Walker. "But I like the way it sounds now, in retrospect. At the time, we were like pretty upset to where we walked out. It just sounded shitty to us. But that's part of the attraction—because it just sounds so raw."

As he'd before with Napalm Death, Peel was immediately taken with *Reek* and added Carcass to his growing playlist of extreme British bands, that now included Napalm, Extreme Noise Terror, Bolt Thrower, Unseen Terror, as well as a pair of acts—Doom and Jeff Walker's old band the Electro Hippies—from the

Carcass at Rich Bitch studio. Photo: Lee Dorrian

Dewsbury-based Peaceville Records, which was initially established in 1981 as a "cassette label."

"I did 51 cassettes," recalls Hammy, Peaceville's singular-named, enigmatic founder. "That's really only getting a bedroom recording from a band and making it available by duplicating cassettes. It really wasn't a big production, very low-key—never had any money or anything. I was totally sold on that and loved anar-

CARCASS
"REEK OF PUTREFACTION"
The debut splatter platter of anatomically correct, bowel corroding, audio-torture from them; amansogoic evisceration of grotesque frenzied brutalization. 22 tracks of fetid fetishes and grisly fates that will make your vitriolic juices burn thru' your stomach wall.

Suggested Retail Price £4.98 U.K.
EARACHE RECORDS. MOSH-6

(bottom left) Former Carcass vocalist Sanjiv captured during his only live performance with the band, 1987. Photo: Andy Barnard

(top) Carcass' *Reek of Putrefaction* album

cho-punk and all of the grindy, crusty life. But that was the start of the Peaceville proper, and then shortly after that we signed Electro Hippies and Doom.

"These were Peaceville's second and fourth 'real' albums that Peel was playing, and they sold like 6,000 copies each in the first week," Hammy continues. "John Peel gave them both a session, so he was playing them constantly on national radio. They became hip to mention in the media and things like that, and Peaceville had instantly become totally successful."

The success afforded Peaceville immediate growth, allowing Hammy to sign Norwegian avant-garde death metallers Darkthrone along with the California-based Autopsy, featuring former Death drummer Chris Reifert.

"I think they just wrote us a letter," recalls Reifert. "The first offer we got was from some label that sent us a couple copies of some records they just put out, and they just looked like a 3rd grader put them out. Even we, who were like stupid teenagers, were like, 'No way.' So the second offer, which we didn't know anything about, was Peaceville, and we said, 'Okay, contract, let's sign it.' And we'd never heard of Peaceville because they were so new and they hadn't done much yet, but it just seemed cool. Later I found out Peaceville wanted us because Jeff Walker from Carcass played our demo for Hammy."

Electro Hippies live. Photo: Pete C.

(top right) Doom. Photo: Lee Dorrian. (bottom right) Hammy & Digby Pearson in Holland

Napalm Death circa 1988. Photo: Ken Sharp

However, it wasn't Walker's A&R skills, but rather his work with Carcass that continued to bring him attention from John Peel. The DJ even declared Carcass' *Reek of Putrefaction* debut as his favorite album of 1988 in the English newspaper *The Observer*.

"Maybe John Peel made it seem more pretentious than three kids in a crazy cheap studio in Birmingham making a racket with bad production," says Walker. "Regardless, he made it more palatable when he gave it the seal of approval."

Part of the attraction for Peel was *Reek*'s stunningly graphic cover art. In fact, this collage of grisly autopsy photos collected from medical journals proved to be an appropriate jacket for songs like "Oxidised Razor Masticator," "Manifestation of Verrucose Urethra," and "Vomited Anal Tract."

Another *Reek* number, "Microwaved Uterogestation," best exemplified the band's over-the-top lyrical approach, featuring the memorable couplet of "Formentatious perflation hydrogenates your foetal cisterna/ Coagulating haemorrhage and your congenital hernia."

"I guess we just wanted to cause some friction," says Steer. "Part of it was that teenage thing where it's fun to offend, but there was also this streak of humor running through it. If it was just some brain-dead guys going on about raiding graves or something, that would have been one thing, but when we threw in these other elements it suddenly became something else."

For Carcass that angle was vegetarianism. Although their implication that animal and human meat were one and the same was often clouded amid the gore of their album artwork, Steer and Walker were both devout vegans, while Owen was a vegetarian.

"At the time we were really hardcore about that," Steer explains. "That was what we were really into and we couldn't see any other way to live, so that was all wrapped in the whole package."

If Carcass was making rumblings in the underground, then the buzz on Napalm Death was louder than a Harris blast beat. Early in the summer of 1988, Napalm reconvened to record their sophomore album, traveling to Birdsong Studios in Worcester with house engineer Steve Bird. They even rehearsed *twice* this time before the sessions, allowing for a smoother recording.

"When we were actually recording the album, it just felt a lot more together and a lot more precise," says Dorrian. "I just remember thinking things like, 'We really gotta make this as extreme as we possibly can, but it's also gotta be a bit more rounded.'"

When the resulting *From Enslavement to Obliteration* was released in September of 1988, the group knew they had written a better, more cohesive record than their debut. That, however, didn't prepare them for the attention that ensued.

"Napalm knocked fucking Sonic Youth out of the number one position in the

Napalm Death *NME* cover, November 1988.

independent charts with *Enslavement*, which sold, straight away, something like 35,000," recalls Harris. "I couldn't believe it."

The record's success was aided by the ever capricious British press, who granted the band extensive coverage in *Melody Maker, Sounds,* and also awarded them a cover story in a November edition of *New Music Express*. Steven Wells, the author of the *NME* cover piece, even said of the band, "This is not the 'next stage' of rock n' roll, this is its grave digger... This is the music metal and punk hinted at. This is the music for which Jerry Lee, The Who, 'Helter Skelter,' The Ramones, Damned, Pistols, Northern Soul, Speed Metal and Speed Core were just practice."

Other British journalists even attempted to christen the band's extreme approach with the term "Britcore."

"The reason *FETO* outsold *Scum* was obviously because it was a second album and its popularity had grown, but also Earache as a label had gotten its act together better," says Pearson. "We knew how to put out a CD, for instance, and make that eligible for the independent charts. That chart is actually quite central to the whole growth, because suddenly these bands were in people's faces and they started going, 'What's this grindcore stuff? Who's this crazy band that are above Sonic Youth and Pop Will Eat Itself?'"

"At that time, when *NME* were covering Napalm, I think people actually loved the fact that we were working-class kids," says Dorrian. "All the music that was trendy was a bit dippy University student and Happy Mondays indie kind of stuff. And we really just didn't give a fuck."

"I guess it's easier to achieve that notoriety in a smaller country," Steer offers. "But Napalm was in a fantastic position, of course, because the band was placed right in between all of these things that happened at once. Looking at it worldwide, there was the underground death metal thing, the underground hardcore thing and the merging of those two scenes, so Napalm was in exactly the right place for that, because nobody could really pin down which side of the fence the band was on."

The attention helped make Napalm Death the hot ticket in town, eventually enabling the band to draw over 1,000 concertgoers at a London show in late 1988.

"It was very mixed," Dorrian says of the Napalm audience at the time. "It was indie kids, school teachers, there were one or two metallers, but not so many, a lot of punks as well—it was just very diverse. I think it was a special time in music in England, because at that time, Britcore, or whatever you wanna call it, although it was an underground kind of music, it was very kind of anti-establishment and it did join a lot of people from different backgrounds together. It was just pretty diverse times."

"It just went ballistic," says Harris. "We were just doing huge gigs and the crowds were going mental. All of these indie kids were into grindcore and UK hardcore. You had loads of bands forming. It was just a big movement. For us, we just wanted to get up there and fucking do it and get it faster and faster and faster."

As Napalm sped onwards, so too did the Earache label. The success allowed (and forced) Pearson to move the Earache operations from his bedroom to a proper Nottingham office in late 1988. The rapid growth of the label also meant that the entrepreneur needed help. One day, in November of '88, Pearson received a call from old British indie label friend Martin Nesbitt. At the time Nesbitt was working for an independent label called Fundamental in Covington, Georgia, just outside of Atlanta. When Fundamental's distributor declared bankruptcy, Nesbitt offered his services to Pearson, who awarded Nesbitt a job as his right-hand man at Earache.

Mick Harris at Kaleidoscope club in Birmingham, June '89. Photo: Mitch Dickinson

"I came back to England in December and started working with him," says Nesbitt. "For me, I just knew nothing of this music until I started at Earache. The first thing we did was work on this big gig, which was filmed for the Arena TV arts show documentary on heavy metal at ULU [University of London Union] in London, which was in January or February. And it was just a big show, with Napalm, Bolt Thrower, Carcass and Intense Degree."

Pearson and Nesbitt knew, however, that fresh product from the bands—especially Napalm Death—was vital for Earache's continual development. In May of 1989, Napalm was commissioned to record their first EP. At Harris' urging, the band booked time at the Slaughterhouse studio in Yorkshire, hoping, according to the drummer, to showcase "a more death metal influence."

"As far as I remember, the reason we ended up going there was because Mick really liked the production on a record by the Sundays and he saw that it was recorded at the Slaughterhouse," says Steer. "There's no particular reason why that sound, however good it is, would translate to what we were doing."

When Napalm arrived, the band was greeted by house engineer Colin Richardson, who previously worked with hardcore punkers like Discharge and GBH. That aggressive music pedigree helped him properly capture the extreme sounds Napalm Death desired.

"The thing was, nobody knew how to deal with that kind of music in those days," Richardson explains. "I think if anybody put in some input, the labels and the bands were going, 'Woo-hoo! Somebody's actually trying to help.' I remember there was another engineer there, and he was like, 'This is just shit. It's just noise.' And I was like, 'No, it's just really aggressive and exciting. You got the wrong take

Napalm Death circa June '89. Photo: Mitch Dickinson

Martin Nesbitt circa 1989. Photo: Mick Harris

on it.'

"I just wanted to get some clarity going and keep it aggressive and in-your-face," he continues. "And I think I was learning about the music the same as the bands were, really, hoping something good came out. I don't think there was a master plan. I just had to make sure that it wasn't embarrassing."

After the resultant six-track *Mentally Murdered* EP was finished, Harris continued to pursue a more traditional death metal direction for Napalm Death, searching out a second guitarist to complement Steer. Harris turned to Carnage guitarist Michael Amott, a Swede with whom the drummer had been tape trading for years.

"I first wrote him a letter in '87," remembers Amott, "and he replied immediately and sent me all these tapes. Mick Harris got me into the whole death metal thing, really, and the whole tape-trading thing. He introduced me to bands that I'd never heard of, like Repulsion and Master, and all these kinds of demo bands, like Obituary before they were even called Obituary.

"I spent a lot of time in England," he continues. "I used to go on my holidays. I used to take a ferry over to England and just travel around with Napalm Death in the back of their van to gigs and stuff like that, and just sit on the side of the stage."

During one of those visits in the spring of '88, Harris implored Amott to join Napalm Death as a second guitarist.

"I came back over and I learned all the songs," Amott says. "I went up to Bill Steer's house in Liverpool, his parents' house, where he was living at the time, and he was showing me all these Napalm Death tunes. And basically Bill said, 'This is great, because this is the window I've been waiting for. When you know the

Napalm Death live in 1989. Photo: Nick Royles

songs you can step in, and I'm gonna get out and I'm gonna focus on my other band Carcass.' I was like, 'Whoa, that's not what I wanted.' I was looking forward to playing with Bill."

"I think it was even more complicated, because around that time I suggested that he join Carcass," admits Steer. "I imagined Carcass sounding really good with a second guitar player, and I think it all just got a bit weird for him."

"When they asked me to join they only had the *Reek of Putrefaction* album at that point, and I thought that sucked," says Amott. "So I was like, 'No, I'll just focus on my own band back home in Sweden. You'll be all right. This isn't gonna go anywhere.' And the whole thing fell apart for me and I just went back home."

More personnel turbulence soon found Harris, not with Napalm but with Ipswich grinders Extreme Noise Terror, who booted Harris from the band in mid-'89.

"Mick was the archetypal hyperactive child," says former ENT guitarist Pete Hurley when pressed for an explanation of Harris' dismissal. "He was an amazing drummer, but to go on tour with such a temperamental beast became a little wearing, to say the least. It was a shame that we had to sack our best drummer, but some things just have to happen. We were definitely much slower before the advent of Mick joining, but the jump in speed was really easy to achieve when you have the percussionist to do it. I really learned the 'a band is only as good as their drummer' lesson there."

"They said I was too metal for the band," Harris explains. "Napalm was getting a lot of interest, and I think it was pissing the rest of them off. Napalm being classed as more of a metal act than hardcore might not have looked too good with ENT having a metal drummer. And I remember [ENT vocalist] Phil Vane coming along at the end of a gig that Napalm Death played with Killdozer one night, and he said, 'I'm sorry, Mick, but the rest of the fucking band aren't down anymore and I've been left to tell you that you're out of the band.' And I thought, 'No problem. No worries, Phil, it's been good.'"

While Harris was enjoying a little more free time, on the strength of a few phone calls, Napalm vocalist Lee Dorrian was busy organizing a brief summer tour of Japan with Japanese punks S.O.B., who had recently toured Europe with Napalm. Though the Japanese scene was miniscule compared with what was happening in England, a few "Japanese hardcore" bands—as they were simply classified throughout the underground—like S.O.B. exerted a significant influence on extreme music.

"We were very into the Japanese hardcore scene, and, again, tape trading," admits Embury. "I traded with some Japanese people, but S.O.B. were one of our favorites. The first time heard we S.O.B. it just totally reminded us of Siege, actually. And we freaked on them. Micky and I just couldn't believe it. Some of the riffs on *From Enslavement* were definitely inspired by S.O.B. Lee Dorrian wrote to their lead singer, and he found out that S.O.B. was into Napalm and that we had influenced them as well. But part of the reason the impact was so small was because almost all of the bands except S.O.B. never made it out of Japan."

Although Napalm's *Scum* and *FETO* albums had only recently been made available in the country via Earache's new licensing deal with Japanese label Toys Factory, the group embarked on the precarious two-week expedition. Martin Nesbitt accompanied the band.

"Three nights in, everybody was going on at Lee, saying, 'This is really badly organized,'" says Nesbitt. "We didn't have hotels to stay at, we were sleeping on

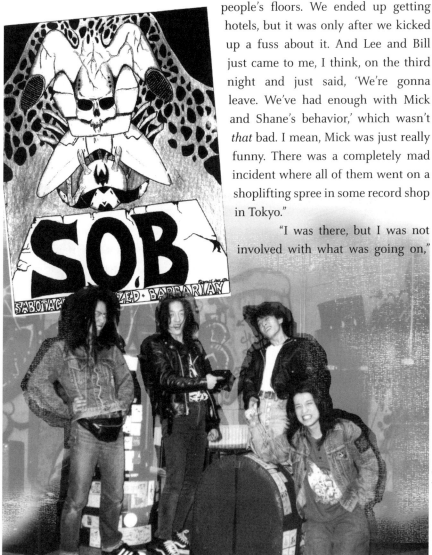

people's floors. We ended up getting hotels, but it was only after we kicked up a fuss about it. And Lee and Bill just came to me, I think, on the third night and just said, 'We're gonna leave. We've had enough with Mick and Shane's behavior,' which wasn't *that* bad. I mean, Mick was just really funny. There was a completely mad incident where all of them went on a shoplifting spree in some record shop in Tokyo."

"I was there, but I was not involved with what was going on,"

S.O.B. circa 1989. Photo: Mick Harris

Harris contends. "Shane and Lee certainly didn't feel bad about it at those prices. They were like, 'These are bootlegs. We are not paying these prices, we're gonna rob.' And they shoved a few down their jackets."

"I remember I arranged to meet up with John Zorn out in Japan and he took us all out for lunch," Nesbitt explains. "Then after lunch me, Bill and John Zorn are just walking down the street, and the rest of the band just come out of the shop with the alarm going off and arms full of bloody records. I was just completely embarrassed and so was Bill. And the Japanese people never stopped them, because they were Napalm Death, so they just got away with it."

Beyond the good-natured antics, Dorrian was now severely disillusioned with the internal state of Napalm Death.

"I thought two people in the band had just turned into rock stars, really, and they were just in it for the money, and to me it kinda defeated the whole point of what Napalm was about in the first place," says Dorrian. "I mean, okay, if it was any other band then it maybe wouldn't be so important, but the fact that Napalm started out with a significant message and stood for something that I always thought to be quite sincere—when I saw that kind of falling apart, I started to lose a bit of interest. Musically, the band wanted to do more death metal, and I thought what we were doing was quite unique. If anything, I wanted to do more slow doom parts, really."

"For me, I saw Napalm Death as an incredibly extreme act that couldn't last forever, and I think Lee maybe felt the same way, but it seemed like Mick or Shane felt like, 'No, this could really last,'" recalls Steer. "And on top of that, they were bringing in a manager, a guy named Mark Walmesley, who had managed punk bands like The Stupids. And to be honest, I didn't really like the idea of that, not the idea of having a manager, but he didn't seem like the right person to me. But the number one thing I really think was just the music. I just thought, 'Well, I'm more comfortable in Carcass.' And Jeff [Walker] and Ken [Owen] were my best friends at that time, and there was a little bit more room for doing my own thing."

"To be brutally honest, back in '89, there was no communication between any of us as a band at all," says Embury. "I think because we were young we let our immaturity show pretty badly. We were drifting apart, but at the same time I don't know if we were truly ever together, because me and Lee often talked about parting company with Micky because he had quite an overbearing personality."

"The deciding factor for me was halfway through the tour in Japan it became apparent that the tour had lost a bit of money—a grand and a half or something like that," says Dorrian. "And just before we had got on the plane to go on the tour we received royalty checks, and I didn't have time to put mine in the bank. I was gonna put it back when I got back from tour but I found out halfway through the

Last ever photo of Embury/Harris/Steer/Dorrian Napalm Death lineup. Photo: Martin Nesbitt

tour, without anybody telling me, that my royalty check had been cancelled to cover the losses of the tour while everybody else still got theirs. This decision had been made behind my back without anyone confronting me about it at all, so I just thought, 'Fuck you, you're supposed to be my friends.' And that was the final nail in the coffin for me."

"Even though Lee arranged all the details with S.O.B. members directly, I funded the trip, so Earache was entitled to recoup such costs back from royalties under the record deal we had with the band," says Pearson. "I guess for that reason I felt it was okay to take such costs back from any royalties due the band—nowadays it would be a simple matter of reclaiming any 'tour support' paid out on the band's behalf. At the time, myself having had no previous record company experience, I guess I probably didn't explain what was happening very clearly.

"Lee wasn't happy to be the one whose check was the one I recouped from," Pearson continues. "Being at that point an ex-member of the band, it seemed easier to recoup from him. After all, the rest of the guys who were still in the band would go crazy if their checks had been withdrawn. Though I was lucky enough to be enjoying quite a few sales, it was still a real hand-to-mouth operation financially. If we didn't get the money back for the flights, we couldn't release the next record. As much as Lee would like to assume it, we didn't exist just for Napalm's benefit."

"At that last gig in Japan, Lee Dorrian actually said to the crowd, 'Ever feel like you've been cheated?'" says Nesbitt. "And me and Bill, we were laughing, and Mick and Shane didn't even know [what was happening]."

"There's a classic photograph that I have that says everything," Harris declares. "It's at some airport in Korea where we stopped off on the way home from Japan. It was me in a pair of crazy Hawaiian shorts, a pair of flip-flops, Shane in a Joker t-shirt, and we're both looking at the camera, but both Lee and Bill, you can see it, it's over. They're not even acknowledging the camera. They are not there. Basically, it's the last photo of the band together. And that was it, we got back and they both announced it. And I think for Shane and I, it was like, 'Shit, what should we do? We're fucking loving this. We've got songs written already and we wanna continue. Where do we go?'"

Mass Appeal Madness

WHILE EARACHE RECORDS WAS ENJOYING SUCCESS OVERSEAS, by 1989, death metal albums finally began slithering out of American record shops, many of them bearing the logo of Roadrunner Records' new death metal imprint R/C. The previous year, Roadrunner signed contracts with Brazilian speedsters Sepultura and Floridian death metal outfit Xecutioner—what the label felt to be their first entries in the mounting death metal sweepstakes. After Xecutioner changed their name to Obituary at the behest of the label, Roadrunner released the band's debut album *Slowly We Rot* and Sepultura's first domestic LP *Beneath the Remains* in May of 1989. While Roadrunner A&R Monte Conner was responsible for signing both bands, he effectively served as the publicity contact for the groups as well.

"You're talking about Roadrunner in 1989—there were five of us [in the U.S.

Sepultura in New York City. Photo: Frank White

Obituary's infamous "hanging" promo photo, circa 1989. Photo: Tim Hubbard

office]," Conner recalls. "As opposed to now, we have 150 people worldwide. And when you work at a small, little label like that you wear many hats, so I did it all. I was actively working the stuff to magazines. To be honest, it was pretty easy at the time, because Sepultura and Obituary both had amazing angles; the whole 'Sepultura are from Brazil' thing—people were really freaking out on that and wanted to write about them. And then as far as Obituary goes, back then they were maybe the heaviest band ever. No one sounded like [vocalist] John Tardy. And to be honest, the whole angle of the death growl and the band not having actual lyrics—people freaked out over that too."

"When we used to write music, it wasn't like I sat down and wrote lyrics and the band would write music so everything goes together," offers Tardy, whose chilling howl was one of the most distinct of the genre. "They would just be jamming and putting stuff together, and then I'd start singing something in the parts that I wanna sing in. It just seemed like, at times, if I couldn't come up with words to go along with the song, I'd just kinda make something up and just fill in something that wasn't maybe a word, but it sounded good and fit in the song so, I'd pretty much go with it. It's really as simple as that. I just couldn't really come up with something that sounded good with an actual word."

The coverage certainly helped propel record sales in the United States. According to the label, *Beneath the Remains* sold over 100,000 copies, while *Slowly We Rot* sold 75,000 units, a somewhat astounding number for a small indie label releasing music once thought to be so uncommercial. Perhaps more surprisingly, Obituary's achievement came without any significant touring effort from the band.

"At the time, we didn't even know it was a success," offers Obituary guitarist Trevor Peres. "We didn't care, we were all just working and playing local shows and smoking reefer. When *Slowly We Rot* came out, I was 19 years old, so I didn't even know to care if it was even selling. We were full of testosterone and we just wanted to play music—that was all we cared about. But apparently it did pretty well."

Sepultura's success was equally unforeseen. Although the band's approach closely mirrored traditional thrash metal, frontman Max Cavalera's gruff vocal delivery suggested that the band might be too extreme for the typical Anthrax and Megadeth admirer. Furthermore, in Sepultura's corner was Scott Burns, the producer whose name would become synonymous with death metal over the next few years. In fact, Burns produced *Beneath the Remains* largely because he was one of the few producers willing to fly to Brazil to record the album over Christmas of 1988.

"I remember getting there, and I had like 500 bucks to get in the country, and instantly, everybody I was dealing with in Brazil was corrupt," says Burns. "I came in with drum heads, sticks, strings, picks, reels of tape to record on—all that stuff I could use—and a lot was confiscated. Basically, Max came out and he had

Scott Burns at Morrisound with Obituary. Photo: Tim Hubbard

bleached blonde hair and tattoos, so he was not looked well upon by the Brazilians themselves, and we just went around to all the customs agents until we found one that would let us in the country with the lowest price, 300 bucks. And I think we had like 500 for everything to get by in the three weeks. So instantly, Roadrunner had to send some more money, so we were starting over budget and things like that. We didn't finish the vocals, so Max came back and stayed at my apartment for a while, finished the vocals and did the mix."

"[Scott] did a great job, and the conditions of that album were horrible," recalls former Sepultura frontman Max Cavalera. "You didn't sleep at night, we spent all night awake recording the album, which is physical work with the drums being so fast and all the riffs. And then in the daytime, it was 100 degrees in Rio in the middle of the summer, staying in a one-star hotel, worrying about your shit being ripped off, tired from the sessions. All of that, I think, contributed to some of the anger of the record. We were kinda on the edge. But at the same time, we were so excited, because we were making our first real album. *Beneath the Remains*, I really think that is the cornerstone of Sepultura, there's where it all started. That was our chance to prove that Sepultura could do something and could make a mark. And when I went to do *Beneath the Remains*, I was just hoping we could make a good record. I would have never dreamed that album would have been compared to anything Slayer would have done. From that point on, it was like we were a real band."

Although record sales were rapidly rising, death metal and grindcore coverage in the mainstream press was still sparse. However, the communities had an invaluable friend in the influential *CMJ Music Monthly* magazine, whose extreme music coverage was spearheaded by Atlanta native and New York City transplant Kevin Sharp.

"Being in a situation where I came from—a really hip radio station called WREK in Atlanta—they were willing to let me do what I wanted to do," says Sharp of his *CMJ* editors. "I did a lot of really cool, weird shit, that when I look back on it now, I'm like, 'How did I manage to sell that after pitching it?' Like, we got an Extreme Noise Terror track right next to a Mr. Big track on a radio sampler CD. I don't know if that could be done now.

"But Sepultura and Obituary were an even easier sell," he continues. "The reason *Slowly We Rot* and *Beneath the Remains* were a hit was because everyone was sick of hearing low-grade [San Francisco] Bay [area] thrash. It lost its fucking edge, and they were looking for something more [extreme], and here's this kid who's not even singing words, just puking into a mic. That was the end-all extreme."

"It was something new to many people, but it's not like those were the first death metal bands ever," says Conner. "Even at the time the Sepultura and Obituary records came out [in the US], it wasn't like they were groundbreaking bands.

Sepultura were influenced by Slayer, and Obituary were influenced by Celtic Frost. So it wasn't like we were inventing it, but these new bands were definitely taking things to a new level. And I don't think all of those early bands, like Possessed and Death, really got a large amount of recognition. And it's at the same time that we started doing Obituary and Sepultura that Digby really had his thing kicking up with Napalm Death."

Pearson, however, was about to get in on the growing stateside action with Earache's first American signing, Florida death metal goliaths Morbid Angel. The band may have already been regarded as a minor legend among underground tape-trading aficionados on the strength of bootlegs of the *Abominations of Desolation* LP and the recently recorded *Thy Kingdom Come* demo, but it was a fervent endorsement from Napalm Death drummer Mick Harris that helped seal Morbid Angel's deal with Earache.

"I made a two-week trip to Tampa in August of '89," recalls Harris. "It was a part special trip and part me treating my girlfriend to a nice holiday. She'd probably say now, 'Oh, yeah, that was Mick's death metal holiday.' It was already decided that we were gonna go on holiday, but I did end up visiting a lot of these bands, and for sure it was good fun. I was just purely out there to meet people for the love of the music. A holiday was not really in the cards. I mean, what the hell was I really going to Tampa, Florida for?"

"[Harris] came down to the Tampa area and met with different bands, and he met with us and saw us practice, and he was really into it," says Morbid Angel

Morbid Angel circa 1990. Live photo: Frank White

guitarist Trey Azagthoth. "We gave him some tapes and he hooked them up with Dig from Earache, so definitely, he was the one."

"There were a lot of labels that we were talking to at the time," says former Morbid Angel frontman David Vincent. "One day I just said, 'I'm getting on the phone today.' So I start making calls [to labels], like, 'What do you think about this?' And I heard, "Well, you know, you need to slow it down a little bit and make the vocals a little more melodic.' And immediately it was like, 'Fuck you,' and the phone got hung up. Then the next person got called: 'Well, we kinda like the stuff, but there are a lot of other Angels out there. There's Death Angel and there's that band Angel Witch, so you might need to change your name.' 'Alright, fuck you,' and there was a hang-up again. So after Mick had spoken in Digby's ear about us, it ended up working out. Dig took a chance on it and we made it happen."

Pearson also turned his attention to the developing scene in Sweden, which by 1989 was clearly led by Stockholm death metallers Entombed.

"I first saw Entombed back when they were supporting Napalm Death," says Pearson. "They were playing in Stockholm and they were called Nihilist at the time. They were just a young band, but they were killer live."

"Napalm Death was coming to town and we were bugging the people who booked it for so long," says former Entombed drummer Nicke Andersson. "We just told them, 'We have to open. You don't realize this. We've got some credibility in the underground scene, which nobody else would give a fuck about. They know who we are, probably, because they trade tapes too.' So eventually we got that gig, and that's when we gave Dig the tapes. That's the first time we met Dig—he was on tour with them."

The Earache owner kept in touch with the young Swedes, eventually offering them a recording contract in mid-'89.

"I remember I still lived at my dad's house," says Andersson, recalling the day Entombed signed with Earache. "I was about 18, I guess. Our guitarist Alex [Hellid] was 17. I remember, because he was so young he had to have his mom's signature to sign the contract."

New death metal bands like Morbid Angel and Entombed required a change from the punk-themed homemade cover art that adorned each Earache release to date. Pearson turned to 18-year-old Nottingham native Dan Seagrave, who a year earlier provided the artwork pro bono for the split album from comedic thrash collectives Lawnmower Deth and Metal Duck.

"Dig saw it in a magazine and he got the word out to me that he wouldn't mind me doing an album cover for Morbid Angel," says Seagrave. "But based on the look of the Lawnmower Deth cover, I don't know why, actually. I think he saw the album and he saw that it was a really indie release, and he'd only done a few records at that point, and because I was local, it got his attention. So I just took some artwork in and I took [what would become] the Morbid Angel cover. I was actually painting it at the time as something for myself. And one of the band members was there, David Vincent. He saw it and he liked it."

Soon Pearson commissioned Seagrave to provide the cover art for other death metal releases from Earache.

"I wasn't really expensive at that point, so they just naturally handed it over to me," Seagrave explains. "I don't think they had any other artists on the books

(top) Original cover art for Morbid Angel's *Altars of Madness*. Courtesy Dan Seagrave

(bottom) Advertisement for Entombed's *Left Hand Path* featuring Dan Seagrave artwork

at that point. All the covers were traditionally very cheap and bad. I was certainly not a professional artist at that point. I look back at a lot of work and see it for what it is—it's not that great, but it kinda worked at the time."

Earache wasn't redesigning the look for all of the label's releases, however. Carcass' hideous autopsy collages remained unencumbered by professional artists for at least one more record, *Symphonies of Sickness*. Carcass' music, however, was becoming slightly more refined. Shortly after his exit from Napalm Death in the summer of '89, Carcass guitarist Bill Steer returned to the Slaughterhouse studio with producer Colin Richardson, who had the unenviable task of making sense of Carcass' frenzied sound—a challenge no other producer or engineer had previously met.

"Before we did *Symphonies* I remember Carcass did a track in this good studio in Liverpool called Amazon, and Dig gave us a decent budget to do one track for a compilation, so it was a real luxury," Steer explains. "We were in the studio for a day and we recorded one song. It was a new experience for us. But when we were doing the mix, I remember Jeff turned to the engineer and said, 'Have you got any suggestions?' And the guy just threw his hands up in the air and said, 'What can I do with this?'"

"We walked in feeling that it was probably gonna turn out like *Reek* again, but Colin really enabled us to iron out all the problems with our playing," recalls Carcass frontman Jeff Walker. "We

Carcass live in Gothenburg, Sweden, 1989

Carcass in Holland circa 1990. Photo: Ingrid Martin

Carcass' first live performance with Michael Amott at Planet X, 1990. Photo: Jim Kitler

weren't the tightest band and we didn't rehearse that much, so he just put us under the microscope. He wasn't hired in specifically to do it. He really made sure the second record didn't turn out to be a disaster like the first one."

As a result of his triumphant taming of both Napalm Death and Carcass, Richardson became Earache's unofficial go-to producer for much of the label's British roster.

"It was really kinda modest at the beginning, because I had done a few records for Earache, and I remember this band Gorefest from Holland contacted me, and it was like, 'Wow, people from other countries!'" says Richardson. "I think I got a lot of work from people seeing my name on the back of the sleeves. And I think Roadrunner just heard some stuff—obviously they heard the Earache stuff—and thought, 'That's pretty good,' because there weren't too many people doing it, there wasn't a whole bunch of choices, really."

The strength of Richardson's recording actually helped Carcass land the second guitarist they had previously coveted. After initially declining the invitation in 1988, Carnage guitarist Michael Amott was now ready to accept the position based on Carcass' obvious improvements.

"When I heard the *Symphonies of Sickness* album, I was just like, 'Oh, no, what have I done?'" Amott says. "So I learned from my mistake, and when I got asked a second time I was just like, 'Okay, I'm leaving Carnage and I'm gonna go and do this.' This was in January of 1990, and I went over to England in April."

Amott's decision effectively ended Carnage, but it allowed Carnage drummer Fred Estby to resurrect his previous band, Dismember, which featured the majority of Carnage's final lineup.

While other death metal bands continued to restructure, Mick Harris was busy searching for his own death metal talent to augment his once again depleted Napalm Death lineup. First, he replaced departed vocalist Lee Dorrian with Mark "Barney" Greenway, who had often served as a Napalm Death roadie—or "humped"—for the band's various UK shows.

"I say humping, but it was basically a case of pretending to carry some cabinets around and getting drunk and just fucking falling around, because I was pretty much a drunken crusty back then," admits Greenway, who was bestowed the Barney nickname for his drunken antics, during which he bore resemblance to the prehistoric "Flintstones" cartoon character. "I was sort of a semi-dirty kind of character."

Like Harris, Greenway's roots were in the country's anarcho punk movement. Despite his heritage, the vocalist was fronting Benediction, a Birmingham-based death metal act, when the drummer asked Greenway to enlist with Napalm in September of 1989.

"Benediction was a time, to be really brutally frank, when I'd actually lost a bit of my passion for hardcore," Greenway says. "I just wanted to do pure death metal at the time, because the whole hardcore/grindcore scene was going through a real weird time, and there were a lot of people stabbing other people in the back because a couple of bands had got a bit of exposure, and it was like

Benediction circa 1989. Photo: Mick Harris

New Napalm Death lineup, November '89. Photo: Martin Nesbitt

there was the sellout fingers a-pointing about Napalm. And I was just really disgusted that people could be like that, people that were friends of the bands and knew them really well and just knew that that was not the case at all. And I was just really fucking disenchanted with the whole thing. I was like, 'Fuck this shit, I'll just do death metal, and fuck this hardcore shit if people are gonna be assholes.'"

Despite his distaste for what he felt the scene surrounding Napalm had become, Greenway couldn't resist the opportunity to join one of his favorite bands.

"I called up Micky one day, and Micky said, 'Bill and Lee left,'" recalls Greenway. "I was like, 'Oh, yeah?' And he said, 'Do you wanna join?' I said, 'Yeah, of course.' I mean, I learned 28 songs in a day and a half, so I was up for it. I was riding my BMX at the time because I didn't have nothing. I was working some shitty fucking job, getting paid fucking nothing, and I was riding on a BMX to get around, and I was so excited, I crashed my BMX into a post box."

Harris and Embury also had their sights set on a pair of American guitarists they were corresponding with in recent years: Mitch Harris, guitarist of Las Vegas death metallers Righteous Pigs, and L.A. native and former Terrorizer guitarist, Jesse Pintado.

"I used to write to Mick and Shane, just trading tapes and stuff," says Pintado. "They just invited me over and it was cool. I mean, Napalm's my favorite band, and I was like, 'Wow, I've never been to Europe.' And they had a tour lined up, so it was like, 'Let's do it.'"

"At this point, me and Mitch had also been communicating for some time," says Mick Harris. "He was also heavily into Napalm. He turned me onto his outfit, Righteous Pigs. And both Shane and I fucking loved Terrorizer. This is the philosophy in Napalm—it had to be someone that understood, someone that shared the feeling."

Pintado was first to depart for England, arriving just a few weeks before Napalm Death were to embark on a brief UK tour as part of the Grindcrusher package, featuring fellow Earache artists Carcass, Bolt Thrower and Morbid Angel.

"It was four or five dates in England, Scotland, and then straight up to Europe, which was just Napalm and Morbid Angel," recalls the drummer, Harris. "Mitch came around for the English dates, so at this point I wanted Mitch in the band. I still couldn't ask. I just didn't have the confidence. Mitch didn't come to Europe. He left us alone. He stayed in England, and when we came back I think I just hit them on it. 'Look, let's get him in, it will sound fucking killer with two guitarists.'"

With Mitch Harris still a spectator, in December of '89, the reconfigured Napalm Death were ready for the first US performance, a show at the legendary New York City rock club CBGB's with Prong and Blind Idiot God. Pearson and Martin Nesbitt accompanied the band to New York in hopes of finalizing a stateside distribution deal with Relativity Distribution and Records subsidiary Combat Records. In the weeks prior, Pearson received a call from Combat sales director Alan Becker at the prompting of new Combat tour promotion director and international licensing assistant Jim Welch.

"I wanted to sign a distribution deal with Earache just because I was always buying their records on import," says Welch. "I was totally into all that stuff, and really, when the first Napalm record came out and started doing well, I was like, 'I gotta call this guy up.'"

"Alan Becker was the first guy to contact me in

(left) Brutal Truth live at CBGB's. (right) Death circa 1987

the States about a distribution deal," says Pearson. "He just said, 'We wanna put out some of your records—Napalm Death is blowing up here.'"

One of the people singing Napalm Death's and Earache's praises in New York was Danny Lilker. The lanky bassist was already quasi-famous in thrash metal circles thanks to his work with Anthrax, S.O.D. and Nuclear Assault, the latter of which were the subject of a protracted label dispute between IRS Records and Combat in 1990. With Nuclear Assault's future uncertain and his interest in extreme music mounting, Lilker formed the blasting grindcore outfit Brutal Truth with *CMJ* music journalist Kevin Sharp.

"I was friends with a lot of the bands, like Carcass and Napalm, and they'd give me shirts and I'd wear them," Lilker says. "Sometimes I'd wear them and there would be a photo session for Nuclear Assault, and the next thing you know, it's on an album cover."

"He was like a walking billboard for Earache at the time," says Pearson. "He certainly helped. So Combat started off buying some records to distribute and they sold quite well, so then they suggested a license deal for the whole label, which was great for me. I had never done any licensing before—I didn't even know what it was. I had to get to a lawyer and find out what it actually meant."

Fortunately for Earache, Combat were no strangers to death metal. By the time the label signed a three-year licensing deal with Earache in 1990, Combat

(bottom left) Death circa 1988. (top left) Terrorizer circa 1989 recording session

Bolt Thower circa 1989. Courtesy Earache Records

had already experienced success with a pair of records from both Possessed and Death in the late '80s. Moreover, when Death released their third record, *Spiritual Healing,* in February of 1990, the album swiftly sold over 50,000 units in the US alone.

"It was great, because we were part of some pretty big, groundbreaking type of stuff," recalls former Death bassist Terry Butler. "We were playing death metal, but it had some melody to it, so it was acceptable."

The Earache label, with their faster, more atonal acts, represented a greater commercial challenge for Combat.

"For Earache, the Combat deal gave us a kind of head start on the other labels in hitting America, because Combat put a lot of time and effort into promoting the bands and touring them, which is very expensive stuff to do, and they set up the label really well in America," says Pearson. "They did exactly what they were supposed to do."

The deal also afforded Pearson the freedom to concentrate more on A&R. But while he added several new acts to the Earache roster in the months prior, such as Birmingham grinders Bolt Thrower, the Mike Browning-led, keyboard-infused death metal act Nocturnus, and the Justin Broadrick-fronted, electronic drum-machine metal juggernaut Godflesh, Pearson practiced what he called "strict quality control" regarding artists he felt were worthy of displaying that spiky Earache logo on the backs of their record sleeves.

"Well, we thought we had the best bands," Pearson says plainly. "We didn't do the normal industry things, because the business wasn't formed in that way—it's kinda out of fandom. In hindsight, now that I'm a bit more experienced in business, it's obvious that we owned that scene for a little while. I mean, we rejected Sepultura's demo for the *Schizophrenia* album. Fear Factory was another band that was turned down. I think we sent them a letter back that said they sounded too much like Godflesh and Napalm Death. We were kinda high-minded really. But, if I had advisers at the time, what we should have said is, 'Let's just sign the whole lot!' Then there would have been no Roadrunner."

Perhaps more astutely, Pearson capitalized on the renewed interest in death metal and grindcore bands that never existed beyond the demo stage. First the LA grindcore outfit Terrorizer—originally featuring current Morbid Angel drummer Pete Sandoval and current Napalm Death guitarist Jessie Pintado—reunited with original vocalist Oscar Garcia to record a proper full-length LP in the summer of 1989. Morbid Angel frontman David Vincent supplied the bass.

"Terrorizer was actually signed to Earache before Morbid Angel was signed to Earache," says Vincent. "When Morbid Angel got Pete in the band, Terrorizer never had the opportunity to make a record. When I was over in England delivering the masters for the *Altars of Madness* record, I spoke to Dig about Terrorizer and said, 'Hey, if you are still interested, put a budget together and I'll find a fucking way to make it happen.'"

"Well, Earache was interested," says Pintado. "But there wasn't a big budget or anything, so Oscar and I just hopped on a bus and went out there to Florida and all the Morbid Angel guys all lived together. So we stopped there for a few weeks over the summer and did the record. And Vincent ended up playing bass, because we didn't have bass equipment. We went in the studio and recorded it and mixed it in three days."

Massacre, the Florida demo band, which featured vocalist Kam Lee and three current members of the now increasingly popular Death—Bill Andrews, Terry Butler and Rick Rozz—were earning attention courtesy of Benediction and Napalm Death vocalist Barney Greenway, who was liberally crediting his vocal influence to Kam Lee's style. It was through a conversation with David Vincent that Lee actually discovered the veneration the contemporary death metal scene had for his former band.

"Dave comes up to me and he's like, 'Man, you have no idea what it's like overseas. So many people love Massacre over in England,'" Lee remembers. "So it was pretty much David sitting down and talking to me and saying, 'Look man, you've gotta get Massacre back together.' And I was like, 'How am I gonna do it? They're all in Death.'"

Actually, Death guitarist Rick Rozz had recently departed the band for Florida metallic experimentalists the Genitorturers in 1990. When he learned of this, Lee proposed the idea of resurrecting Massacre to Rozz one night after a Genitorturers show. Rozz immediately refused. That wasn't enough, however, to deter Earache's Pearson from pursuing the matter.

"Digby calls me, and he started asking about the chances of Massacre ever reforming, and I said, 'Right now it doesn't look like it's gonna happen,'" says Lee. "'Bill and Terry are still in Death and they're over in Europe,' and I said, 'I don't see

Massacre in the studio with Cronos circa 1991

how it's gonna happen.' And he said, 'Well, give me Rick's number.'"

"I think money motivated him a little bit," Pearson says of his initial conversation with Rozz. "I do remember having to make them join up together again by giving them the pep talk, telling them that all of Napalm Death were singing the praises of Massacre, and all the tapes were going around the UK and Europe and the US, but they never made their classic album, which they need to do. I was like, 'Get it together. I'll give you money and buy equipment to help things.' I remember having to buy Rick a whole Marshall cabinet. I was on the phone with a credit card, buying it from some Florida music store, and then sending Rick to go there and pick it up, along with guitars and strings. But I didn't mind, because we needed the record by Massacre."

Andrews and Butler eventually rejoined Massacre as well after a difficult European tour with Death, but that wasn't enough to keep the group together for very long. Tensions between the band members eventually escalated during a European tour of their own, and by 1992 Massacre folded once again.

"They made their *From Beyond* record and did a bit of touring, but then they imploded again pretty quickly," says Pearson. "I still don't know, to this day, what their actual problem with each other is."

There was one final seminal grindcore act that Pearson was intent on unearthing—Flint, Michigan's Repulsion. Surprisingly, there was already interest in signing the group from Carcass' Jeff Walker and Bill Steer. The pair hoped to sign off welfare by starting a record label and exploiting England's Enterprise Allowance Scheme in the same fashion in which Pearson launched Earache only a few years earlier.

"Initially, I got a tape of the Electro Hippies' first recording and took the idea to Revolver, the label that distributed Earache in England," recalls Walker. "Revolver would basically pay for the pressing of the records and sleeves, they'd distribute it as well, and all you'd have to do is provide the recordings. You'd have to be an idiot, really, not to make money back. As long as you thought you could sell 1,000 albums, you'd be laughing. So we discussed doing Repulsion with Revolver, and Dig found out and he started shitting himself, because he thought we were trying to do what Heresy did, which is walk away from the label and start our own thing, and that really wasn't in our mind at all. We just wanted to get some financial breathing space while we were still in Carcass."

As it turns out, Pearson had already sent Repulsion into the studio to remix their 18-track 1986 *Slaughter of the Innocent* demo.

"Repulsion kinda became a pawn, and Dig was like, 'Well, I wanna do this Repulsion too, but I don't wanna do it on Earache,'" Walker remembers. "So he said, 'Why don't you just put it out through Earache on a sub-label?' And we really weren't too bothered either way, so that's what happened."

Both pre-Cannibal Corpse bands, Beyond Death and Tirant Sin, circa 1988

The Repulsion demo was rechristened *Horrified* and released through Walker and Steer's freshly minted Necrosis label in late 1989. The debut LP from the now-defunct Carnage quickly followed as well.

"They were a little after the fact," says Walker, "but still obviously worth releasing."

While Earache had already earned a reputation as the world's first exclusively death metal and grindcore label, already established American metal labels began turning their attention toward the genres by late 1989. In their first eight years in business California-based indie Metal Blade never signed anything more extreme than Slayer, although the label did license early European thrash bands like Sodom, Kreator, Destruction and Celtic Frost to the US market.

"Almost all of our stuff at that point was the Flotsam and Jetsam and the Sacred Reich element of things, which was straight-on thrash," explains Metal Blade president Mike Faley. "But we were aware of what Earache was doing over there. They had that article in *Sounds* on the label, and *NME* was talking about Napalm Death and all of these grindcore type of bands, and that was pretty interesting to me to see what they were doing."

A native of Buffalo, Faley was also aware of what was happening in his own backyard. In December of 1988, a new death metal band called Cannibal Corpse rose from the remains of Buffalo's two largest metalcore groups, Beyond Death and Tirant Sin. When he wasn't growling his guts out with Cannibal Corpse, vocalist Chris Barnes worked in the warehouse of local record chain Cabbages. Fortuitously for the group, the head buyer at the chain, John Grandoni, was actually old friends with Faley and sent him a copy of Cannibal's five-song self-titled demo.

"When Cannibal came in," remembers Faley, "I was like, 'Okay, let's take a shot at it. Here's something that's pretty cool and something much different.'"

The band's lyrics, exclusively penned by frontman Chris Barnes, weren't exactly your typical horror movie-inspired paeans either. In addition to the now almost requisite gore and murder themes—rape, incest, sexual torture and a general violence against women—were recurring subject matter in early songs such as "Butchered at Birth," which featured the lines, "Mother ripped apart/ Smashing her face/ My knife cutting holes/ Fucking her remains."

"I was kinda shocked the lyrics weren't picked up on more," says Barnes. "It's some pretty fucked-up shit that I wrote, and I'm surprised that it hasn't gotten more attention—you know, negative attention, which is good to me. I kinda

Cannibal Corpse's Chris Barnes. Photo: Frank White

thrived on it. But that was all set up by the record company, because the press eventually picked up on it a little and wanted to talk to me, because they wanted to know what kind of sick fucking idiot wrote that shit."

In February of 1990, the freshly signed Cannibal Corpse made the nearly 1,300-mile journey by van from Buffalo to Morrisound Studios in Tampa to record their debut album with producer Scott Burns. "It was rough," recalls Cannibal bassist Alex Webster. "I got really sunburned on the way back up north. I was driving through the snow and we didn't have heat in the van. I was getting the chills."

"Scott was really the person that we looked at when it came time for Cannibal to go in there," says Faley. "They were looking at Obituary, they were looking at Death, they were looking at Morbid Angel, and they were seeing the quality of the sound that was coming out of those records, and that's what they wanted to have on their records. So it was important for them to enter that same realm."

Roadrunner Records was busy raising its own death metal profile, thanks largely to Monte Conner, who continued to recruit new talent in the rapidly developing genre. But sometimes, as in the case of Amon, the Florida-based death metal band fronted by the flamboyant Glen Benton, the artists came to him.

"I was sitting at my desk one day, and Glen Benton storms in, walks across the room, throws a tape on my desk and says, 'Sign us, you fucking asshole!' And storms out," recalls Conner. "I was on the phone, and I literally didn't even get off it. I see the tape on my desk and it was a six-song demo, and of course it was done at Morrisound with Scott Burns, and I'm just thinking, 'What is this crap?' I put it in and I was blown away."

"I was in New York City at the time, and I figured, 'Fuck it, I'll walk in there and introduce myself and give him a copy of the demo,'" Benton explains. "I figured if I went in there and scared him good enough he would at least listen to it. And by the next day I got a call and they said, 'Hey, we've got contracts coming to you.'"

After a name change to Deicide (meaning "the killing of God" or "one who kills God") in late 1989, Benton and his band of not-so-merry men were signed and began preparations to record their debut album. Released in 1990, *Deicide* was an instant success, thanks in part to Benton's overtly Satanic image. Burning a three-inch inverted cross into his forehead and spewing lyrics such as, "Kill the chosen righteous son/ Claim the cross inverted one," and ",Suicide Sacrifice/ Destruction of holy life/ Blood of unholy knife/ Satan!" Benton attracted a storm of controversy.

"The UK press was just going crazy over Deicide," recalls Conner. "The whole cross in the head thing—they ate that up."

There was one particular interview with British mainstream weekly *NME*,

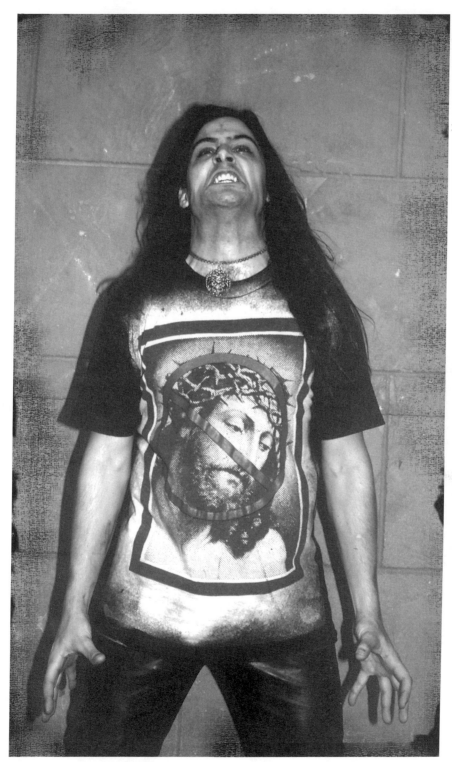

Deicide's Glen Benton, 1990. Photo: Frank White

however, which brought the frontman some undesired publicity. During the interview conducted on his property, Benton shot and killed a squirrel—an incident the author included in the final version of the story.

"The next thing you know, I was getting death threats from animal rights activists," says Benton of the sharpshooting fallout. "I killed the fucking squirrel because it was in my attic chewing the fucking electrical wire on my fucking air conditioning unit, and I was trying to get the last one out of the house so I could block the hole up so they couldn't get in anymore. But there was this one squirrel that every time I'd see his ass he'd jump back in the fucking hole. So I'm sitting there doing the interview, and the motherfucker comes trotting out on the clothesline, sitting there watching us. So I was like, 'You stay right there, I'll be right back.' And these guys were like, 'What the hell's going on?' I come back and *Bam*! Clip the fucking squirrel off the clothesline. They just looked horrified. I mean, it's just a rat with a bushy tail, man."

Despite such antics, it was ultimately the aural brutality of the first Deicide album that captured the dark hearts of death metal fans. Recorded at Morrisound Studios with producer Scott Burns, *Deicide* was the latest in a successful string of death metal albums laid down at the studio. In fact, by 1990, Morrisound was *the* place to record for such American death metal bands as Death, Morbid Angel, Cannibal Corpse and Obituary, who all tracked their latest albums in the studio owned by Jim Morris.

"There weren't a lot of high-quality recordings for the fast bands," Scott Burns explains. "Even if you listened to some of the Earache Records, they were extreme, but I don't think the early ones sounded so good. So I think the one thing is perhaps that there was a little more definition and clarity with what we were doing. And for the American bands, the drums were very important to them, and playing correctly and being able to blast, and no clicking your sticks on tom fills, and not cheating—things like that. You could always tell on one of my records or one of the records that we did—if like the sound or not—it was always a cleaner recording to a point. The bands liked that."

Already desiring more death metal influences, Morrisound seemed like the logical place for Napalm Death to record their third album.

"It was a decision for probably more me and Shane," says Napalm drummer Mick Harris. "We were very much into what Scott was producing. It's got to be [Death's] *Leprosy* record—I loved that production. So we were like, 'Let's go there.' We got out of England. A more death metal influence was certainly coming into the songwriting. The pair of us—Shane and I—couldn't keep writing the 30 to 40-second long songs. There was only so much. It was also my way of getting to play drums. So it was a conscious decision, definitely. We had to move on."

"We decided we'll do death metal, still with the hardcore ethos," says Greenway. "The ethos never died, because it never does—a principle is a principle. Our musical approach just changed because we were just sick of getting fucking hassled by punks. We just had enough. We were getting shit—shit from people that were supposed to be our fucking friends and we thought would support us, and they turned their backs on us."

"Napalm came down, and they were more into the Kam Lee/Massacre/Death scene and things like that," recalls producer Scott Burns. "They were definitely into the whole Florida scene. So I think that's what they wanted to try, because that's where everybody recorded and that's the sound they wanted to capture. It was a weird predicament, because they were a grindcore band but yet they picked up metal players.

"Mick's more of the traditional European grind player, and he definitely has a style, but I guess when you put it under a microscope and really try and get a good recording of it, you see some things that aren't so good," Burns continues. "From American players versus European players, perhaps some of these things weren't as tight as they should have been. And that really didn't fly with Mick at all. He was the man, and no one tells him what to do. Basically he'd tell me, 'Who the fuck is this guy? I'm the king of grindcore.' Which was a valid point. So these were some of the dynamics that were going on. For instance, spending some time doing drum tracks, Mitch and Jesse would be saying, 'Really, the timing isn't so

Napalm Death at (and outside) Morrisound circa 1990. Photos: Tim Hubbard

good on these things.' And no one could really do too much, because Mick was the deciding vote on everything, so that was both difficult and strenuous."

"It was a fucking team," Mick Harris explains. "That's how we worked and we played. But for sure, there was a tension there. I had a big problem with the fact that Jess, Mitch and Shane were partying a lot. I'm not a party pooper; we all have our vices. If people wanna abuse themselves, then let them. But I think it was a new thing. We were away from home and at this famous studio. Mitch had friends that were turning up at the studio, and for sure he's gonna go out with them. But it just continued. And I felt a bit of pressure that the record was just left to me. This built up, and one night Jess and Mitch were out, and the next day they didn't show up, and I was thinking, 'I'm fucking here being told that this is noisy and do it again. I'm not doing the drum track again. I think it's good. This is the way I like it.' So I remember one day I just lost it under stress and I snapped at Scott and I called him a fucking cunt. Straight away, he walked right out of the studio and goes into Tom Morris' room and he tells Tom. Basically, they called up Earache, and Scott was ready to pull the session and pull the tapes and send them back to England.

"Tom comes back and has a word with me," the drummer continues. "He was like, 'Mick, if you know somebody around Tampa, you should call them and get away from here for a few days.' So first I spoke to Dig on the phone and he said, 'Mick, please.' And I said, 'Dig, it's not fucking working. It's not sounding right. It's not going to be Napalm.' He said, 'Come on, you can make this right. There's a lot of money [invested] in this [recording],' and sweet-talked me, and it helped me get out of there for a few days. And I remember phoning David Vincent up, and he said, 'Look Mick, you've gotta get out of there and clear your head.' So Dave took me in. And then two weeks later, I went back and I felt fresh."

"Ultimately, I don't think those guys had a real vision of what kind of sound they wanted," says Burns. "They just wanted something heavy. And it definitely sounded too clean for them, and I just remember when we were done, listening to an Entombed tape, and Mick was very disappointed because he wanted it to sound more like Entombed. And hell, a lot of people would probably like that sound. They wanted to be extreme but in a death metal way, and that album didn't make them sound extreme. I definitely think as far as they were concerned, it was a big disappointment."

"We spoke again at the end when the album was finished," says Harris. "It was all pats and there were no hard feelings. It was everybody's fault but nobody's fault."

Napalm's death metal-infused foray, however, would be their first formal introduction to US fans. Released in tandem with Morbid Angel's *Altars of Madness*, Entombed's *Left Hand Path*, Godflesh's *Streetcleaner* and Carcass' *Symphonies of*

Sickness on December 7th, 1990, Earache's first official Stateside releases were an immediate success.

"Obviously, the records were released in the UK before Combat was releasing them," reckons Pearson. "So there was some kind of time delay, which meant that we were putting out more records in a shorter space of time in America, which might have added to the intensity of releases. Nine months' worth of titles would come out in three months in America, because Combat had the finances to press all the records in one go. I mean, we were still struggling and waiting for the money to come in for one record so we could make the next one. We were still pretty much hand-to-mouth then, even though it was bigger numbers. But I think Combat shipped roughly 30,000 to 40,000 [initial copies to record stores] of the major league bands, like Morbid and Entombed and then go up to like 60,000 over time."

With distribution secured, touring was the next logical step for many artists. Obituary, in particular, had some work to do. Despite not setting foot beyond their home state of Florida to support their debut album, the group was back in Morrisound recording their second record, and was now in need of a guitarist to replace the departed Allen West. James Murphy, who had officially left fellow Floridians Death in late March of 1990, after relationships soured during the group's North American tour, was unexpectedly drafted to fill the position.

"I had no idea that Obituary was even looking for a guitarist," says Murphy. "I called Scott Burns just to tell him what had happened with Death, because I had

Obituary live circa 1989. Photo: Tim Hubbard

(left) Immolation circa 1990. Photo: Frank White

(top right) Suffocation circa 1990. (bottom right) Incantation circa 1989

become friends with Scott. Basically, he said, 'Dude, I'm working with Obituary right now in the studio, Allen left the band and they need a guitar player. Let me talk to them.' So he called Trevor and the band, and I actually never even spoke with them until I arrived in the studio.

"We all sat down at the table in the lounge at Morrisound, and they just told me, 'Here's the way it is: Allen is leaving because his wife is having a baby.'" Murphy continues, "They said that he might return one day and that he was their bro' from way back, and that if he did, they would consider taking him back. Basically, they were just covering their bases so I wouldn't be mad if they did take him back."

With the album nearly complete and his position within the band established, Murphy recorded his guitar leads and Obituary officially wrapped up the recording of *Cause of Death* in the spring of 1990. That summer the group would embark on their official US tour.

"We opened up for Sacred Reich; that was our first real tour going beyond Ft. Lauderdale or Tampa—the only places we ever played," says Obituary guitarist Tevor Peres. "We called it Rotting Slow in America, because *Cause of Death* was getting ready to come out pretty soon, but we hadn't toured our first album. Then we went to Europe, and the *Cause of Death* album dropped. So we basically did that one tour in America, and then we went to Europe and started touring for *Cause of Death*—we literally had four days off in between the tours for basically two albums. It was awesome, because we didn't know that people knew who the fuck we were and people knew our songs. We didn't even realize it at that point, I think. I look back at it now, and I go, 'Wow, that's pretty fucking crazy that people knew our shit.' Something was happening."

Indeed, the death metal groundswell appeared to be spreading into new territories throughout the United States. The movement had been festering in the New York/New Jersey region, in particular, for the past few years. The area's robust thrash scene, anchored by speedsters like Revenant and Ripping Corpse, provided a fertile breeding ground for heavier and faster outfits influenced by the extreme sounds in the underground tape-trading network. As Revenant were restructuring their lineup in August of 1989, guitarist John McEntee departed the group to start his own brutal death metal band, Incantation.

"There were some New Jersey death metal bands, like Hatred, Savage Death, and Regurgitation, that I knew about before us, but they didn't really play out a lot," McEntee explains. "We were a lot different than most of the other bands in the area at the time. When we first started playing shows, people would either be going sick, or just look at us and try to absorb it all."

By then, McEntee had already forged a bond with New York City neighbors Immolation—the death metal band that helped Morbid Angel put together their first mini-US tour in October of 1988.

"We were ready to do a demo, and right before that, in May of 1988, we had our first show at this [New York] club called Blondies," recalls Immolation front-man Ross Dolan. "John McEntee called us up and said, 'Hey guys, wanna do a show with us?' So our very first show was supporting Revenant, Ripping Corpse, and a band called Deranged. That was the first time that I met John and the guys in Revenant, and, of course, we had another dilemma. We used to rent a rehearsal room, which was 20 minutes from where we lived. Now the night before the show we were gonna get our equipment out and we went and the studio was closed. The guy who owned the studio was playing a gig that night so we couldn't get our equipment. So we called up John McEntee and we were like, 'All right, listen, we're not gonna be able to get our equipment.' And he was like, 'Oh, don't worry about it, there's plenty of equipment here.' So right away there was that brotherhood, and they were like, 'You can just use our stuff, no problem.'"

After some initial interest in the group via Earache Records in 1989—largely generated by lobbying from the band's friends in Morbid Angel—had waned, Immolation signed their first record deal a year later with Roadrunner Records. They weren't alone either.

"When we got signed, we thought it was such a special thing," says Dolan. "We were like, 'Wow, we're finally signed. We finally have this under our belts.' And it was something really special to us. And then in that same breath, Roadrunner signed like ten other bands. And we got no attention. We got no focus. It was just like, 'Okay, here you go. The album's out—go for it.' So we were disillusioned really quick."

By 1990, willing labels like Roadrunner had plenty of death metal artists from which to choose—especially in the New York/New Jersey sector where other suffix-friendly acts like Long Island's Suffocation and the Yonkers-based Mortician joined Immolation and Incantation in cultivating a healthy Northeast death metal scene.

"When I first started getting out and playing in the scene with the band, all of those bands came and played shows with us," recalls guitarist Terrance Hobbs, who co-founded Suffocation in early 1989. "To this day, the majority of all of those people are still playing and they're still holding up their end of the bargain."

The New York/New Jersey bands often acted equally as enthusiastic as their fans. Clad in the familiar uniform of jeans, sneakers and black band t-shirts on stage, death metallers didn't present themselves that much differently from their admirers in the audience. With no true hierarchy, the new prospect of organizing exclusively death metal shows and day-long festivals was relatively challenging. One of the earliest, the Michigan Death Fest, included Virginia-based death metallers Deceased in the lineup.

"It was us, Morbid Angel, Sacrifice, Nuclear Death—it was bands like that that were coming up and, to me, it was real live death metal is here. After that, all the Earache bands, like Entombed and Carcass, had

(top left) Deceased circa 1989. (below left) Mortician circa 1990 just started to break out and you just kinda realized that this shit was taking off."

Mortician's Will Ramer, who played the Buffalo Day of Death festival in October of 1990—the first of such high-profile death metal events—remembers the excitement of the period.

"We were only together about a year before we played that show," Ramer explains. "The speed and aggressiveness of these new death metal bands blew me away, and I figured I could do something like that. Also, I was heavily into horror movies at the time, and I wanted to combine horror and death metal and grindcore together. I have about 800 to 900 horror movies, so I thought, 'I'll never run out of ideas—there are so many movies I can write about. I can put out 50 albums.'"

"When a lot of the Roadrunner and the Earache death and grindcore releases started getting released in the US, things really started to take off in New Jersey," says McEntee. "Soon after that, bands like Putrefact, Human Remains and Deteriorot started brutalizing over the Northeast. It was cool, because it exposed a lot of new people to death metal."

As more death metal bands began rising, so too did new underground record labels willing to release their music. Tiny 7-inch and demo operations like, Thrash Records from France, Gore Records of Germany and Cleveland-based Seraphic Decay, had been pressing a few hundred copies of their releases for several years. Meanwhile, a new generation of labels, spearheaded by Relapse Records in Colorado focused on releasing legitimate compact disc recordings from underground American acts, such as Mortician, Deceased, Incantation and Suffocation—even gaining proper stateside distribution through Important Distribution, which would later merge with Relativity.

"Besides the stuff that Roadrunner was doing, which was already huge, there weren't many underground labels that were doing a lot of stuff like that," says Relapse founder Matt Jacobson. "And we, at least from my perception at the time, were working with bands like Incantation and Deceased and Mortician; the bands that had the biggest buzzes in the underground. Those bands in the tape-trading and the fanzine circles were the most well-known bands."

The new breed of brutality even affected Germany. Though its actual death metal and grindcore output was limited, the country produced a pair of the fastest-rising extreme music labels in the scene. First came the Donzdorf-based Nuclear Blast Records, which was officially founded by Markus Staiger in 1987. Although it began with a concentration of hopelessly obscure punk and hardcore releases, Staiger began moving in a more metallic direction by 1990.

"I always loved the extreme stuff," Staiger explains. "Righteous Pigs' *Live and Learn* was the first grind album on Nuclear Blast. Guitarist Mitch Harris called me and sent some demos and I really loved the stuff. The second death grind album we released was Defecation, which we also got through Mitch Harris, which [at the time] was the biggest success for Nuclear Blast. Soon we signed other successful death metal bands like, Dismember and Pungent Stench."

Staiger also had a close friend named Robert Kampf, who had been playing guitar for a technical thrash band called Despair since the mid-'80s, but had yet to find a suitor for his group's music.

"We talked to Roadrunner and several other labels, but I didn't like them that much at the time and thought that it was better—coming out of the hardcore scene—to basically go the do-it-yourself way and start a label," says Kampf. "So I convinced my bandmates to put trust in me and let me just do it, instead of giving it over to someone else where we were just band number 15 or 20 on the label."

Staiger actually helped fund the release of the first Despair LP, pitching in

(bottom right) Carcass' Jeff Walker and Death's Chuck Schuldiner backstage in Pittsburgh, 1990. Photo: Terri Heggen

Carcass background image by Joy Lambert. (middle right) At the Gates circa 1991

Napalm Death circa 1991. Photo: Frank White

one-third of the money for what would become Century Media Records' inaugural release in early 1989. Kampf's first official signing to the label, however, was Morgoth, whose Floridian death metal bombast belied their German heritage. Within a year, Kampf turned his attention to Sweden, signing the death metal trio of Unleashed, Grave and Tiamat.

British label Peaceville also continued to evolve, assembling an imprint called Deaf Records in early 1990. Although Deaf would only survive for a year, in 1991 the label scooped up At the Gates, who had just recorded a five-track EP, *Gardens of Grief*, with small Swedish indie Black Sun. In fact, the band actually formed only a few months prior out of the ashes of cult Swedish death metallers Grotesque.

"Grotesque ended up in this big mess, and we went to form At the Gates straightaway," says former At the Gates frontman Tomas Lindberg. "The death of Grotesque was the birth of At the Gates. We were really happy with how far we'd progressed and were ready for more people to hear us."

Earache, of course, was still the toast of the scene. In fact, they had the weight to send a band like Carcass to the US, even though, at the time, the group had no material available domestically.

"Combat wanted to have Entombed on the tour," says Carcass' Jeff Walker of the 1990 late summer trek his band eventually carried out with Death. "They had planned to release [Entombed's] album, but since Entombed couldn't do it we were, as usual, second best."

After the December release of the label's product in America, Earache wisely began dispatching more of their artists stateside. Hoping to mirror the success they'd experienced in Europe, the label organized a US Grindcrusher tour in April of 1991, featuring Nocturnus, the American debut of Godflesh, and headliners Napalm Death.

"It varied quite a bit, but generally we had about 200 to 300 people at most shows," recalls former Nocturnus drummer/vocalist Mike Browning. "There were a few very small shows, like in Virginia and South Carolina, with like 30 or 40 people, but then some very large shows in California that even sold out with like 800 people."

Combat's Jim Welch helped supervise the 45-date tour.

"The first show at Sundance out in Bayshore [in Long Island, New York] was all fucked up, actually," he says. "Godflesh couldn't get into the country the first date because they had work permit problems, which was a fucking nightmare with all these bands all the time. Finally, we got them in for the second date of the tour, which was Lamour in Brooklyn, and they get up on stage to play and the place was jam-packed, and their fucking Roland RA drum machine blanked out, and they couldn't play the show. I remember we drove to Boston overnight, it was Sunday morning, and we had to try to find them a new drum machine, which we actually ended up doing, and they sat on their bus and programmed in four songs. So their first real show was at the Channel in Boston on a Sunday afternoon, and it was fucking packed, and it was insane."

Before the tour's opening, however, Napalm Death drummer Mick Harris began reconsidering his future with the band.

"I'll be honest, I had some new ideas for Napalm," says Harris. "My first sampler was bought in '89, and I started to work with loops, and I wanted to introduce some loops into Napalm. Shane said, 'That's not gonna happen. If you wanna do that, do a project.' So I said, 'I wanna move on with Napalm, Shane. I'm not saying I wanna change things, but I wanna bring in some loops. I wanna play along to some loops. Let's still keep it brutal, but let's try and do something and move on a little bit.' That's all I can say, and I'm being honest there. I was listening to lots and lots of stuff. Things were influencing me. I don't wanna say I got bored, I just wanted to experiment."

"He was totally into his Killing Joke stuff, which we all were," Embury recalls. "But it was like, we just did *Harmony Corruption,* and all of a sudden the blasting didn't have an interest for him anymore, which I found quite difficult of Micky in some ways, because he did tend to leap from one thing to another without trying to let things grow and mature on their own."

Harris' troubles swelled in late 1989 during a particularly vexing Italian tour with recent Earache signing Hellbastard.

"I remember Barney started to have a few ups and downs emotionally," Embury explains. "And Micky really started to give Barney his typical 'Mick,' and I just said, 'Look, man, pack it in or otherwise you're out of the fucking band.' Which I can't believe I actually said now, to be honest."

"It was a particularly fraught tour," agrees Greenway. "We played this one place where they were slaughtering horses and stuff, and that really did my head in. Things got a bit fraught, and Micky just got outta control. I mean, none of us dealt with it particularly well, but Micky just started freaking out. Towards the end, Micky was very much a 'Jekyll and Hyde' character. I'll never say that I didn't love the guy, but beyond that Mick who was a real good guy, there was a real fucking sinister side to him. He would turn people in the band against each other by saying something to one person, getting a reaction from that person, and going back to another person."

"I was rocking the boat, because I can be a fucking bastard," Harris admits. "I know what I'm like, and I'm a bit of a tease. I was rubbing things in. I was playing a lot of music that was grinding them. I was being a bit of a bastard. I won't deny it. Rubbing it in: 'I like this. I like this.' I remember Shane saying, 'I've fucking had enough, Harris. Get it together. If you wanna play that shit, go off and do it. This is fucking Napalm and this is what we're doing.'"

Napalm survived the tour intact before taking a well-deserved Christmas break. After reconvening in early 1991 to record the *Mass Appeal Madness* EP with producer Colin Richardson, the band set out on the Grindcrusher tour of North America. By then, however, it was clear that the "human tornado" had blown itself out.

"'This is a six-week tour,'" Harris thought. "'This is my last chance. It's the biggest thing that we've done together—go and do it.' Towards the end, you could see it. You could see that I wasn't into it. I did what I had to do, and I remember those last few gigs—those last seven/eight gigs, I sort of just went into machine mode and played and just really cut down on the fills. It was, get it done, get off."

After the tour's final show in Trenton, New Jersey at the Trenton Gardens, the band returned to England, where a few days later Harris wrote three letters—one to Earache, one to Mark Walmesley, the band's manager at the time, and one to Shane Embury.

"I sent everything registered so that they would have to sign for it and so they did receive it," Harris explains. "I couldn't face them. I wanted to see Shane, but it was a hard thing. Even though I knew Napalm was gonna read it, I put in the letter to Shane to come with me. I just said, 'We've worked so long with this. I know Jess and Mitch are your friends. It's not firing. It's not sacking. But let's get some-

thing new together. I still wanna work with you.' He'd had a day to think about it, and he phoned up and he said, 'Come on, Micky, you're just tired.' And I said, 'No, that's it. I can't do it anymore, Shane. It's just not there.' And he said, 'Yeah, but we all want changes. You've just gotta work at things, but we can't just change like that.' I said, 'Shane, I just haven't got the feeling anymore. I'll be honest with you, I left in November of last year. I just want you to come with me. Jess and Mitch are my friends, but me and Barney have grown so far apart. Me and Barney can't be in the same room now.' And he said, 'Mick, I can't leave Jess and Mitch, they're my friends.' I said, 'No problem, Shane. Respect to you. Just do what you've gotta do. I'm sorry.' And that was it."

"It was a surprise on one hand, and on the other it wasn't," says Embury. "We had just started to widen out. We'd just been to America for our first tour, and it went down really well, so of all the times, why now? He'd tell us that when we wanted to do the next album he wanted to do blasts where there shouldn't be blasts, really weird, strange things. And it was like, okay, you wanna progress, we can appreciate that, but I think we wanted to go a little harsher after *Harmony*. So we had differing opinions, which was a bit of a blow, really. For as much as anyone could be a pain in the ass, it was still losing a member."

While Harris began the experimental electronic outfit Scorn—ironically with former Napalm Death bandmate Nick Bullen—Napalm Death were not only forced to fill one of the most demanding positions in extreme music, but to also replace the most visible drummer of the genre. Pintado remembered a friend from LA named Danny Herrera. Without a proper audition, Herrera was asked to join the band, and flew over immediately to begin rehearsing for a German festival show, followed by a six-week tour of the United States with Sepultura, Biohazard and Sick of It All.

"Danny's first show was in front of 3,000 kids in Germany," says Embury. "We were setting up for a line check, and he had never line-checked before, so we said, 'Give us your kick drum.' And he hit it once. Then on the first track of the first show in Germany his stool broke. I said, 'Danny, don't even worry about anything else then, because nothing worse can possibly happen to you.' But he pulled through."

Napalm labelmates Entombed also suffered through a tumultuous 1991, which began when drummer Nicke Andersson dismissed popular vocalist L-G Petrov from the Swedish band.

"I was pissed off, because I thought he was hitting on my girlfriend," recalls Andersson. "I'm not even sure if he did or not. If he did that's probably a reason to be pissed off, but not a reason to kick him out of the band. I was so pissed off, I just said, 'You're fucking fired.' And the other guys were like, 'Are you serious about this?' And I was like, 'Yeah, I am serious.' Looking back on it, I'm laughing about it. Like, what did I have to do that for?"

Andersson drafted former Carnage bassist Johnny Dordevic as Petrov's replacement, but when it came time to record Entombed's sophomore LP *Clandestine,* the situation changed quickly.

"Johnny was gonna be the singer, but we were rushed to the studio," Andersson remembers. "He didn't have the time to learn the songs, because we had to finish the damn album and go out on tour, so since I knew the words, I sang it. And I don't know why, but we figured no one has to know. Looking back, it's kinda funny. I don't know why you'd do such a thing. We probably had a good thought behind it. We did get a lot of questions about it, like, 'Is this really Johnny singing?' And we're like, 'Oh, sure, yeah.'

"But then it turned out that he wasn't such a good singer after all," he continues. "He didn't have the heart. He really wasn't dedicated."

Dordevic performed on half of Entombed's first US tour, with Morbid Angel and Unleashed, in 1991—guitarist Uffe Cederland provided vocals for the second half of the tour—before the band officially asked Dordevic to leave.

"Afterwards, we were like, 'Why did we do it like this? Why did I get rid of L-G?' But then I met L-G again later in the year, and I said, 'Sorry, let's just not talk about this anymore. Let's forget it ever happened.' And he came back."

While Napalm and Entombed regrouped, so too did Earache. In July of 1991, Earache's stateside distributors Relativity folded their In-Effect Records imprint, along with the Combat Records imprint that had been carrying the Earache titles. That left Jim Welch without a job and Digby Pearson without a proper label in the

Inside Jim Welch's office (pictured: Danny Lilker, Kevin Sharp)

US. The pair worked out a deal where Welch would run a US division of Earache, and Combat's parent company, Relativity, would resume distribution of Earache's titles. For the next two years, Earache's US offices were run through the kitchen of Welch's West 4th Street studio apartment in the West Village of New York City.

"I can't express how tiny it was," Welch says. "There was a doorway for the kitchen, but there wasn't a door that shut. The kitchen had a stove in it and a refrigerator in it and a big desk, and the cabinets of the stove and the desk, and that's where all the promos were kept instead of dishes."

Surely that wouldn't have mattered to the mounting number of young consumers purchasing death metal albums; 1991 proved to be the best selling year in the genre's brief history. Media played a more prominent role than in the past, finally giving death metal's vicious audio clear visuals. US publications such as *Metal Maniacs* and *Rip* awarded death metal the generous coverage it received for years prior overseas, while MTV's heavy metal specialty program *Headbanger's Ball* began playing videos from Sepultura, Morbid Angel and Napalm Death with increasing regularity.

"I always believed that the Ball needed to play death, hardcore, grindcore— whatever you call it—I just call it the really heavy shit," recalls Riki Rachtman, the former host of the US version of *Headbanger's Ball*.""Rock like Soundgarden, Pearl Jam and Stone Temple Pilots were played during the day, so why not give time to the heavy shit? I got a couple hundred letters in praise of that music getting played on 'the Ball'. Unfortunately, there were a lot more Poison and Ratt fans at the time. I was always butting heads [with MTV] because I knew what we should have been playing, but all my whining had fallen on deaf ears. We did, however, have Cannibal Corpse, Napalm Death and a few of those types of bands on as guests. Although their fans hated me, I always knew we should have given that scene more airplay."

With death metal and grindcore's heightened profile came a greater possibility of censorship. Much of the controversy started in England, where Earache Records was the first target of the UK's Obscene Publications Act, a law created to prevent the sale of material designed to "corrupt or deprave."

"As we opened up one morning in early 1991, about eight policemen and policewomen barged into Earache's office, totally out of the blue," recalls Earache founder Digby Pearson. "They proceeded to ransack the place, including smashing open a locked steel filing cabinet with crowbars. They were looking for all things 'offensive' they could lay their hands on—they seized Carcass albums, but also Cadaver's *Hallucinating Anxiety*, Filthy Christians' *Mean* and—get this—a huge poster we had on the wall of Alice Cooper holding aloft a severed bloody head, theatrical style. They took away many bags full of 'offensive' LPs and CDs and posters as evidence."

Dismember. Photo: Lena Granefelt

A few days prior to the raid, British customs seized a package containing the artwork for the new album from Painkiller, the experimental noise outfit from avant garde instrumentalist John Zorn. The record, *Guts of a Virgin*, featured a gruesome photo of a dead woman with her stomach cut open to reveal a fetus inside. The police were immediately alerted.

"I was fucking in shock," says Pearson. "Obviously I knew the bands' album covers were meant to be repulsive, but the fact they could be illegal as well never occurred to me. I had encouraged these bands to make the offensive sleeves in the first place, buying Jeff Walker the *Forensic Pathology* medical textbook to use its images for Carcass' *Reek [of Putrefaction]* cover. Basically I wanted the bands to have record sleeves that pushed back the boundaries, using real-life gore, as opposed to the fake horror movie stuff that other death metal bands had at the time."

As the months went by, the chances of a successful prosecution against Pearson and Earache dwindled until, nine months after the raid, the case was formally dropped.

"And I never did get that Alice Cooper poster back," says Pearson.

Swedish death metallers Dismember also came under fire—not for album art, but for the lyrics to the track "Skin Her Alive" from the band's Nuclear Blast debut, *Like an Ever Flowing Stream.*

"The English customs went through a package from Nuclear Blast Records to the distributor, and found our *Like an Ever Flowing Stream* album," recalls Dismember vocalist Matti Kärki of the 1991 incident. "They read the lyrics for 'Skin Her Alive' and decided that this was 'Indecent and Obscene' and declared that the album should be banned from England."

The trial, which made headlines in UK music publications such as *NME*, ended with Dismember's record deemed neither "pornographic, obscene or indecent." The band's UK distributor Plastic Head was awarded court costs of £7,500.

While death metal's commercial breakthroughs often centered around sensational storylines like these, independent record labels such as Roadrunner and Earache were obviously great success stories, boasting sales figures comparable to other indies specializing in "mainstream" music.

"When I was running Earache [in the US] we pretty much knew that when we put out a record in America it would sell 20,000 copies or sell like 6,000 of an EP, no matter what it was, barring a fucking Lawnmower Deth record," says Jim Welch. "The two years that I ran Earache independently out of my kitchen we sold about 600,000 records each year. And that's why the major labels started calling by 1991, because they were like, 'What the fuck is going on here?'"

Despite the label successes, personnel turmoil continued to plague artists on the Earache roster. Shortly after one of the label's commercially strongest outfits, Morbid Angel, released their second album, *Blessed Are the Sick*, guitarist Richard Brunelle was dismissed from the band, leaving Trey Azagthoth the group's lone guitarist.

"I think a lot of it was that they were just progressing more than I was," admits Brunelle. "I should have worked harder. I kinda took things for granted a bit. And Trey was a really talented writer, and he kinda engulfed me. By the time I learned one riff and was trying to write something, he'd have ten more riffs ready to go. He was just way ahead of me. So the band got together and made the decision for me that it was best [for me] to move on."

The loss didn't dissuade Morbid Angel manager Günter Ford from testing the band in deeper commercial waters. In September of 1991, Ford began a dialog with several major labels. By the spring of the next year, he was in negotiations

Morbid Angel circa 1991

with Giant Merchandising CEO Peter Lubin and legendary music industry power-house Irving Azoff, founder of the Warner Bros. subsidiary Giant Records.

"I have always been interested in supporting artists who are pushing the envelope in some way. I never worry about what others may think," says Azoff. "They had developed a rabid grass-roots following with only the resources of a smaller label. I was intrigued with what they could accomplish with the larger resources Giant had to offer.

"We didn't think in terms of a specific goal," Azoff continues. "We never expected a mainstream audience. Rather, we felt we could help the band and, in the process, support a band that was out of the mainstream. That was the point."

"The actual negotiations took ten minutes," recalls Ford, who orchestrated an agreement with Giant, giving them the rights to release Morbid Angel records in North America before Earache negotiated a deal of their own for Europe. "They were done in an ice cream store in California. Irving asked me what kind of ice cream I wanted, and we finished the deal. I think that probably started other people looking at the genre."

Of course, there was no precedent for death metal bands and major labels. Giant, whose hit record at the time was from pop vocal group Color Me Badd, approached their Morbid Angel relationship tentatively, presenting the group with a one-album deal that included options for five more records. Ford made certain, however, his artists would not be pushed around by corporate muscle.

"We totally trusted him to take care of us," says Morbid Angel frontman David Vincent of the manager's approach. "He got in a conference call with the A&R people over there who were 'producers' or who would want to have a 'say-so,' and he literally told them, 'You guys are not allowed in the studio when they're making the record, and you're not allowed to call them, and if I find out you did, I'm gonna fly out there and kill you.' He shielded us from any kind of corporate business and all the stuff that I know today is just the worst part of the business."

Unfortunately, not all of Earache's artists had Ford in their corner.

Corporation Pull-In

BY LATE 1991, MAJOR LABELS WERE WARMING TO THE IDEA of signing atypical rock bands, thanks to the colossal commercial achievement of "alternative" rock acts like Nirvana and Pearl Jam. Such success proved no musical exponent too peculiar for commercial consideration. Yet, it was the search for the next metal megastar—not the next grunge god—that brought many major labels to Earache Records' doorstep.

While Morbid Angel's signing to Warner Bros. subsidiary Giant established death metal as a viable commodity in the eyes of the majors, it was, ironically, Lee Dorrian's post-Napalm Death project, Cathedral, which first caught the attention of Columbia Records—and, more specifically, Josh Sarubin—in early 1992. Freshly promoted from retail marketing to an A&R position by head of the department David Kahne, Sarubin was encouraged to discover new talent in the emergent underground metal scene. Cathedral's Sabbath-induced doomy groove ultimately had a far more marketable appeal, partly because it was the polar opposite in terms of Napalm Death's velocity. After Sarubin played Kahne a copy of Cathedral's recently recorded four-track *Soul Sacrifice* EP, Columbia immediately began pursuing the group.

"At that time," Dorrian recalls, "I suppose they saw us as being the most commercially viable. When the *Soul Sacrifice* EP came out it was a bit more melodic than the other stuff that Earache was putting out—a bit more catchy, and it was a new crossover in the death metal thing. We were adding different influences to the heavier side of music at that time, and I thought they just saw us as being a bit fresher than the other bands of the time."

By the summer of 1992, Earache and Columbia had agreed on a North American licensing deal to distribute Cathedral. Word traveled fast in the tightly linked major label assembly, and soon labels like Atlantic, East/West and Def American Records were also courting other Earache artists.

"We spoke with Mark Geiger, who worked for Def American," explains Earache Records founder Digby Pearson. "He told us that [high-profile producer] Rick Rubin was madly into our stuff, particularly Godflesh—that was a key thing for the other labels. Godflesh were the prized asset, it seemed, even though they weren't the biggest seller."

"Even before the Columbia thing happened, Atlantic were interested in Godflesh," remembers former Godflesh frontman Justin Broadrick. "We went to meet the big guy at the time, who was Danny Goldberg, and we were treated like royalty for a day. He flew into London, and we had a stretch car with all of this bullshit pick us up from Birmingham and take us [to London] and back. And he

(bottom) Cathedral circa 1990. Photo: Jules Leach.

(top right) Godflesh's Justin Broadrick. Photo: Frank White

186   CHOOSING DEATH

basically told me, 'I want Godflesh, I don't want the other bands. But Earache are claiming that they'll only let us take Godflesh if we do take the other bands.' The labels knew they could get sales out of all the stuff, but they really thought that Godflesh could be the next Nine Inch Nails and that we would be selling out fucking stadiums. The buzz at the time was ridiculous. It outweighed the sales, obviously. It was all hype."

"It was nice to be wanted," says Pearson. "At the time, it came as a reassurance that Earache had something that was doing well, and in the bigger music industry it was sought after and could well be the next big thing—that's what my lawyers used to say anyway: 'If there's a new Metallica, it's coming from Earache.'"

Clearly Columbia already had a crucial chip in place with Cathedral—whose *Soul Sacrifice* EP had already sold a respectable 15,000 copies—but Earache's own US label manager Jim Welch was giving Columbia even more leverage in the developing bidding war for the Earache label.

"When we started selling all of these records in America," says Welch, "all these major labels started sniffing around, going, 'What the fuck is going on here? How is this label selling so many records with just a distribution deal for all of this extreme music?' So I was getting calls from one label about Fudge Tunnel, one label about Godflesh, one label about Napalm Death, one label about doing a label deal—there were just all of these different possibilities. So at one point, Dig came over and we just started taking meetings with all of these people, and when people found out that I actually didn't own Earache, they started offering me jobs. So basically I decided, 'Let's see how far we can take this whole thing.'

"I knew Dig was gonna be okay, because he was gonna get a deal out of this, so basically I said, 'I think I wanna go to Columbia,'" Welch continues. "Because I really liked the people there and I thought some of the people in their metal department, who I knew really well, could do a really good job with this music. So Dig said, 'Do your deal—we obviously wanna be with you where you go. Then I'll do my deal.'"

Shortly after Welch left Earache for a position as director of A&R at Columbia in April of 1993, Earache entered into a three-year North American licensing deal with Sony Music on July 13th, 1993.

"I made the decision to do the whole label and keep everything together, rather than license Godflesh to that company, Napalm to that company or Entombed to that company," Pearson explains. "It was quite unusual at the time to have enough bands that a major label wanted to do a label deal."

One of the contract's stipulations was that Columbia had free rein to specifically choose which albums to release from the Earache roster. In addition to Cathedral—whose existing contract with Columbia continued separately from the new deal—Columbia would eventually select forthcoming titles from Fudge Tun-

Cannibal Corpse circa 1994. Photo: Michael Mulley

nel, Carcass, Napalm Death, Godflesh, and Entombed to distribute. Earache artists not selected for release by Columbia would continue to be distributed through Relativity in the US.

Earache, however, wasn't alone in its major label association. Though it was never highly publicized, much of the Metal Blade Records catalog had been distributed through Warner Bros. since 1990. Conversely, Metal Blade had the power to decide what records they would offer to their major label distributor.

"One band that we didn't put through Warner Bros. was Cannibal Corpse," says Metal Blade CEO Brian Slagel. "We felt at the time it was just a little too extreme for Warner Bros. And it's probably a good thing we did. I remember we put out a GWAR [record] and, of course, [Warner Bros.] came back to us immediately and said, 'Okay, you need to take this song off the record. You need to change these lyrics.' And I said, 'That's not gonna fly.' I can't imagine what they would have done with Cannibal."

Other mainstream outlets, however, weren't so afraid to endorse Cannibal Corpse. One afternoon, Metal Blade president Mike Faley fielded an unlikely phone call from the Morgan Creek film production company regarding a new comedy called *Ace Ventura: Pet Detective*.

"Out of the blue," says Faley, "a gentleman from there called and goes, 'We're looking for a death metal song for a movie that Jim Carrey is working on. He really wants to use one in the movie.'"

To that point, Carrey was recognized for his role on the popular sketch comedy television show *In Living Color*, but was hardly an established draw at the box office. He did, however, own records by Napalm Death and Cannibal Corpse.

"I said, 'Okay, we've got 'Hammer Smashed Face' by Cannibal Corpse—you can use that,'" Faley explains. "They were looking for any band to go in there and headbang to Cannibal's music. So I offered them Cannibal."

"Mike told me, 'Jim Carrey, the guy who's doing this, is a fan of yours, he likes your music,'" says former Cannibal Corpse vocalist Chris Barnes. "And I was like, 'Jeez, this guy must like death metal or something,' which really kinda freaked me out, and I told the other guys, and me and Paul were like, 'Oh, that's fucking cool as shit.' So we got there and we pulled up to the shoot, and [Carrey] came out and we were talking to him between scenes, and he was so cool, man, he was just so fucking cool. He was goofing around with us, and I was just like, 'Dude, whatever you do, do not do that thing with your neck, that Fire Marshall fucking Bill thing,' and he was like, 'What? This? This grosses you out? All that shit you write and that little thing grosses you out?'"

While Cannibal were shooting what would become the number one movie in the United States a year later, Roadrunner Records worked out a licensing deal of their own with Sony label Epic Records. Their deal, unlike Earache's or Metal Blade's, was exclusively for the label's most commercially successful act, Sepultura. The group's *Chaos A.D.* record, released through Epic in the autumn of 1993, eventually went on to sell nearly 300,000 records, perhaps because Sepultura had abandoned their death metal roots in favor of a more palatable blend of thrash and punk.

"We were pressured by the band to make the deal," says Roadrunner A&R chief Monte Conner. "They felt that just being on Roadrunner they would never be able to step up to the next level and sell as many records as they wanted to. As it turns out, the guy that brought them to Epic wound up leaving the company a week before they signed, so their main champion was gone. So a guy named Michael Goldstone, who signed Rage Against the Machine and Pearl Jam, was assigned to be their in-house A&R person at Epic. And at the time *Chaos A.D.* came out, they were heavily promoting other metal bands like Prong and Fight and just didn't give a fuck about Sepultura, and the band got very little attention. They quickly realized that they were better off being the big fish in a small pond."

More often, however, with label distribution deals the artists themselves have little say in the matter. Fortunately for them, Carcass were one of the few acts that supported Earache's deal with Columbia.

"We were chuffed," admits former Carcass frontman Jeff Walker. "We thought, 'Fuck it, let's give her a go.' The bottom line is, we were doing this band and we weren't doing it as a serious career thing, so moving to a new level helped us keep it interesting for ourselves."

"I thought that it was totally fabulous that we were gonna get some prime

(left) Entombed's *Wolverine Blues*

(right) From Entombed's "Wolverine Blues" video

international distribution," says Carcass drummer Ken Owen. "The label had a lot more selling power than what Earache had, and at the end of the day, we wanted as many people as possible to hear it."

Other acts, like Napalm Death, weren't as pleased with the prospect of major label affiliation.

"I couldn't believe it," says Napalm vocalist Barney Greenway. "I was thinking, 'What is this guy doing?' Digby signed us to Columbia. We had nothing to do with it. I remember one day he just said, 'Oh, yeah, by the way, you're signed to Columbia Records in America and that's about it, really.' And I was like, 'What? No fucking way.' I don't remember if I came out right with it, but I remember thinking, 'This is the end of the band.' I was so disgusted. I just did not want to be on a major label, it went against what was my vision of the band. The other guys in the band weren't happy either, but they sorta took it on the chin."

Some bands, such as Bolt Thrower, who weren't selected for release through Columbia, welcomed the decision with a sense of relief.

"We thought the Earache/Columbia collaboration was the kiss of death for Earache, and we were extremely happy we weren't a part of it," says Bolt Thrower bassist Jo Bench. "When major labels get involved in a scene they usually end up killing it; luckily Bolt Thrower weren't dragged down with it."

The Columbia marketing team knew these artists already had significant fanbases upon which to build. Slick videos and aggressive advertising campaigns would help, but to reach beyond the underground death metal disciple, they would need to work more exotic angles.

Entombed had already determined that *Wolverine Blues* would be the title of their next LP, so Josh Sarubin contacted Marvel Comics, attempting to arrange a tie-in with the record and one of Marvel's most popular characters, Wolverine. To their astonishment, Marvel agreed, not only allowing the label to use an image of Wolverine on the initial pressing of the record's cover, but also permitting a lavish, partially animated video to be filmed featuring Wolverine for the LP's title track. Not everyone, however, was overjoyed with the turn of events.

"It was like we were run over by a tank or something," recalls Entombed drummer Nicke Andersson. "We had nothing to say about it. The actual song 'Wolverine Blues' was taken from a James Ellroy book about this killer that was obsessed with the animal the wolverine. And Sony was like, 'Oh, the Wolverine— Marvel Comics.' And none of us had, personally, ever read it. But they came up with this great marketing idea that they should include the comic and the video. We were like, 'Is this really a good idea?'"

For Carcass' impending *Heartwork* record, the label commissioned prestigious artist H.R. Giger to provide a cast aluminum sculpture for the album's cover art. Similarly, Columbia hired high-profile artist Antonio Serrano to direct a promotional video for the first single from what would become Godflesh's more rock-oriented *Selfless* LP. Although the arresting clip for "Crush My Soul" cost over $75,000 to film, its powerful religious imagery was deemed "too offensive" by MTV, and the video was never shown on the channel.

As the time drew closer to enter the recording studio, the temptation to craft a more commercial record loomed heavily over some of the artists. While each would record their most accessible albums to that point, to be fair, all of the Earache bands that released material through Columbia claim to have felt no pressure from the label to manufacture a more sellable album.

(left) Carcass *Heartwork*.

(right) From Godflesh's "Crush My Soul" video

"I wanna say right now that we never told the bands to change their sounds at all—ever," Pearson also stresses. "That's not Earache's way. Deep down, it was never actually said, 'Well, we're on Columbia so let's make a record that's gonna break.' But it was kinda inherent in the artists themselves—something to force them to do this and do that. Obviously, there was a little bit of pressure, I think, from Columbia. Jim Welch might disagree slightly, but from what I remember he would tell me, 'I've got to go to radio with something by Carcass, I've got to go to radio with something by Entombed.'

"I think it just came to the bands from within," Pearson continues. "After making so many albums on no budget—the Earache indie budget—they were like, 'Wow, we've got something real to work with now.'"

After Fudge Tunnel released their Earache/Columbia debut *Creep Diets*—a sludge punk metal amalgam that stylistically differed little from its predecessor—in the summer of 1993, Entombed was the first death metal band to step forth with a new LP. Although still heavier than anything even approaching mainstream, the aggressively marketed *Wolverine Blues*, released in January of 1994, delivered a crushing midtempo groove that was more akin to traditional rock and metal than brutal death

Carcass circa 1992. Photo: Joy Lambert

metal or grindcore.

"We didn't know it would be on Columbia when we wrote it," emphasizes Nicke Andersson. "It was absolutely not written for them."

Although the deal was finalized after they had finished recording the blatantly melodic *Heartwork* album, Carcass were acutely aware while still in the studio that their new LP could be distributed with major label muscle.

"I think that Carcass would have probably made *Heartwork* regardless of the Columbia deal," offers Welch. "But I think the Columbia deal pushed them a little further. It was just like a great steppingstone. I think that one thing inspired the next. I don't think that it was a conscious thing that Bill Steer woke up one morning and said, 'I think we can be Megadeth.'"

"We'd done three brutal albums by then, and although they had worked for us, we wanted to work with something a bit more accessible—something that you could listen to for more than one or two tracks without getting totally bored with it," recalls Ken Owen. "And although *Heartwork* made us a lot more accessible, we still thought of ourselves as an underground band, regardless of the fact that we were on a major label. I don't think any of us thought we were gonna sell millions—I don't think we were that naïve, really."

"Although it was never spoken about, in our heads we all made the decision that this band was gonna progress, so we tried to make each record different and better than the previous one," says Steer. "When you reach a certain point, are you gonna stay at that plateau or are you gonna try and take it further? There were no qualms about it because there was some frustration in the band because there were a million bands doing similar things out there, and rightly or wrongly, we wanted to stand out, and it just didn't seem to be happening. In other genres of music it seemed like other people would be respected as having innovated or achieved certain things before other people, but in the world of death metal, everything just seemed like this big mess of bands, and no band seemed to be coming out ahead of anybody else—nobody got any more respect than anybody else, whether you were around for three years or three months."

Other circumstances within Carcass, however, wore on guitarist Mike Amott, who, despite the band's position, left the group immediately after *Heartwork*'s recording was complete.

"By that time, everybody in Carcass was bitter and twisted," recalls Amott, who was quickly replaced with guitarist Mike Hickey. "They thought everything was bullshit, and maybe the combination of the close-mindedness of the fans and their own negativity just wasn't working for me. So I thought, 'I wanna do something fresh and get away from this.' If I would have had my head totally screwed on straight, I would have just hung in there. But I was young and emotional, and I said, 'Fuck this, I'm out of here.'"

Napalm Death was the final death metal-inclined act to begin recording their Columbia-distributed album. Entering the studio in October of 1993, the band tracked what would become the far less grinding *Fear, Emptiness, Despair,* eventually released in May of 1994.

"To be really brutally honest, the direction was fractured in the band because, after our last record [1992's *Utopia Banished*] there were a few reviews that said, 'Well, this band is treading water,'" says Napalm's Greenway. "And I think, without naming names, there were a couple of people in the band that were like, 'Hmm, maybe we should start doing something else.' So I got to rehearsal one day and I'm hearing all of these like real midpaced songs, and I just kinda turned around and went, 'Hang on, guys. Where's all the fast stuff?' I was just really confused, and thereafter my mood dipped, and that whole writing session for me was fucking agony. And the writing period had a knock-on effect to the recording period. We ended up in these studios, and we had to use the engineer on the previous album to produce it to save money, and it was just disastrous. The studio where we were at was too fucking warm and my throat kept drying up and I couldn't get the vocals recorded. If I was to go to bed tonight and have the worst nightmare I could ever have, you could describe it as the *Fear, Emptiness, Despair* nightmare."

"It was a massive learning process," remembers Napalm's bassist Shane Embury. "Shortly after we got involved in recording the record, it became apparent that there was just far too much bullshit involved with what we normally do—remixing, rerecording, and God knows what else. We'd say, 'Look, you're dealing with a band like Napalm. You don't have to spend stupid amounts of money on this record to make it sound good.'"

Although Pearson and Earache were pleased with Columbia's considerable capital helping promote their artists, ultimately, with six full-length LPs to work in the space of a few months, it was becoming clear that even a behemoth corporation like Columbia had its hands full.

"If it was up to me, I wouldn't have released so many bands through Columbia at once," says Welch. "I would have released Carcass, Entombed and Godflesh. Look, you gotta understand, I didn't know shit about working at a major record

Columbia Napalm Death promotional photo. Photo: Matt Anker

label. Everything I learned was trial and error. Columbia was the biggest major record label in America, so I went from working at this tiny little label by myself in my kitchen to working at the largest. So I couldn't have necessarily raised the red flag when the Earache deal was done and say, 'Hey, don't put out six records at once,' because I didn't know that that's just too much for somebody to bite off."

That sentiment was ultimately reflected in the album sales. In their first year of release through Columbia, Carcass, Napalm Death and Entombed each failed to SoundScan over 40,000 copies in the United States within their first two years of release, a slightly lower number than what their previous albums managed to shift. Titles from the ostensibly more commercial Godflesh and Fudge Tunnel didn't even crack the 15,000 plateau.

"I wasn't trying to reach a mass audience with this stuff," says former Columbia head of A&R David Kahne. "I was hoping we would sell 100,000 copies of at least one of the bands. If you sold that many records and you had a scene going around it could continue to grow. If you sold 100,000 Carcass records or if you sold 50,000 Fudge Tunnel and the band was touring, and then there was another band in the scene that you would sign, maybe they would take it a little bit farther. You're looking for that kind of vibe. I think part of the reason that I eventually got fired from Columbia in 1995 was that I was trying to take chances with new genres and it wasn't working."

Soon some of the bands were becoming equally disappointed with Columbia and their perception of how they were treated by the label.

"After a while it was becoming clear that Columbia just wouldn't commit to actually giving the band any real funding," claims Carcass' Walker. "At first, you think, 'We've gotten signed to a major label. They've got a shitload of money and they can do what they want.' But unless you get the support from inside the company or the funding, nothing happens. They basically wanted us to just get back in the van and just constantly tour, and we thought, 'Fuck that, we've done that for five years now.' Obviously, you've got these other bands that have got nothing more, and they're in it for a career and prepared to tour and tour, but, I'm sorry, we were just lazy. We weren't prepared to do that. We would have been quite happy if Columbia were willing to put some tour support and get us on a big tour, which they never did. It would have been nicer to play some theaters or get on a support tour, but it just never materialized. Sony was always kind of dangling the carrot that, 'We can get you this tour or that tour,' but they just never did. They always made empty promises."

The commercial folly of these Earache titles was further perplexing in light of the obvious success Giant was enjoying with Morbid Angel's *Covenant* record, an album that was actually more extreme and uncompromising—musically and lyrically—than any of the Earache titles that Columbia released.

Giant Records' Morbid Angel promotional photos. Photos: Alex Solca

Napalm Death live. Photo: Mitch Carpenter

"We had laid a lot of groundwork touring, creating a global business and connecting to the band's fans through the years," says Günter Ford, head of Morbid Angel's modestly named management company World Management. "Our deal was direct to Giant/Warner and had nothing to do with Earache. The Earache deal was with the label, and with that there were too many bands and no focus. When you have a label deal, you have a tremendous amount of infighting between the bands, and the labels each think that they were the reason that the label got a deal in the first place. And I think Columbia came to the conclusion very early on that this wasn't gonna blow up. This wasn't the next big thing. And they weren't gonna get the types of sales that even we were getting with *Covenant*. And the other part of the problem was that Columbia is a company that has historically been all about songwriters. The types of songs that would be necessary to work weren't really on the records that they were delivering at that time."

By early 1995, Columbia started cutting its losses and began dropping the Earache bands one by one. In a matter of only a few months, Columbia had severed all ties with the label it had courted so aggressively just a few years earlier.

"It didn't seem like a purging," says Kahne. "We were still trying to look at the different bands, and the time ran out on the deal, and as I remember, it just got weirder with Digby and the bands. So then you get the bands calling, trying to get around Digby, and he was a real key guy because he was supposed to set up marketing, and he was supposed to be working in Europe through his distribution over there where there was already a following. And it seemed like their bands and Digby were always just screaming at each other."

"David Kahne is quite right about the problems we encountered with the bands," says Pearson. "In hindsight—and it seems petty and irrelevant now—Earache had five bands all caught up in the race to become the first platinum death metal band in the world. It was hellishly difficult to keep five or six driven bands toeing the Earache company line. You gotta remember, they were all selling well, all working with ambitious managers, all had their own agendas. Plus, even though the bands were all on Earache, they were also somewhat in competition with each other at the same time, so if one band got $25,000 tour support from Sony for a US tour, the next one wanted $35,000. It must have driven Sony nuts, and I know one Sony product manager *did* quit at that time, citing the stress of dealing with the Earache bands' demands."

"One of the other problems was that Dig didn't really hold up his end with some stuff," says Columbia A&R man Josh Sarubin. "Once he got the deal with Columbia, he was kinda like, 'Okay,' and he just didn't do his part in a lot of it. Be-

Entombed live at a Sony showcase gig circa 1993

cause he would be obviously more hooked into the underground than we would be, we were supposed to take it once the band had gotten to a certain level, then we would grab it and take it to the next level. And slowly stuff came out that the bands didn't like him or wanna be under contract, and that whole part of it turned into a little bit of a mess."

"Josh is right about them not *wanting* to be under contract," offers Pearson. "Though, of course, they all were signed to Earache, a couple of managers saw fit to try to wriggle out of their Earache deals, presumably for their own financial gain. It was a real battle to counteract this, and quite unexpected on my part, through a lack of experience in judging certain people's capacity for greed, I suppose. My relationship with the bands and their managers changed dramatically. Most bands developed a plan to snag a major deal of their own, some commencing legal wrangling for the sole purpose to get out of the Earache deal. Naïvely, it never occurred to me that the bands wouldn't be happy to be part of the label deal. It quickly became evident that some bands' managers would prefer to discuss their touring or release plans in the US with Sony directly, circumventing Earache in the process. We were powerless to stop this. Up until that time pretty much everything in the bands' careers had been planned and carried out by Earache, but after Sony, we became more distanced from their plans through no fault of our own.

"In hindsight," Pearson continues, "I don't think anything too unusual was happening. It's human nature, after all. Crudely put, why talk to the little guys in Nottingham when you can talk directly to the guys in the huge Sony building in NYC—the ones bankrolling the operation and who held the key to all your ambitions? It's actually a common scenario played out regularly in the music business, every time a band signed on an indie has interest from a major, some maneuverings go on so the band can cut out the indie to sign directly to the major—the difference between indies' and majors' finances is just so vast, it's nothing peculiar to Earache's experience at all, it's standard practice, even."

If neither Columbia nor Earache were responsible for the unproductiveness of the deal, then one must confront the artists and their records. If, as most of the bands contend, they were simply progressing as artists, the first impressions of the groups for largely unfamiliar audiences were the bands' "mature" records. That might have been too much to ask of new listeners.

"I think the whole Earache/Columbia thing alienated a lot of the kids that were into the underground scene," says Cathedral's Lee Dorrian. "In some ways, it made things brighter and stronger for the bands, but in other ways, they pulled these bands out of the underground scene and tried to throw them out into the mass market. By doing that they're almost too glossy for the underground kids to like anymore, but they're still too heavy for the commercial kids to like, and it kinda got lost in the cross fire somewhere."

Seemingly, the bands had every conceivable factor in their favors. Each artist had a considerable and devoted fanbase, which they established through, in many cases, cultivating their own unique sounds. They had the deep pockets of a major label. And although there were no radio singles from the artists, Columbia and Earache even had the vital support of MTV's *Headbanger's Ball*.

"We had a really strong relationship with Columbia, so it was good for those bands," says Eva Nue, former co-producer of *Headbanger's Ball*. "They were one of the labels that really stood behind their bands. So if you were on Columbia, you were getting heard and played."

But ultimately, the product wasn't right for Columbia.

"Money was certainly spent," recalls Sarubin. "Don Einer, who was the president of Columbia at the time, definitely wanted to go for it. Maybe it just wasn't the right time for that stuff. I don't think any of them commercially had the track, maybe there wasn't that radio single."

Carcass live. Photo: Joy Lambert

"The ambition to be a rock star was blatant," Pearson concludes. "We were all on the same page. We all wanted to make that breakthrough. We were kinda caught up in our hype slightly. It's pretty humiliating that not even one of the six bands broke through. The sense of failure was pretty palpable. Sony, to their eternal credit, had taken a calculated gamble on the heavy/extreme Earache sound, throwing up the next wave of platinum rock acts. For the record, I have no regrets personally or problems about how things were handled by Sony at the time. Everything had gone so well for all the bands on Earache. The next album they sold more than the one before, and everything was on an up slope. The next stop was platinum albums—that was the plan. And everyone went along with that plan."

Well, maybe not everyone.

"Personally," says Napalm's Greenway, "when the deal was done, I breathed a fucking ten-minute-long sigh of relief."

Fall From Grace

SINCE EARACHE RECORDS HADN'T DELIVERED any new product to Sony Music since the autumn of 1994, Sony formally terminated its North American distribution deal with Earache in September of 1995—just two years into a three-year agreement. Sony concluded that all Earache material should again be released through RED, Earache's one-time exclusive US distribution company, which was now owned and operated by Sony Music. Although this didn't threaten the future of his company at the time, the public failure to bring his artists to a greater audience profoundly affected Earache label chief Digby Pearson.

"I was deflated," he admits. "We'd only known success as a label. Then you reach a major label and you expect [your records] to go gold or platinum—maybe unrealistic expectations, but we were having them—but it didn't happen, and the bands were dropped. Yet, at the same time, I was getting bored with death metal, to be honest. I was looking for something more exciting."

The end of the Earache/Sony deal was symbolic of something larger: the dramatic plunge of death metal's underground popularity. Of course, symptoms of the descent were surfacing in the years before the Earache/Sony deal was even completed. In the early '90s dash to sign anything that grinded, grunted and growled, labels indiscriminately handed out recording contracts to bands based often on a single demo recording. Unlike genre progenitors such as Death, Morbid Angel or Napalm Death, who had developed their approach for years prior to getting a deal, many bands of this second wave of death metal lacked the sufficient time to hone their craft into something unique. By 1995, the international death metal scene was clearly oversaturated with a glut of uninspired, unoriginal acts.

"These bands popped out and flooded the scene," says Suffocation's Terrance Hobbs, guitarist of one of the period's most often plagiarized acts. "That's kinda flattering that they were trying to imitate what we were doing back then, but there were *so* many bands doing what we were doing. We went down [to Morrisound] to get the Scott Burns production like all the other bands had been doing, because that's what Roadrunner wanted us to do. Stick a Dan Seagrave cover on there and it was like the instant Roadrunner package."

"I got caught up in it," admits Roadrunner A&R head Monte Conner of the mid-'90s feeding frenzy. "I signed some bands that maybe shouldn't have been signed. But soon we pretty much decided to get rid of the bands that we didn't feel had a future—bands like Gorguts and Sorrow, who should have never really been signed, and Immolation who, at the time, took four years to write a record. We got rid of those bands, but we kept Obituary and Deicide, because they were such important bands for the label at the time and they really helped break the label. Maybe at the time we realized that those bands were never gonna be any bigger, but at the same time they were workhorses for the label and we made a profit on them and so forth, and it's like, how can you drop those bands? It was really important, because if we would have just dropped all of the death metal bands there would have been an identity crisis."

Perhaps an even greater concern to the labels was the sharp sales decline death metal albums were experiencing. Even the principal genre movers like Deicide, Entombed and Obituary were selling between 30% and 40% of what they had in the early '90s.

"The prime directive of Roadrunner," says Conner, "has always been to sign a band, try to sell 10,000 or 15,000 on the first record, and then try to branch that out to 50,000 or 100,000 on the second and 200,000 on the third. After a while it just became no fun to sign these death metal bands with ceilings on them and know that no matter what you did, no matter what kind of record the band made, no matter who produced it, no matter how much money you spent promoting it, you were gonna sell this amount of copies, because this is what the market was. So it was like a combination of hitting that brick wall in terms of sales, as well as the genre completely stagnating, that made us get away from it and turn our attention elsewhere. So for me, when death metal got boring, all of a sudden I heard Pantera and Machine Head, and I was like, 'Fuck, this is something new. This is different.' And I started focusing my efforts on that sound."

While Conner actually signed genre luminaries Death to a one-album deal, and Obituary and Deicide remained with Roadrunner, the mid-'90s also saw death metal acts Malevolent Creation, Pestilence, Suffocation, Cynic, Gorguts, Immolation, and Sorrow either being dropped from Roadrunner or disbanding altogether.

Such aesthetical shifts signaled a decrease in employment opportunities for producer Scott Burns, the American death metal specialist. Along with the Road-

Obituary circa 1994. Courtesy Roadrunner Records. Photo: Michael Mulley

runner label, Nuclear Blast and Metal Blade stopped shipping many of their death metal bands south to Burns' primary working studio, Morrisound in Florida.

"There was work, but there wasn't the glut of bands coming out," says Burns. "I think everything was just starting to flatten out. Back in the day, Monte would say, 'Well, we expect to sell so many units.' And then he started realizing they're only gonna sell a certain amount of units with these kinds of bands.

"In my experience, there were very few bands that on their third and fourth record were putting out better records than their first or their second or even a demo," he continues. "I mean, everybody got more money, everybody spent more time in the studio, and maybe technically things sounded better. But looking back on things, for the $5,000 that was spent on the Deicide demo or the first record compared to when you spent $45,000 or $50,000 on [1997's] *Serpents of the Light*, it may sound better, but I can't tell you that it's a better record than the first Deicide record. Or even the first Obituary album, which was done on an 8-track tape machine for 500 bucks, compared to [1992's] *The End Complete*, which cost tens of thousands more to make. They sounded better and they were all good albums, but in my opinion, death metal bands weren't coming out with better records later on in their career than earlier in their career."

"The way it works in this business is that once a producer gets tagged as being such and such a producer, very few people are ever willing to give them a chance and let them do anything different," says Conner. "So we started pulling away from Scott simply because it became so trendy and it was just like assembly line stuff to go to Scott Burns, and to be quite honest, Scott's sounds were just never really that great. I think Obituary's *Slowly We Rot* record sounded good and [Sepultura's] *Beneath the Remains* sounded good, but other than that, Scott just specialized in mud."

"In my defense, it's pretty hard when you've got a week to get the best, heaviest guitar sound in the world, and the [artist] walks in and he has no earthly idea how to get that guitar sound," says Burns. "I'm not a miracle worker. I probably did 80 death metal records, but you've got drums, bass, guitar, they're all playing double bass, they're all downtuned and they're all barking, so how many ways can you make it sound different? Eventually, everybody gets used to doing things

(top left) Scott Burns works with Death at Morrisound Studio

(bottom) Deicide circa 1995. Courtesy Roadrunner. Photo: Alex McKnight

the same way. So part of it's my fault, but then part of it isn't. And I probably got big for my britches at the time and would tell some people 'whatever.' But it was pretty hard when everybody just walks in and they expect miracles on shoestring budgets and they really don't have a defined sound."

"Everybody wanted their band produced by Scott so they could sell a lot, but they didn't wanna spend a lot," recalls guitarist James Murphy, who worked with Burns as a member of both Death and Obituary. "So he had the unenviable task of working at this studio where they had a very high hourly rate for what bands could afford back then. He had to try to work fast to get something done and he had to cut corners wherever he could. So basically he tried to help the bands, and he bent over backwards. I think he was just under a lot of pressure to do a lot of records in a short period of time and make them all sound professional quality. So if that happened to you, you'd fall back on some habits too that are tried but true."

"Scott is one of the coolest human beings alive and he used to do this stuff for pennies," offers Conner. "People liked his vibe and he got along with the bands. But we just stopped using him because we overused him and we realized that there were better people to do this stuff."

Burns went on to engineer a handful of heavier mixes for industrial-flavored rock acts Gravity Kills and KMFDM, but was ultimately unable to shake his stigma as a death metal producer. In 1995, he returned to school, pursuing a computer programming career before leaving Morrisound and the record business a year later.

"You walked in a studio and everyone was like, 'Oh, you're the death metal guy,'" Burns says. "So it was pretty hard to get other work without moving to New York or LA to have a shot. Maybe if I hung around something would have happened in Tampa, but I was lucky to be in the middle of a great scene for a while, and it's better to be lucky than good sometimes."

Fearing his own luck with death metal and grindcore was running out, Earache's Digby Pearson turned his label's attention in a decidedly un-metallic direction.

"I'd say '94 to '95 onwards is when I personally became a massive fan of electronic music," Pearson explains. "In England, that music sorta took over—well, the harder stuff didn't, but techno in general, dance music was inescapable. It struck me as a really radical, interesting form of music. At the time, I preferred programmers to guitarists and drummers. I think a hell of a lot of art goes into that, and it's underestimated in the rock fraternity."

While the hard techno sounds of D.O.A., Scanner and Delta 9 were a minor hit in the underground dance community, they clearly left a negative impression with Earache's metal contingent.

Entombed circa 1997. Courtesy Music For Nations. Photo: Mez

At the Gates circa 1994. Photo: Lisa Halmshaw

Carcass during the *Swansong* sessions. Courtesy Earache

"The thing was, we never had any focus," Pearson says. "It was kinda whatever I liked that got released on Earache. This new genre was extreme techno, so I thought it was still extreme, so I thought people would like it because I liked it for that reason. So releasing this kind of music did alienate a hell of a lot of metal kids who were the bread and butter and the whole staple of what Earache's about."

After the Sony deal expired, Pearson's Earache roster appeared to be in tatters. Although there was never an official announcement, Fudge Tunnel disbanded in late 1995. Entombed also jettisoned the label, signing an ill-fated contract with East/West in 1996, only to move again to UK-based Music for Nations a year later.

The uncertainty of the band's future also took its toll on Nicke Andersson. The Entombed drummer and founder would eventually leave the band in 1997 to pilot The Hellacopters, the garage rock band he initially formed as a side project in November of 1994.

"There are, like, 20 reasons why I quit," says Andersson, "and I have to say that The Hellacopters is not a reason for quitting—I would have done it anyway."

The Earache body count rose further when, shortly following their extraordinary Earache debut, *Slaughter of the Soul,* intra-band tensions tore At the Gates apart in late 1996, after a successful North American tour with Napalm Death.

"I think the pressure was really hard on us for the next album," recalls former At the Gates frontman Tomas Lindberg. "Straight when we came off the tour there was pressure on us to do the album really quick, and there were musical differences mounting, along with tension between us. We were still pretty young, so we had a problem with the situation."

There was also the complicated matter of one of Earache's most identifiable acts, Carcass. Thanks to a curious clause in their record contact, with the release of their *Heartwork* LP Carcass had fulfilled their recording commitment to Earache.

"There was a clause in their deal at the time that said Earache could have two more albums if we got a record of theirs in the top 40 albums or singles charts," Pearson recalls.

"Before *Heartwork* came out, I said, 'We could go nuts and kinda force you into the top 40,'" he continues. "But because they were on a profit-share deal, which means they take 50% of all profits of their recordings—which is an incredibly unusual deal—I asked them, 'Do you want us to waste all of your money by plugging it into independent radio promotions to get you into the top 40?' I think it would have been worth doing, because it would have been so fucked up to have a band like that in there. But they said, 'No, don't bother spending all that, it will be okay.' And we eventually charted at 54. Then they turned the tables on me slightly and said, 'Okay, we're not gonna record for you anymore, because you couldn't get us in the top 40.' And I was like, 'You told us not to bother!'"

Only a week after *Heartwork*'s release, Carcass was on the market. The band's manager, Martin Nesbitt, was already taking steps to position the band for a record deal directly with Columbia.

"I did definitely tell Carcass to make no secrets that we were out of our contract just to get Sony to actually take a look at us," Nesbitt says. "We did have interest from East/West here in the UK, which to me was unheard of. Suddenly a UK major was interested in what Carcass were doing, and that just felt mad. But, hand on my heart, I never had any intention of signing to them. There was no point. Columbia were already working *Heartwork,* so what's the point of doing a bloody deal with somebody else? But I did have to have someone else to drive up the deal to bid against them. And the powers that be at Sony said, 'You'd better get Carcass signed, because we're not working this record just to find out that they're gone.'"

The strategy worked. On April 3rd, 1994, Carcass signed directly to Columbia Records throughout the world. Just a few months later, the band replaced recently departed guitarist Mike Hickey with 20-year-old Liverpool local Carlo Regadas and began working on what was to be their major label debut.

"The time came for us to try and start writing stuff, and Bill turned up at my house and had a drum machine and a four-track [recorder] and we were gonna start getting some ideas together," recalls Carcass bassist/vocalist Jeff Walker. "My attitude was, at that point—and I'm not just saying this to look cool now—that this album's gotta be even more extreme, more intense than *Heartwork*. But Bill just said, 'Look, I haven't got any of those riffs in me.' And he started playing these less aggressive riffs that he had, and I thought, 'Cool, I can handle that, if that's the way he wants to go, because it's his band as much as anyone's.' But at the outset, being a simpleton, I thought this album's gotta be really brutal. Somewhere along the line I just fell under Bill's spell of, 'Okay, we'll do this.'"

"I think some of the things I wanted to do were just not compatible with Carcass and the timing was all wrong," says Steer. "I think if we'd gone all out making another really crushing record like *Heartwork*, which was superheavy and it had guitars everywhere, and it was, in that world, very produced—if we carried on in that direction, who knows what might have happened? But I didn't really feel like doing that."

The recording sessions for what would become the band's *Swansong* album were particularly arduous for the group's members. After spending over two months in the studio—with the money coming out of the band's own pockets—Walker and Steer were clashing over the direction of the album with increasing regularity.

"They were butting heads constantly," remembers *Swansong* producer Colin Richardson. "But Bill was really hard on showing his feelings, so he would rather leave the room and be on his own for like three or four hours and come back rather than actually having it out with the rest of the band. He didn't know how to communicate a problem, because he was an inherently shy guy."

"The atmosphere was so bad in the room that I just knew our days were numbered," offers Steer. "We wouldn't socialize unless a band thing was happening. I wasn't even sure if we'd make it through the record. Everything felt wrong."

The band survived long enough to present rough mixes of the new material to Jim Welch at Columbia in early 1995. Welch wasn't exactly enthusiastic about what he heard.

"It was me basically saying to the band, 'I really think that you can do better. You've done better, and by better I don't mean more commercial,'" says Welch. "They already had some really commercial songs. But just because they were more commercial didn't necessarily mean they were better. I would have much rather had three songs that were heavy but still better, just more memorable. I don't care if it sounds like *Reek of Putrefaction*. I remember Jeff got really pissed off at me for saying what I thought. But especially being the first record you're gonna put out as [a] strictly Columbia [release]—I mean, come on, it should be their best record."

"Jim was a bit cold about it, and I started to hear things like, 'Maybe Jeff should go for singing lessons,'" says Walker. "Obviously I put my back up, thinking, 'What the fuck is he going on about?'"

"Jim said, 'I just think the vocals aren't accessible enough,'" recalls Richardson. "But I just think when you sign a band like Carcass you kinda know what you're gonna get. It's extreme vocals. I think they made an attempt to slim the songs down to three-and-a-half, four minutes and put in a chorus. But looking back, for me, the album never had the excitement or the classic riffs that *Heartwork* had. With the band pulling in different directions it ended up to be a little bit of a hodgepodge. What happens to certain bands is you wanna please everybody—you wanna please individual members of the band, you try and please the label, the management, and it just ends up not knowing quite where it wants to go."

It was becoming apparent that Columbia wanted no part of Carcass' new death/heavy metal direction. Sensing that the label would never provide the band with the funding to finish the album, Nesbitt proposed the idea of cutting Carcass loose from their deal with Columbia.

"It got to the point where they didn't wanna change it, and I didn't feel totally comfortable putting it out," says Welch. "We gave them back the record, they made money, and they were free to go."

Carcass used much of the money from the settlement to complete *Swansong* in April of 1995. By then, the band's members knew the record would be their last.

"That fatalistic attitude definitely set in after the album was in the can," says Walker. "We'd spent so long in the studio that I think we were just sick of the sight of each other."

"Parts of the recording were like a nightmare for me," recalls Carcass drummer Ken Owen. "Yeah, it was just a clash of personalities between Bill and Jeff. There was no malice, but I often had to mediate."

"I was really determined to see it through, because I didn't know anything else," says Steer. "But I did have this feeling that there was no way forward for the band. For me, it was a musical thing, because I had been pursuing a certain direction in my head for a few years, and then suddenly I was doing stuff and wanted to do stuff that just wasn't compatible with Carcass. I didn't wanna record four guitar tracks for each rhythm. I didn't want that wall-of-guitar sound. I didn't want the solos to sound overproduced. I wanted things to have a rock vibe to them, which is kind of crazy, thinking about the band's background. But that's

(bottom left) Six Feet Under. Courtesy Metal Blade. (top right) Napalm Death circa 1995. Courtesy Earache

just how I felt at the time. In some ways I was happy with the riffs I was bringing in, but more often than not, I was spending the day thinking, 'Fuck, this is not happening.' And I just knew that there wasn't any more mileage in this."

"Bill made the decision that I didn't have the balls to make, to be honest," says Walker. "He said to me that he didn't wanna do it anymore. And with Bill doing that, I let out a sigh of relief, because there was no way I was gonna carry on without him. I was not gonna let Bill walk away from it and me carry on like a complete loser with other musicians."

With a record but without a band, Nesbitt brought *Swansong* back to Earache despite the band's differences with Pearson. The record was eventually released in May of 1996 to lukewarm reviews and disappointing sales figures.

"I don't think that's what anybody wanted from Carcass," offers Steer, "whether it was the old fans or the new fans, the record label or whatever, we weren't delivering what people wanted."

High-profile death metallers Cannibal Corpse may not have been breaking up, but they certainly were experiencing turbulent times of their own. The 1995 recording sessions for the band's fifth LP hit a snag when vocalist Chris Barnes' touring commitment to his newly formed death metal side project Six Feet Under clashed with Cannibal's recording schedule.

"The Six Feet Under thing may have been the breaking point for them," Barnes explains. "But when I got into the studio with Cannibal, everything was cool. I remember writing [lyrics for] one song, 'Absolute Hatred,' I think [former Cannibal Corpse guitarist] Rob [Rusay] wrote it, and Rob was like, 'Oh, yeah, this is fucking killer.' He was all about it, and there were a lot of things like that. At rehearsal, when I'd bring stuff up, they all liked everything I was doing, but then when we got into the studio, I was being ripped apart by the producer, Scott Burns, about certain timings, vocal patterns, and I just couldn't agree with him. It just accelerated in the studio to right before I left for the first Six Feet Under tour. They were talking about things like, 'No, that ain't working, and this ain't working.' [Cannibal bassist] Alex Webster just wanted to get so much more technical with the music, and that's great, but I don't think that's what death metal was, I don't think that's where we started from; it was more like raw energy and just brutalness straight out—not worrying about doing a million notes in one fucking measure. So it pissed him off that when I wrote stuff, and it didn't really go along with what he was wanting from it. So when I was getting ready to leave for the tour, they were like, 'Look, we're gonna need to redo stuff when you get back, and talk about what we wanna do,' and I was like, you know, 'Whatever.' And so I left for the tour, and got back, and Alex called me and just said, 'We're gonna have to let you go. We got another singer and we're gonna rework everything.'"

Personnel tumult similarly plagued Napalm Death. With inner relations

Napalm Death circa 1995. Courtesy Earache

already precarious from the band's decision to incorporate more progressive elements into their grinding approach, Napalm's marathon 65-show, 68-date European *Diatribes* tour in the spring of 1996 only further strained affairs between the band's members.

"I was like a fucking zombie after that," remembers Napalm vocalist Barney Greenway. "I could barely walk. And then we immediately did a Japanese tour after that, which, ironically, was the most stress-free part of the world tour, but I was just really down at that point—inconsolable, almost. And I said to the guys, 'Man, I'm fucking sick of this shit.' And [guitarist] Mitch Harris turned around to me, and I remember this quite clearly, and said, 'Man, will you shut the fuck up?' And I was like, 'Fuck you,' and I was shouting in the middle of the street. I was majorly unhappy and knew something had to give. After we came home from *Diatribes* we had a few weeks off, and I never saw the guys. I never spoke to them. Then we had a meeting one day, and they came and decided that my heart wasn't in it and they should try another vocalist. And I was fucking pissed off. Although I was unhappy, by the same token I was like, 'You know what? You guys are pricks.' So they kicked me out, and so I thought, 'I best start integrating into regular life again,' which seemed really strange."

What happened next was even more peculiar. First, Napalm Death replaced Greenway with Extreme Noise Terror co-vocalist Phil Vane. And with Vane entrenched in the Napalm camp, Extreme Noise Terrorists Dean Jones and Ali Firouzbakht propositioned Greenway to fill ENT's vocal slot that Vane had vacated.

"They asked me to join full-time, and I was like, 'No, I'll do an album, but

I ain't joining,'" says Greenway. "I knew that Dean and Ali—no disrespect to them—but I knew that they were the leading lights in that band, and their opinions came first and foremost. And I've strived for fucking democracy, which was one of the things I felt was lacking in Napalm during that period. So I did the ENT album, and it was all right. And that was it. I actually did try and get another band together with the drummer from Cancer, Carl Stokes, and a couple of other guys that had never been in any bands before. The aim was to play something that I felt at the time Napalm had turned its back on, which is like fast hardcore, but what I was trying to do wasn't quite working out. We did a couple of cover songs, and that was about as far as it got, really."

Still more troubles awaited Earache. The label's other high-profile act, Morbid Angel—who were still under contract with Earache throughout Europe—were nearing the end of their relationship with Warner Bros. subsidiary Giant Records. After 1993's hugely successful *Covenant* record, the band followed it up with *Domination* in May of 1995. By then, MTV's *Headbanger's Ball* had been pulled from the airwaves in the States, leaving the band without the promotional tool that had been so vital in their recent commercial achievement. Despite still selling an impressive 70,000 copies of the record in the United States, Giant did not even consider picking up the option on the band's next full-length due to serious restructuring within the label.

In the summer of 1996, Morbid Angel were about to undergo some reorganization of their own. Longtime frontman David Vincent decided that the band's upcoming fall European tour would be his final venture with the group. Out of respect for his bandmates, he kept the decision to himself until the completion of the tour.

"There were a lot of things that were changing," says Vincent. "Some things in my mind were changing. There were just things I was unhappy about, not necessarily with the band; it was time for a change. Sometimes you get up, and you've just had it. I'm the kind of person that if I get to the point where I've had it, then I shift—I shift into something else, and that's where I was."

"At that time, I was kinda dissatisfied with some of his ideas and where the band was going," says Morbid Angel guitarist Trey Azagthoth of his former bandmate. "I always thought Dave was an incredible artist, but I could just tell that he was not really into it, because I was into the spiritualism with the music and being ritualistic, so it became difficult to relate to where each of us was coming from."

After recording four full-length LPs and spending ten years fronting Morbid Angel, death metal's allure was simply beginning to fade for Vincent.

"The last tour that we did, I wasn't getting the reaction out of the crowds that I was used to, the power, and people just going mad," Vincent recalls. "I thought maybe there was something wrong with the soundman. So I walked out during

Morbid Angel's David Vincent. Photo: Alex Solca

soundcheck and I stood at the mixing board and I listened to the band, including myself playing along at the desk. And sure enough, it was killing. We had all the technology, we put triggers on the kick drums so we didn't have to worry about the fluctuation of different mics or temperature or bass drums going out of tune. Everything just sounded tight and powerful and totally in-your-face, and I was like, 'Why is this not going over?' I could feel a difference. It wasn't the band. We were on top of our game more than anybody. But what I just realized was that everybody was doing this now. We'd go out on tour, and there would be four bands, all of them being death metal bands, all of them having blast beats and double bass and raging vocals, and people were numb. After four hours of listening to this stuff, you can only take so much. There's nowhere you can go from there."

That notion is central to the genre's demise. When bands like Napalm Death started playing as fast and heavy as possible, it was seriously intended to be the end of the line in terms of extremity. Realistically, you can't progress and expand on something that was meant to be a conclusion.

"You can look at every label's roster from that period and see hundreds of bands that really shouldn't have been putting records out in the first place, but they were part of the machine," offers Morbid Angel manager Günter Ford. "And that culminated and peaked with the Earache/Columbia deal, and with Giant/Warner and Morbid. When you have a mountaintop, either the mountaintop goes to another level and it gets bigger and bigger, or it collapses. And in the case of

Morbid Angel circa 1995. Photo Alex Solca

Darkthrone circa 1991. (with Mayhem's Euronymous)

death metal, these people underneath in these small labels really glutted up the marketplace, and not enough new, young talented bands were given the opportunity to develop properly inside the genre. And let's face it, the genre is extreme, so for it to even sell the amount of records that Morbid Angel did at the height of their career is, in fact, a minor miracle—it's just not pop music.

"In terms of commercial effort, *Domination* was a tremendous record," Ford continues. "We did get to another level. We sold over 200,000 records with that fucking thing worldwide. No one else can say that. Unfortunately, we were not able to continue with the original lineup into the next album. I do think that would have made a great difference as to what we would have done moving forward."

As the stagnating death metal genre appeared to be meeting its own commercial and creative end, black metal clearly became the underground's extreme music of choice by 1995. A first cousin of death metal, black metal took death metal's aggression and high-velocity playing, and married it with grandiose symphonic melody, in some cases, while stripping down the production and musicianship to atavistic levels in others.

Darkthrone was a perfect example of the latter. After debuting with the angular, dark death metal of *Soulside Journey* via Peaceville Records in 1990, the Norwegians quickly traded in their sweatpants and white high tops for spiked armlets and black-and-white corpsepaint. With 1991's *A Blaze in the Northern Sky*, Darkthrone became the first high-profile death metal act to publicly switch allegiance from death metal to the black metal camp.

"For me, playing black metal offered more soul and feeling," explains Dark-

throne drummer and lyricist Fenriz. "We sacked our bassist and went for the jugu-
lar around '90/'91. In retrospect, it seems like a subconscious strategy—I know,
perspective is everything. But I am sure we just followed our hearts and angry
minds at the time. Death metal became more about musicianship than message.
This was a time when people actually liked Death's *Spiritual Healing* album. Need
I say more?"

Moreover, many black metal bands in Scandinavia were generally antagonis-
tic towards death metal bands, some black metal artists even sarcastically refer-
ring to death metal as "life metal."

"The black metal movement was, at some point, hostile to parts of the death
metal scene," recalls Samoth, former guitarist and co-founder of the Norwegian
black metal band Emperor. "Certain people were opposed to the idea of death
metal becoming so 'normal' and 'mainstream' in many ways, and with the so-
called 'trend' of death metal, we also saw a lot of prototype bands that offered
little spirit and excitement. Black metal, in a way, became the opposition—it was
all about the real death and darkness, and being true to the underground cult.
However, there were still many people who enjoyed death metal, especially bands
that seemed to embrace the dark side with a real dedication, like Deicide and
Morbid Angel."

Most Scandinavian acts, however, such as Marduk and Immortal, quickly
abandoned their death metal rehearsal roots in favor of black metal's more extreme
image—and in some cases—ideologies. Varg Vikernes, of the one-man Norwegian
black metal jam Burzum, is undoubtedly the most prominent figure among them.
Prior to his murder and arson exploits—which made front-page news in Norway
and in music publications throughout Europe in the early '90s—Vikernes' crude
black metal sounds actually caught the attention of Earache Records.

"At first, we wanted to sign Burzum and I think he wanted to sign with

Emperor circa early 1990s

Earache," says Earache's Pearson. "He flew over and stayed at my house—this is before the murder. I thought he was a very interesting character, very charismatic. Of course, I had no idea what was going to happen in the future. But the main reason we didn't get involved with him is because of his racist views. I remember we were having pizza, and he was just coming off with total Nazi stuff, and we were completely shocked. After that, we wanted to keep black metal at arm's length, because we were exposed to the more unsavory elements. I mean, black metal's music is great. And maybe we gave it too wide a berth, actually. We got involved with Varg and it left an unpleasant taste in our mouth, so we thought, 'We'll leave that alone.' As a label boss, I'm kicking myself, because of a bad experience with Burzum, we basically turned our back on black metal. We shunned it when it was the most exciting music in the world, and just watched that explode right in front of our eyes."

Other labels didn't make the same mistake. Soon black metal bands such as British sensations Cradle of Filth, and Norwegians such as Emperor and Dimmu Borgir were selling the hundreds of thousands of records throughout Europe and the US that Obituary and Deicide did only a few years earlier.

"It's rather ironic," says Samoth, "that black metal probably ended up being even more 'mainstream' than death metal in the end."

Such divergent popularity further stretched the rift between the genre's artists, even if, as Günter Ford points out, there was such an obvious similarity between the two movements.

"It should have never been separated," he offers. "How different is black metal from death metal, really? They're not reinventing the wheel. Fundamentally, it borrows heavily from death metal. In the '90s, the bands that did come along that were innovative got lumped into a new genre instead of being kept in their own genre. If they had been kept in the death metal thing, it would have been like, 'Wow, this is a new death metal band called Emperor that's doing this cool thing with makeup and keyboards.' You would have had an explosion of new bands coming in and feeding the genre, and you wouldn't have had a downfall in the mid-'90s."

Back From the Dead

TERRORIZER MAGAZINE'S 1996 YEAR-END ISSUE served as a clear snapshot of death metal's evaporating presence in the underground. At the decade's onset, the genre was perhaps the lone recognized form of extreme music, but only a few years later, just a pair of death metal records—Arch Enemy's debut album *Black Earth* and Vader's *De Profundis*—appeared in the magazine's top 30 records list for the year. Other forms of extreme music—though partially or largely derived from death metal—had taken the genre's place in the extreme music pantheon.

While black metal continued its commercial ascent, doom metal bands gained widespread acceptance, passing on death metal's speed yet embracing its subterranean qualities while marrying them with the keyboard swaths of '80sflavored gothic rock. The first such group to move in such a direction was British quintet Paradise Lost, who made the transition from sloppy death metal act to gothic and doom metal progenitors with their 1991 album *Gothic*.

"We were listening to extreme metal music many years before it emerged from the underground—it was and still can be very exciting music," says Paradise Lost vocalist Nick Holmes. "But it does have its limitations. I think we explored every area we could, and grew out of it artistically and wanted to try other angles.

"After a point, I mean, how heavy or downtuned can it get—until the guitar strings are literally hanging off the neck?" he continues. "The gravel growl had worn a little thin for me, besides I've burst enough blood vessels in my eyeballs barking like a rabid dog. You can only take it so far before you think, 'Hang on, I've got another 60 shows to do and already I feel like my throat has been cut.'"

"We felt we had gone as far as we could with our style," seconds Paradise Lost guitarist Gregor Mackintosh. "So it was time for a little branching out to see if we could become more melodious but retain the dark edge."

"In the early '90s, we were into Morbid Angel and all the Napalm stuff and the early Roadrunner stuff, like Obituary's *Slowly We Rot*—the classics, as we call them now," recalls Calvin Robertshaw, former guitarist and founding member of fellow British doomsters My Dying Bride. "Once we became a band, I started to filter out a lot of the death metal I had been listening to. A lot of it just got tired, so we started to move in a different direction. We just wanted to let these death metal songs develop and breathe by building on them. We didn't want to set boundaries for ourselves by just being a death metal band, but the influence was still apparent in our music."

Similarly, groups clearly rooted in underground hardcore, such as Converge, Bloodlet and Earth Crisis, adopted death metal's sheer ferocity as the perfect

My Dying Bride circa 1990

Earth Crisis circa 1994. Courtesy Victory Records

vehicle for both their personal and political views.

"Our idea was to meld all the different styles of music together that we liked," says former Earth Crisis vocalist Karl Buchner, whose band militantly professed of vegan and straightedge lifestyles. "Me and Scott [Crouse], who wrote the majority of our guitar work, were into was those bands, like Bolt Thrower and Obituary and Carcass and Napalm Death. We liked how they had those superslow, heavy breakdowns. We loved those bands, and we always wore their shirts and we always tried to play with them. But you obviously wouldn't call what we were playing death metal."

These developments were all clear to then-*Terrorizer* editor Nick Terry, who wrote in his editorial accompanying the magazine's 1996 year-end list, "At the start of the year, nothing seemed so ghastly and tedious to our reviewers as penning a few words on a death metal album. And since every writer who voted this year has been, at one stage or another, a death metal fan, we know what we're talking about."

"Definitely in '96, there wasn't much out there," says Terry now, reflecting on a list that featured no death metal albums in its top 10. "You look at the big death metal record that came out that year, Carcass' *Swansong*—it sucked. And what else was there? There wasn't an Obituary or Deicide or Morbid Angel record that year. Most of the records had come in '95, so the problem, in a way, was actually the two-year album cycle. It just happened that there were very few full-stop death metal records that year, and most of the ones that came out were shit. Also, a lot of the death metal bands that had made death metal records had decided to 'progress out of the genre.' By the end of the year, there were pretty much examples of almost every type of death metal band having gone in that way, or bands that had previously more of a death metal element having decided to become more gothic, progressive or black metal."

There were, however, also signs of hope for conventional death metal in the coming year.

"But by the autumn," continued Terry in his notes, "it was clear that a remarkable turnaround had taken place. Vader and Arch Enemy were the bulldozers that blazed a path back to artistic greatness."

"Clearly, the Arch Enemy record was great, the sort of mainstream thing that Carcass should have made after *Heartwork*," Terry explains now. "It was the Carcass record that *Swansong* wasn't."

"I was enjoying not having anything to do with that kind of music and just playing everything else that I could do after Carcass," says Arch Enemy founder and former Carnage/Carcass guitarist Michael Amott. "Then, after a year or two, these Carcass-type riffs just started coming to me—I guess that's a sign that it's in my blood. I just kept taping them, and I ended up with a hundred riffs. Then I got Arch Enemy together and we recorded the first album, which actually contains a few riffs that were originally intended for Carcass."

"Then you had Vader at the other, less melodic, more traditional end of the spectrum," says Terry. "Vader was coming practically on the heels of the news of David Vincent leaving Morbid Angel. It completely filled that hole. You had Cryptopsy, whose *None So Vile* was something

(bottom left) Cryptopsy circa 1994

(top right) Michael Amott's Arch Enemy. (bottom right) Vader circa 1997 different. It was fresh and new and just more extreme. It was progressive and challenging. It wasn't one of these typical sludgy Suffocation-type things."

Expanding on the progressive tendencies of later Death, Holland's Pestilence and Florida death metal avants Cynic, who released only one album, *Focus*, in 1993, Cryptopsy added complex twists and turns into their arrangements that would challenge even accomplished jazz musicians.

"The way we started was more along the lines of typical death metal and grindcore," admits Cyptopsy drummer Flo Mounier. "Then we got to a point where we could tweak it and play around with it, because the musicianship got really serious. I'd say it was towards the end of *None So Vile* where we really started tweaking things. At that time, I was growing out of just listening to metal altogether and just listening to different types of music, and trying to soak up different ideas so we can bring it back to the band and meld it into Cryptopsy, and it's just been growing ever since."

Still, a complete recovery wasn't fully under way.

"To be honest, the early part of '97—just from the release cycle—it was just fallow," says *Terrorizer*'s Terry. "But then before long, there was an Obituary record, and Deicide put out a record as well—two of the flagship bands had returned. Then Brutal Truth followed as well. And then I'd definitely say that Vital Remains' *Forever Underground* was also a key record in terms of demonstrating that a death metal band that was ultimately second or third division a few years earlier could rise up and make a great record."

Perhaps even more crucial than death metal's recovering health was the reality that black metal's stranglehold on the underground was finally loosening. Ex-

Early Nile promo photo

periencing much the same saturation death metal did years before, black metal's popularity subsidence meant a level playing field where death metal could coexist with other genres of extreme music. Though it wasn't quite the commercial or artistic force it had been in previous years, by the end of 1997, death metal had visibly regained some credibility on the extreme music landscape.

"Clearly I'd call it a rebirth," says Relapse Records founder Matt Jacobson. "I could see this, because a lot of things work in cycles, and frankly, a lot of times bands' best albums are within their first three records, and so by the time they come around to their fifth record, they're either broken up or they suck. And on top of that, although there's no way to define them or see them, there are somehow breaks in generations. A death metal band is on the rise and playing shows, and therefore all the kids can totally feel it and are a part of it and are excited about it. But you give it five years down the line and those people are out of it or there are only a few left, and then new kids aren't into that rehashed old band that sucks. They're into the next new band that's the rise, so I think that's what happened to some degree, because people felt that death metal died.

"You'll notice that Relapse was basically the only label that continued to release death metal records during that mid-'90s period," Jacobson continues. "A lot of the other labels that had been mainstays in the past, whether it was Roadrunner or Nuclear Blast or even Earache, almost all of them moved away from death metal and signed up all of these goth metal bands or power metal bands and black metal bands, but they all kind of abandoned death metal. And then when things started to cycle around again, they were like, 'Oh, shit, we'd better jump back on board again.'"

To their credit, Relapse unearthed one of the bands that helped bring death metal back from the dead. In 1997, the label signed Nile, a South Carolina-based act founded by guitarist Karl Sanders in 1993. Although Sanders' formal link with the death metal scene dates back to 1987, when the guitarist briefly resided with Morbid Angel while the group was living in Charlotte, Nile was, in fact, the first brutal death metal band Sanders officially assembled.

"Well, if your connection to death metal is Morbid Angel, that's pretty untouchable," Sanders explains. "To me, it's unthinkable. I'm gonna do this thing and not even be a fucking speck, not even coming close to what I saw these guys do right in front of me. Why would I wanna try to do their gig and do it half-assed? It would just be laughable. How on earth can you touch that early Morbid Angel? You can't. Even the playing technique was not evolved enough to the point where I could have done anything that I felt was worthy of standing on its own and having respect. I had to be my own guy for a while.

"Death metal had already peaked and had taken a plunge by the time we actually formed Nile," he continues. "I knew guys back in '92 that would take their paycheck every week and buy five or six death metal CDs, but that wasn't happening anymore. All this stuff was sitting on the shelf, and bands were getting dropped like crazy. So all of a sudden it was really not cool. But we were like, 'Yeah, but we like it.'"

Following a pair of self-released EPs, the band's debut LP *Amongst the Catacombs of Nephren-Ka*, released in April of 1998, combined Sanders' fascination with Egyptian culture and lore with the ferocity of time-honored death metal. And like Morbid Angel a decade prior, Nile's epic compositions were imbued with a symphonic, neoclassical element that separated them from the streamlined bru-tality of other bands of the genre.

"Out-weirding Morbid Angel is no easy task," wrote *Terrorizer* for the magazine's year-end issue, in which *Amongst the Catacombs of Nephren-Ka* placed 12th, "but Nile pulled it off with 1998's best brutal death metal debut, Ancient Egypt was

Nile's Karl Sanders. Photo (top right) Scott Kinkade

evoked back from the dead as these Americans went into battle, piling up hands and fans as they went."

"It's kinda like a dichotomy," says Sanders of the band's Egyptian-tinged death metal ethos. "I think the music stands alone. If you didn't put any words in it at all, it would still be interesting music. But the words kind of give a point to it—they tell a story. When I was a kid, my dad would have big epic flicks on all the time, like *Ben Hur, Sodom and Gomorrah, Land of the Pharaohs,* and *The Ten Commandments.* So I thought it was just this amazing kind of thing, and I always had a personal interest in it. Ancient Egypt seems a lot more fascinating to me than driving down the street in Anytown, USA, where there's the Fast Fare, there's the McDonalds, and then there's the Quickie Mart. Nowadays, you wanna talk about religion in America, you go to a church. We have entirely dull lives and surroundings, and even our beliefs are fucking mundane. So it was just a much more interesting place for my head to be."

"The Egyptians were a totally pagan culture," Nile guitarist Dallas-Toller Wade

(left) Nile in the studio

(top right) Trey Azagthoth. Photo: Alex Solca. (bottom middle) Morbid Angel circa 1998. Photo: Alex Solca

adds succinctly. "It's perfect death metal material."

1998 also saw the return of the reconfigured Morbid Angel. With an album's worth of material already complete, guitarist Trey Azagthoth recruited gravel-throated ex-Ceremony bassist/vocalist Steve Tucker to replace the departed David Vincent.

"It wasn't easy," says Tucker, of replacing the very popular Vincent. "Death metal's a weird genre. The fans, for as brutal and as loyal and as great as they are, at the same time, there's a lot of them who are very goofy. I think, a lot of times, if it isn't exactly the way it started out, then people have a problem dealing with it, which is very funny because a band like Morbid Angel is all about nonconformity. The fact of the matter is, David Vincent left. He didn't believe it anymore. So many people talk about David coming back, and I've got no problem with David, but I think these people are fucking ignorant. David is so far from it, it's unreal. What makes the whole situation so ironic is the fact that these are the same people that are supposedly nonconformist, and they have a complete lack of ability to accept change.

"To be honest, I think that when I came in, it was an injection of excitement and hunger." Tucker continues. "I'm not David and I've never been David. I think, in the beginning, I really shunned any idea or acknowledgement of David. But the fact is, I've always thought that he was a great singer, but I do this music because of me."

In direct contrast to its major label predecessor *Domination*, the exclusively Earache-distributed *Formulas Fatal to the Flesh* was a largely uncommercial death metal juggernaut.

"I think *Domination* was lacking a little bit of what makes death metal death metal, says Azagthoth. "It was getting a little too smooth or too straight or too orderly. This album, though, is all about Morbid Angel death metal. It's brutal. It's unruly. It's dark. It's heavy.

"Some people thought Morbid Angel couldn't move ahead without Dave," Azagthoth continues. "People always said in the past, 'That Trey guy—he's the guitar player and Dave is the main brain behind the band.' [Vincent] was the brains behind the vocals and the singing, but he wasn't the brains behind the music that I wrote. With Steve, he's a really hard worker, but I felt bad for him with that album. I didn't wanna write the lyrics like today's lyrics. I wanted to write it like ancient writing, so it was really tough to sing."

"That's bullshit," says Tucker. "He didn't feel bad for me. He may feel bad now, but at the time, he didn't feel bad about it at all. He said, 'Well, dude, you just gotta do it.'"

"I wanted it to be just sick," says Azagthoth. "With David, he only had a couple of songs that he sang really fast; he usually had it more spread out where he could

Morbid Angel's Trey Azagthoth. Photo: Frank White

say each word with power. It was just kinda tough for the lyrics on *Formulas*—
they were just like a tongue twister."

Those lyrics clearly reflected a new spiritualism, which Azagthoth had embraced in the years between Morbid Angel albums. Discovering self-help authors
such as Tony Robbins and Deepak Chopra, Azagthoth interpreted their new age
philosophies for his own "spiritual growth" and "personal power."

"The thing that has always really helped Morbid Angel beyond the music was
the message," Azagthoth explains. "Even in the darker days, like *Altars of Madness*
,where it seemed like we were just Satanists, it was always positive. It's always
about freedom. I mean, the band has grown. I don't think the same way as I did
back then. It has happened that someone says, 'Oh, you guys have changed, and
that's so bad. You're not Satanists anymore and you're not talking about killing
Christ.' I try to show them the growth in how we really haven't changed.

"That said, I'm definitely not trying to smash everybody down with music
anymore," he continues. "I just wanna write music and just make it really special
and do our own thing. But back then, I did wanna kill all of the other bands, not
literally, but I did wanna just devastate everybody—that's what drove me. I'm not
gonna say that's the right way or anything, but I'd be lying if I didn't say that I
really wanted to just corner the market and be the only real band.

"I looked into the whole philosophy behind that. In other words, studying
Tony Robbins, and it's basically as simple as tearing down to build. A lot of the
lyrics in *Formulas* are about others' concepts that will limit you and the whole
idea about what is reality and what's real. Every new second is a new day, and it
doesn't have to be based on the past. We only carry the past into the present in
our minds. And our basis of reality is all based on our interpretation and based on
our experiences and previous interpretations that have happened. Things happen
and we think we understand them and we have those as reference points. I always
wanted people to go after it themselves, not to just listen to what I say, because my
words are my interpretations. They might mean one thing to me but something
else to someone else. If the idea is rebelling, the idea is breaking free from the
chains of other people's ideas—to be free, to be neutral, to be zero, to be just pure
potential. Then once you're free, there's no reason to do that anymore. Now you
want to build. It's not just the paradigm shifting, it's not just following the inner
voice, it's not just trying to make the music on *Formulas* have this special feeling,
it's also about this philosophy behind it."

More importantly for Earache, *Formulas* helped fuel the label's metallic
rebirth. Curiously, however, the label that helped trigger the extreme music explosion formed a sub-label to release extreme underground metal. In 1998, with
longtime Earache publicist Dan Tobin serving as the label's chief of A&R, Earache
officially launched the Wicked World imprint.

"What I did really resist, to my slight shame, was Earache's whole techno thing," says Tobin, whose only Earache signing prior to the Wicked World label was At the Gates in 1995. "I got the extremity, but I just didn't see the point of it. I didn't see any musicality in it. I didn't see anything challenging in it. So I was continually bitching, as Dig would say, and one day he just turned around to me and said, 'If you think you're so fucking great at this, then you do a label.' But it worried me that if I was gonna sign metal bands to Wicked World, then what did that mean for Earache? Did that mean no metal bands would go on Earache, and Earache would totally go in a techno direction?

"And that's a question I always got immediately asked," Tobin continues. "To me, I just wanted to get some more metal on Earache. And although the name Wicked World was there and the logo was there, as I told all the bands, it was all the same people working it—it was all the same money and distribution. But to be honest, I think Dig saw the Earache label going in a slightly different way at the time, with the techno and the rock like Dub War, which he was committed to breaking. And we already had the biggest death metal bands in the world—Napalm Death, we had Morbid Angel and Carcass and Entombed, and this was a way of admitting that he didn't quite appreciate what was going on in the metal scene at the time. It was myself complaining and Dig admitting that he didn't have perhaps the full grasp on what was coming through, and he just got sick of me moaning."

"Dan must take a lot of credit for the rejuvenation of Earache's A&R," says Pearson. "There was no other A&R until Dan, and that was a big fault, partly through my own pride. I thought, 'I discovered all of these bands, so I'm gonna discover the next wave.'

"What brought it home to me was when we were talking recently, Dan said early on he brought bands like Dissection to me and I was like, 'It's not as good as Morbid Angel.' He said, 'You should have listened to me, we could have signed this band.' I'd become immune to new bands somehow. They just didn't have much of an impact on me, because I had already been working with some of the best, and it's actually not the best way to do A&R—jaded, I think you'd call it. I was jaded, but I've now taken steps to get people who weren't so jaded with extreme metal to do my signings for me. That's basically what has happened. It takes me back to how I used to feel, just getting excited about new bands and the possibilities."

Tobin didn't need to look far for one of his earliest signings. In 1998, he met Morbid Angel guitarist Erik Rutan backstage at a Morbid Angel show in Sheffield, where Rutan, who officially joined Morbid as a second guitarist in 1995, slipped Tobin a copy of a demo from his other band, a blindingly fast death metal outfit dubbed Hate Eternal.

"Morbid Angel being Trey's band, after the *Domination* tour, I realized that

I really had so much more that I wanted to express than I could fully express in Morbid Angel," say Rutan, whose original Hate Eternal lineup also included Cannibal Corpse bassist Alex Webster and Suffocation guitarist Dough Cerrito. "I always wanted to front a band. It was always this underlying feeling for my whole career."

The rest of Florida's death metal scene still struggled to regain its footing. Although Obituary and Death each returned from a self-imposed three-year hiatus delivering new records, for both acts it would be their final bow.

"We wrote it during '96 and '97," says Obituary guitarist Trevor Peres of the band's *Back from the Dead* LP, "and according to the music industry's standards, we were getting old at this point. So we were like, 'We had better come up with the heaviest, most brutal thing we can think of.' I mean, it probably could have sold more, but this whole scene, at that point, I didn't realize how small it had gotten for death metal. You could only sell so many copies, and that's all you can sell."

"We never got huge, where we were playing arenas or anything, but you hate when you get to the spot where you're playing to a couple thousand people one night, and then you go out again and you're back down and the scene is just not

Erik Rutan's Hate Eternal. Top live photo: Aaron Pepelis

there," offers Obituary vocalist John Tardy. "It was hard to maintain even doing a tour unless we wanted to go straight back to driving around in a van, which, as we were starting to get a little bit older, wasn't what I wanted to do anymore."

"Basically John was just getting frustrated with touring, and that's why we really took a hiatus after [1994] *World Demise*," Peres continues. "We felt that that was hurting us, because the scene was so difficult at that point—you've gotta tour your ass off to even survive. So it was either we have to get a new singer or stop jamming. And we weren't gonna get a new singer, so we just said fuck it. Maybe we'll do another record in five years or something just for fun, just because we like to play and make a few people happy that like our music, but to me it just became more of a pain in the ass."

For Chuck Schuldiner's Death, however, a new album meant yet another new lineup of session musicians and a new label, this time Nuclear Blast. 1998's *The Sound of Perseverance* incorporated the most of Schuldiner's progressive rock influences on any Death album thus far.

"It's an album on which melody and aggression are fused," he told Italy's *Metal Hammer* that same year. "Of course, there are some extreme metal elements typical of Death, yet there are some parts that are the living proof that Death is a band with heavy metal roots, but always wanting to show, in the end, something new and fresh."

After the touring cycle for *Perseverance* ended in 1999, Schuldiner shifted focus onto his other band, Control Denied, a progressive power metal outfit he initially formed in 1995. Just after the recording of the Control Denied debut was complete in May of 1999, Schuldiner began experiencing pain in his upper neck, which he initially attributed to a strained muscle or pinched nerve. Doctors recommended an MRI, which eventually reveled a cancerous tumor on Schuldiner's brain stem.

While he began aggressive radiation therapy, Control Denied's *The Fragile Art of Existence* was released and greeted with an overwhelmingly positive reception.

Obituary circa 1997. Photo: Richard Boswell

Throughout much of his treatment, Schuldiner concentrated more on writing material for Control Denied's sophomore LP.

"It's on hold indefinitely," he said of Death in a February 2000 interview with *Metal Edge*. "I don't want to do two bands at one time. Whatever I'm into, I concentrate one thousand percent on. I've seen people try to juggle two bands at one time, and I don't think it's very sincere."

Sadly, Schuldiner never got the chance to relaunch Death or finish another Control Denied album. As his health continued to decline throughout 2001, cancer claimed Schuldiner's life in December of that year. He was 34 years old.

"One thing I do remember about Chuck," says Kam Lee, Schuldiner's former founding bandmate in both Mantas and Death, "is that even though we became rivals and everything else, I cherish those days when we were forming [Mantas and Death], because those were the purest times for me and I'm sure it was for him as well. I do remember those times as being the best."

"I remember interviewing Chuck for the Control Denied record at the end of 1999, when he had already been diagnosed with the tumor," recalls former *Terrorizer* editor Nick Terry. "I was struck by how calm and mellow he was, which was quite a contrast to the Evil Chuck of old, who always seemed to be complaining and bitching in interviews about problems with the Death lineup or his management or whatever. He didn't seem to have been an easy person to work with in the Death heyday, but that had obviously changed. So it was just an appalling tragedy to hear 18 months later that he'd lost his battle with cancer, when this meant the end of not just one, but two bands. It's all the more tragic because it was history repeating itself: Roger Patterson of the Florida band Atheist had also succumbed

Death circa 1998. Photo: Alex McKnight

The late Chuck Schuldiner. Photo Alex McKnight

to cancer back in the early '90s after they'd made just one record. I suppose because the very first death metal record I'd bought was *Leprosy* by Death, it hit hard, because here was someone dying not from rock 'n' roll stupidities, but from one of those fates that can affect anyone's family."

Before Schuldiner's untimely death, however, other death metal artists were clearly rebounding. Cannibal Corpse replaced the departed Chris Barnes with former Monstrosity frontman George "Corpsegrinder" Fischer. The group's 1996 "comeback" album *Vile* proved to be their most successful out of the gate, actually

Cannibal Corpse. Metal Blade

debuting at the 122nd position on the *Billboard* album charts—the first death metal band to infiltrate such territory. Meanwhile, Six Feet Under, Barnes' death metal side project with Obituary guitarist Allen West and former Death and Massacre members Terry Butler and Bill Andrews, soon became a successful full-time shtick for all participants.

"We purposely set out from day one to be a different type of death metal band," says Butler of Six Feet's initial intentions. "We wanted to be a groovy, back-to-the-roots type of death metal band instead of trying to be a technical blast band. There were just so many bands doing that at the time, and we wanted to go the opposite way. And so, when the first record came out, people were thinking, 'Oh, this is a big death metal supergroup', with Chris, Allen and me in the band, pulling influences from all these other bands. But when they first heard it, it was like, 'All right—this isn't what we thought it would be, but it's still cool.'"

Indeed, many other extreme music fans agreed. Six Feet Under's third full-

The commercially successful Six Feet Under. Photo: Joe Giron

length LP *Maximum Violence*, released in 1999, sold over 100,000 copies worldwide, reaching a barrier that hadn't been crossed since Morbid Angel, Deicide and Obituary accomplished it nearly a half-decade prior.

Other genre progenitors, however, weren't quite as successful. For the members of Napalm Death, it was clear their shotgun marriage with former Extreme Noise Terror vocalist Phil Vane wasn't working out. Without hesitation, they called on Mark "Barney" Greenway, the longtime vocalist whom they'd expelled from the band just four months earlier.

"Out of the blue one day, I just got a phone call from Mark Walmesley, our manager at the time," says Greenway. "And he was sort of making rounded, backwards comments about, 'Just giving a call to see how you are, and Shane had been mentioning your name, and they'd like you to go down to the studio and perhaps, could you do a few vocals on the new album?' And I was like, 'What the fuck are you talking about?' And he was like, 'You know, the new Napalm album?' I was like, 'Hang on a second, are you forgetting something? I was kicked out of this band. Are you asking me to rejoin?' And he was like, 'In a nutshell, yeah.'

"It turned out that they'd done all these rehearsals and made their merry way into the studio," Greenway continues. "It just seemed that Phil just couldn't cut it in the studio. I mean, Phil was a great vocalist in ENT. I absolutely loved ENT back in the day, but he just wasn't cutting it in the studio. So I rejoined Napalm, and the album was already written, so I just got past it, but I was happy enough. There were certain things on the album that might have raised my eyebrows a little, but I was happy to go with it, to be honest, because I was relieved to be back in the fold."

Reunited with Greenway, 1997's *Inside the Torn Apart* and 1998's *Words From the Exit Wound* albums followed the similarly spirited experimental path of Napalm's other mid '90s releases. But the often angular recordings failed to ignite fan interest, especially in the United States, where both albums failed to eclipse the 15,000 sales mark.

"We were on the verge of splitting," Greenway explains, "because we couldn't afford to physically go on."

"Some bands reach a point in their career where they have to do a turning point, so we reached ours," adds Napalm bassist Shane Embury. "Once we managed to get through the personal stuff, it came to our attention that people who were supposed to be looking after us weren't really doing a great job."

Napalm took out their frustration on Earache and label owner Digby Pearson, fueling a very public war of words between the parties that ultimately led to the label dropping Napalm Death in the spring of 1999.

"We were kinda dropped by Earache, but we weren't, really," says Greenway. "They just chose not to take up an option, and the option was almost perfect for us, because it meant that, yes, the advance was quite high, but it certainly wasn't into a six-figure sum, as [Pearson] suggests, and not anywhere near it. Can you imagine Earache paying that six-figure sum? I mean, if they say they dropped us, fine, they technically did, but it wasn't like they turned around and said, 'Right, you're dropped.' One of the reasons we were still even under contract with them was because after the *Harmony Corruption* album we signed a seven-album deal with Earache. Dig saw that we were desperate for cash. Each one of us in that band was desperate for cash—we were totally fucking broke. And Dig knew he could get his fucking claws into us if he slapped a fucking elongated deal on the table; he knew that we would sign it, because we had no other option. At the time, most labels wouldn't go anywhere near Napalm, they were too afraid of the extremity of the band, but Digby would, of course. We did re-sign for another two-album option, but that was on the advice of our manager who has since been fired.

"Earache didn't do shit for us," Greenway continues. "We had fucking no support. We never took tour support from them. I mean, it was never on the table anyway, but we never asked for it, because it would have made us pig sick to have to go Earache and start asking for tour support, because we hated the fucking way they were anyway. Why the fuck would we wanna lower ourselves and go ask Digby for extra money? We've got more pride than that. To back up my statement, it's always gonna be Digby's word against ours, but all I can say is, if people wanna

Napalm Death live in Brazil circa 1997. Photo: Denis Pereira and Joaquim Ghirotti

Napalm Death live, 1997. Photo: Mitch Carpenter

Napalm Death, live in London 1998. Photo: Naki

find out more about it, get yourselves out on the Internet, or if you can't, go to a gig, ask a former Earache band, and they will fucking tell you exactly what I'm telling you. And we have no reason to be in some grand conspiracy, because all this shit actually happened."

"Frankly, this is the sort of distortion and coloring of past events that makes me pretty annoyed," says Pearson. "Why the incessant sniping at the label that supported them for a decade or more is beyond me. I'll suggest: sour grapes, perhaps? The facts are, Napalm Death were dropped because their next personal advance under the contract was £6,500 payable each month—that's £78,000—and when you add the usual recording costs of £25,000, it makes a total of £103,000, or approximately $150,000 we would have to pay in advances to get the next album. So Barney is quite incorrect.

"That is in the ballpark of major label-type advances," Person continues. "So in the light of their steadily falling sales during the '90s, we told them straight up that we still wanted to work with Napalm, and would they consider a reduction, but they refused, which was fair enough—I agreed to the large numbers, after all—so we had no option but to be realistic and formally drop the band. Official explanation: disappointing sales didn't warrant the advances due in the deal.

"As for the tour support, it's true that Napalm never needed any. They have been an established touring band, playing in every corner of the globe under their own steam for a decade. So, why do they need support? It's a little contradictory when Shane, after being dropped, criticized us in interviews saying that Earache wouldn't give Napalm any tour support for a [November/December 1998 European] tour supporting Cradle of Filth unless a proposed video clip was scrapped to pay for it, which is exactly true, as we didn't feel comfortable funding both items, when Barney subsequently [says] they never asked for any tour support from Earache anyway and would never lower themselves to ask for any money like that. The truth is, when Napalm Death really needed it for the Cradle tour, tour support was actually paid, but it was a really rare occurrence, since it was hardly ever needed on all their other tours for a decade.

"When we dropped Napalm Death, it was also prompted in no small measure because of the massive confusion in the band's 'support team', because their longstanding manager Mark Walmesley—who dealt with all [of] Napalm Death's affairs with us on pretty much a daily basis for nine years straight—well, he just literally quit his responsibilities and disappeared out of the picture one day in 1999. And, crazy as it sounds, the band have never spoken to him to this day, greatly adding to the confusion, not to mention the air of suspicion that his sudden disappearance has fostered within the band. Because of this, Earache has been dragged through the mire with wild accusations and finger pointing for a couple of years—all such accusations are unproven and categorically denied, but have been immensely damaging to the label's reputation nonetheless."

In early 2000 free agents Napalm Death signied a one-album deal with UK-based label Dreamcatcher Records. To that end, the title of the group's first post-Earache studio LP, *Enemy of the Music Business*, is self-explanatory. Clearly

Napalm Death live in London, 1998. Photo: Naki

inspired by their preceding tumult, Napalm produced their fastest and most vitriolic album since their seminal early recordings.

"I think all the shit we went through was a good basis for inspiration," agrees Embury. "We also went through our experimental, maturing stage, and I think some people liked it and some people didn't. It was just time for us to start doing what we're known for again. I think everything we learned from those experimental records has been mashed into this record. Obviously, it's far more extreme than the last few. It's probably the heaviest album we've ever done."

The same can be said of Nile, who also returned in 2000, delivering their second full-length album, *Black Seeds of Vengeance*. By incorporating more of their traditional Middle Eastern elements with instruments such as tampuras, arghouls, sitars, gongs and kettledrums alongside their metallic savageness, the band's connection to Egyptian culture grew deeper and darker.

"Branching out to this degree will, of course, spawn detractors and imitators," declared *Terrorizer* in its October 2000 review of the incendiary *Black Seeds*, "but the exceptional authenticity of Nile's experiment cannot be questioned. Neither can the fact that this is probably the best death metal album since *Necroticism*."

"I haven't seen anybody that would say they gave a crap about doing what we're trying to do," offers Nile's chief songwriter Karl Sanders. "I'm still not sure what to think about that. On one hand, I think, 'Well, maybe people just don't like what we're doing and so why bother trying to copy it?' Imitation is supposed to

Nile live at the Dynamo Festival. Photo: Maria Oullette

be the sincerest form of flattery. Well, if no one is trying to imitate us, that's kind of unflattering."

By the end of 2000, *Terrorizer*'s annual album of the year issue awarded Nile's *Black Seeds of Vengeance* the pole position honor and Napalm's *Enemy of the Music Business* a second place finish, besting black metal godfathers Mayhem and heavy metal progenitors Iron Maiden.

"I've been playing metal and listening to metal for a long fucking time, and there are a lot of influences, and they are all part of the stuff swimming around in my brain," says Sanders. "There is a lot of stuff in that soup, so there's not one overriding, dominating influence that slaps you in the face and you go, 'Ah, this is obviously Cannibal Corpse,' or, 'Ah, this is Suffocation,' or, 'Ah, this is Morbid Angel.'

"Why in the world would anyone give a fuck about me if I were to just regurgitate old death metal point-blank? There are so many other bands that are doing that exact same thing, and we'll be another one? No—fuck, no. I don't see what the fucking point is there. I think we've got to move forward and perhaps stop looking at the past in a golden years kinda way. If death metal's gonna have a future, I think we gotta look forward."

Altering the Future

OVER THE COURSE OF TWO DECADES, death metal and grindcore's models of blast beats, guttural growls and detuned guitar riffs remained largely unchanged despite the addition of literally thousands of new bands to the underground. A new generation of Swedish death metal acts, however, seemed intent on following the leads of early innovators such as Death and Carcass. Traditionally the most melodic and tuneful of death metal and grindcore's original genesis points, Sweden's second wave of young death metallers were also expanding on the influences of their own countrymen. Their beginnings, however, were simply clear reflections of the Swedish scene's progenitors, such as Nihilist, Carnage and Dismember.

"Those guys are a couple of years older, but they were the big guys, and they put out demos and had gigs and stuff while we were just rehearsing," recalls Stockholm native Mikael Åkerfeldt. "And obviously, they were the first death metal bands who got record deals [in Sweden] and influenced the world, so we were looking up to all of those bands.

"You didn't know anything about the Stockholm scene until Entombed got their deal," he continues. "Then it kind of escalated from there, because after Entombed put out *Left Hand Path*, there was this Stockholm sound, and every band went to Sunlight Studios to get that guitar sound. I was a big fan of all those bands, like Carnage and Entombed. They were my idols."

Åkerfeldt proudly wore those influences on his long sleeves, playing in a number of local death and thrash metal groups, including Eruption, before co-founding the fledgling death metal band Opeth with guitarist/vocalist David Isberg in 1990.

"We had long songs back then, but they didn't have any kind of symphonic

or progressive elements," says Åkerfeldt, who moved from bass to guitars and vocals upon the departure of Isberg in early 1992. "It was just grind, midpaced and
doom back then. I incorporated everything into a song since I was influenced by
everybody, as long as it was extreme. I didn't actually think too much about the
quality. If they had an extreme logo, I was like, 'Yeah, this is fucking cool.' It was
not until maybe a couple of years later that you found out that some bands were
crap, while bands like Entombed and Morbid Angel, their records are timeless."

Opeth's Mikael Åkerfeldt live. Photo: Frank White

Opeth circa 1992

Within a few short years, Opeth weren't just incorporating Åkerfeldt's extreme music tastes into their approach, but also his love of obscure '70s progressive rock acts such as Camel and Caravan, resulting in a strangely sinuous blend of protracted compositions averaging nearly ten minutes in length. By the band's third full-length LP, 1998's *My Arms, Your Hearse*, Åkerfeldt had successfully implemented choral vocal lines into nearly every one of Opeth's songs, ultimately crafting some of the first traditional "hooks" brought forth in the death metal or grindcore genres.

"I think we are definitely still a death metal band," offers Åkerfeldt on the potentially thorny subject of categorization. "And to many we are nothing but a death metal band, and we still cling to those roots. We still have the vocals, and I'm still very much into the aggressive and brutal arrangements. And to me, there's not much in the world that's so aggressive and still has the finesse that death metal has. You can go and listen to grindcore and industrial and noise, and it's brutal and all, but it just has no punch. It's not that we tried to pay our dues to death metal, but for us death metal is as important a music style as pop and rock. We just wanna make Opeth the band that expanded from being a death metal band to something else, but still having those roots."

Although born in the city of Gothenburg, the roots of fellow Swede Anders Fridén weren't planted far from Åkerfeldt's. Fridén was an early underground obsessive, trading tapes and attending any death metal show that came through town after forming his own death metal act Dark Tranquillity [sic] in late 1989 at the age of 14.

"I'd say it was the traditional start-with-covers kind of thing," says Fridén of the earliest Dark Tranquillity material. "Then we get tired of that, and we started working on our own stuff. We listened to a lot of Swedish death metal, but we also listened to a lot of German thrash. As far as the influence, we wanted to do something different. We didn't wanna sound like [other Swedish death metal bands]. We did wanna have their heaviness, but with the twist of speed and melody."

That Swedish death metal influence was apparent in the band's earliest recordings, but it was the twin guitar harmonies, directly inspired by traditional heavy metal heroes Iron Maiden, that set Dark Tranquillity far apart from their blasting brethren, defining—with help from In Flames and especially At the Gates—the blatantly melodic "Gothenburg sound."

After recording a pair of demos, a 7-inch and 1993's long-player *Skydancer*, Fridén left the band in the summer of 1994 due to an unwillingness to commit to the group on a full-time basis. Six months later, he reconsidered his dedication to music, joining In Flames, while former In Flames vocalist Mikael Stanne actually filled Dark Tranquillity's vocal position, which had been vacated by Fridén. By 1999's *Colony*, In Flames' songwriting evolved to produce more tradi-

In Flames circa 2002. Courtesy Nuclear Blast Records

tional verse/chorus song structures, complementing Fridén's emergent melodious singing.

"It's never been In Flames' goal to be a death metal band," says Fridén, whose death metal rasp still dominates his vocal delivery. "In some people's eyes, we're not at all, but to some other people we might be just because we scream. I don't know and I don't really care—I hate labeling music. We just write good songs, but of course, we belong to the extreme side of music.

"You have to do something with the music," he continues. "You just can't write the same albums with the same riffs over and over. You have to incorporate new ideas and new styles. That's why we are here today. I admire those that are just into death metal and they just play death metal, as long as they don't complain about other people's choice not to do that. I mean, how much more heavy and extreme can it get?"

Former Carnage and Carcass guitarist Michael Amott asked himself the same question when he founded Arch Enemy in 1996. Down-tuned ferocity would obviously be a key component to his new band, but songwriting was equally important. To his credit, Amott has been able to craft catchy death metal songs without relying on traditionally sung vocals to deliver the hook.

(top) Angela Gossow live. Photo: Aaron Pepelis. (bottom) Arch Enemy circa 2003. Photo: Adde

"It's kind of the beauty and the beast—the contrast and the tension between major and minor keys," says Amott. "I mean, we're all music nuts in Arch Enemy, and we love playing brutal and fast, but we also like putting in melodies and harmonies and creating different atmospheres. There are a lot of bands that have the same kinda influences as us, but there's really no other band that does it exactly the same way that we do it.

"I think we *do* have death metal elements," he continues. "We used to call Carnage brutal death metal, but I've kinda moved away a little bit from categorizing stuff. We didn't even do that with Carcass. We didn't call that death metal then. And when I joined, they just wanted to call it metal. But I guess that's typical of every musician—you don't wanna categorize your music. You don't wanna put it in that box. That said, there will always be death metal in Arch Enemy, because that music is in my blood."

Arch Enemy further separated themselves from the death metal pack in 2000 with the addition of death metal's first high-profile female vocalist, Angela Gossow.

"I'm very emotional and I've got a lot of anger, and I think it's a way I can relieve my anger in a way without hurting anyone else, including myself," Gossow explains. "I've been raised a very free spirit. My mom never told me, 'You're a girl. You're not supposed to do that.' I've always been more like my brothers, climbing up trees, falling off. I've never played with dolls, I was racing toy cars.

"When I became a teenager, I was a bit different from other girls," she continues. "I didn't like the mainstream music. I didn't like the clothing that people were wearing around me, and I kept away from the typical school parties. I was just looking for something that fit me, and then I discovered a metal channel on the radio one day, and that basically changed my life. Then I got into the death metal scene, which my mom wasn't so happy about because of all the dark religious imagery. She was a bit afraid of me getting into Satanism and stuff like that, but that didn't happen. I just joined a band. I was 17 and I started screaming and growling my head off."

Not just another pretty face, Gossow's vocal delivery is nothing short of vicious. Sporting a deeper and altogether nastier voice than most of the male vocalists Amott has performed with, Gossow is determined to never soften her approach.

"I take vocal lessons, but that's basically for myself, because I'm a music fan and I should get as much education as possible, and that includes clean vocals, as well," she says. "But adding the clean female voice in Arch Enemy's sound would make it totally cheesy. I shouldn't have to do that just because of my gender."

In fact, the German-born vocalist is still only one of a handful of women playing extreme music.

"It doesn't surprise me; I guess it is an acquired taste [for women]," says Bolt Thrower bassist Jo Bench, the first woman to gain notoriety playing death metal or grindcore. "I think there are more women in the scene now than when I started out in '87, but I never thought, 'Oh, no, I'm the only girl.' If I did, I don't think I'd have lasted five minutes. I found it easier just to get on with it and let the music do the talking."

Still, such music isn't appealing to most women, in many cases, for the simple fact that a number of death metal bands seemingly advocate gruesome violence against women—most notably Cannibal Corpse, who with song titles such as "Fucked With a Knife," "She Was Asking for It," and "Entrails Ripped from a Virgin's Cunt," immediately alienate a good portion of any possible female audience.

"I loved Cannibal Corpse's [1990 debut album] *Eaten Back to Life,* because it was so extreme at the time when I was a kid, but I didn't sing along with those lyrics," Gossow admits. "It's somehow just a bit intimidating. It's so much about violence against women. It's not a guy who's being totally shredded—it's always women. It's usually a sexual thing too, like rape, then murder, and I don't think you should promote that. You don't wanna have your girlfriend raped, strangled and ripped apart when she was pregnant. I still don't get it when so many of the people out there that sing about that [subject matter] have girlfriends—I just don't know how they can justify that."

Despite such obstacles, Gossow's done her part in exposing a new generation of female fans to this extreme form of music.

Arch Enemy's Angela Gossow live. Photo: Aaron Pepelis

"Arch Enemy has tons of female fans nowadays, and we never really had that many before," says Gossow. "They're fond of me, because they see a female who's not afraid of being strong. I think it encourages guys as well to maybe get a female in a band. In fact, I'm in touch with lots of females getting involved with this music. I am totally against competition and cat fights—we support each other."

Further support for death metal even came from the once candidly hostile black metal factions. By the end of the '90s, not only had black metal bands proclaimed their fondness of old school death metal bands such as Cannibal Corpse and Deicide, some black metallers, such as Marduk, actually joined the bands on lengthy European and United States tours. The Norwegian group Zyklon, however, spoke the largest of the genre cross-pollinations. Formed in 1998 by Samoth, the then-guitarist of black metal's most popular act Emperor, Zyklon has evolved from an Emperor-esque black metal act into a pure death metal band over the course of a pair of records.

"With Emperor we wanted to do something more back to basics, and we were totally influenced by bands like Celtic Frost, Bathory and Tormentor," recalls Samoth, who, with former Emperor frontman Ihsahn, actually played guitar in the pre-Emperor death metal band Thou Shalt Suffer. "Later on, as Emperor

Zyklon circa 2003. Courtesy Candlelight Records

Akercocke circa 2003. Photo: Paul Harries

progressed and formed a sound of its own, we did take certain inspirations from death metal. Especially on [Emperor's third album] *IX-Equilibrium,* you can hear strong death metal elements in certain songs.

"I started out with death metal," he continues. "And that's the type of music that got me hooked on extreme music in the first place, so it feels very natural for me to take influences from that genre. Today I just feel more comfortable with that style. I love the brutality and aggression of death metal, that 'bad ass' feeling. However, I do not see Zyklon as an A4 death metal band at all. We're taking influences from black, industrial and thrash metal. In general, I don't see such a big difference, really. Now it's pretty much all the same type of people basically playing the same type of music with more or less the same goals. The scene is stronger if [it's] united."

British extreme band Akercocke further exemplified this idea. Like most extreme metal bands of today, Akercocke formed out of a traditional death metal band—in their case, Salem Orchid—yet over the years they've managed to combine the black metal and death metal genres in a elegant blend of brutality.

"We certainly never contrived to create a hybrid; we all listen to lots of different kinds of music, and all of our influences get thrown into the creative crucible," says Akercocke drummer David Gray, who formed the band with frontman Jason

Mendonca in December 1996. "It is important to some people to be able to classify a band, but we don't mind what people call us, I suppose we have our own sub-genre of 'Satanic' metal, if you like."

While other "Satanic" bands in the death metal scene, like Deicide and early Possessed often come across as cartoonish and juvenile, Akercocke are surprisingly refined and articulate. And although their album covers may be adorned with the well-worn Satanic metal clichés of naked women and gigantic pentagrams, Akercocke's presentation of practicing Satanists who perform exclusively in suits shatters numerous preconceptions of how a metal band—let alone a Satanic one—should appear.

"Generally speaking, Joe Public knows absolutely nothing about Satanism whatsoever, which in theory is no problem; unfortunately he frequently pretends that he does," says Gray. "Such urban myths as goat or baby sacrifice and Ouija boards influence the general public's opinion to some fictional, 'dangerous' sort of cult that just does not exist. Looking at pictures of Possessed in 1985, when they wore inverted cross-studded wristbands and such, dousing themselves in fake blood, any rational, intelligent individual can see that they are harmless kids just expressing themselves, albeit in a rather absurd fashion. The scariest things about Possessed are their outrageous fringes, but the music is absolutely magnificent. Lots of bands who are quite clearly not Satanic have produced great work based on the general themes and ideals."

While death metal and grindcore's late-'90s resurgence appeared modest by commercial standards, the influence the genres left on a new generation of musicians raised on its extremities was greater than anyone could have expected. Having forced its way into popular culture over nearly two decades, the reverberations of the movement could be felt as far as the great corn and pig state of Iowa, where Joey Jordison was raised on rock and commercial thrash metal bands such as Metallica and Megadeth in the college town of Des Moines. At the age of 14, Jordison made the transition from commercial thrash listener to underground death metal obsessive, and didn't look back for several years to come.

"Basically, death metal, as a musician on my part, it just changed everything, as far as the technicality and where you could take music," says Jordison, who began playing drums and guitar just a few years before. "Roadrunner Records had an old ad back then that had Sepultura's *Beneath the Remains* and *Slowly We Rot* by Obituary, and that helped me delve into it to where that's all I did—death metal. And that's where I learned basically all my skills from the drumming that I do—most of my style comes straight from death metal."

Still, living in the musical nothingland of Des Moines, Jordison found it difficult locating records from death metal and grindcore bands in local retail stores. Moreover, the thought of his favorite bands coming to his hometown seemed even more unlikely. The young teen took matters into his own hands with the help of a willing local rock club called Hairy Mary's.

"This is how desperate I was to get death metal into fucking Des Moines, Iowa—I started booking shows," says Jordison. "I brought in Unleashed, Broken Hope, Cannibal Corpse, Entombed, Sinister and Cynic. At the time, I was in school, and I couldn't go out of state. And I was losing shitloads of money, working my fucking ass off at a local music store just to make enough money to then bring in these bands that had guarantees and tour riders. But that's how I got to see it, by just bringing it into Des Moines."

The masked metal marauders of Slipknot. Courtesy Roadrunner Records

(right) Slipknot's Mick Thompson's Immolation tattoo

Jordison's thrash metal act Modifidious opened for the majority of the death metal bands he helped bring to town. "It was more just traditional thrash," says the drummer, "very dated sounding at that time, because at that time thrash was so dead and death metal was getting big."

Soon, however, Jordison moved on to heavier and faster sounds. First joining underground Minneapolis-based grindcore provocateurs Anal Blast on drums before starting his own death metal band, the short-lived Body Pit with Des Moines friends Paul Gray and the Immolation-tattoo-sporting death metal head Mick Thompson. During the same period, Jordison fashioned another band with Gray and Thompson they christened Slipknot. In its earliest incarnation from September of 1995, Slipknot's predominant stylistic focus was nü metal, the amalgamation of down-tuned heavy metal thunder, hip-hop groove and pop hooks that genre flagship bands such as Korn and Limp Bizkit helped popularize, packing arenas across the globe just two years later.

By then, Slipknot had crafted an elaborate image as a nine-piece, mask and boiler suit-wearing modern metal outfit. But more importantly, the band infused their music with strong influences from the death metal and grindcore records that shaped Jordison's youth. That provided enough attraction for former death metal powerhouse Roadrunner Records, which signed the band in late 1997. Despite its overtly aggressive nature, the band's self-titled label debut, released two years later, netted Roadrunner their first platinum release before going on to sell over two million copies in the United States alone.

Such commercial success placed Slipknot in an awkward position. Although their occasional pop hooks and sometimes traditionally sung vocal lines immediately disqualified the group from the death metal faction, Slipknot's members—most notably Jordison—took every opportunity to express their fondness of the genre whenever the topic would surface during interviews. When the group released their third full-length LP, 2001's *Iowa*, it debuted at #3 on the *Billboard* album charts, despite boasting a few measures of blast beats and double bass drumming in addition to vocalist Corey Taylor's deep, death metal-inspired growls.

"When *Iowa* came out, it was basically the heaviest album that's ever charted that high," says Jordison. "I was very proud of how heavy it was and how uncompromising [it was]. It wasn't watered down like a lot of metal is.

"People lump us into the nü metal category, and there might be a hint of that stuff, but if you really listen to a nü metal band and then listen to Slipknot, it's so apples and oranges that it's retarded," Jordison continues. "People just sometimes need to realize that, and that's what we're trying to do. The way I play drums is straight fucking grindcore and death metal, with a little bit more of the rock backbeat that we do. I like to think that our influences will shine through the music, even though it's not strictly death metal. But it definitely plays a huge card in the way that we write songs, and me, for just the way that I play."

Some underground fans, however, interpreted such constant championing as an attempt to gain credibility from fans of extreme music. Slipknot's public praise even raised eyebrows from former members of grindcore progenitors Napalm Death.

"The first time I read a Slipknot interview, they credited Napalm Death and Godflesh as big influences, and I just thought, 'That's hilarious,'" says ex-Napalm

Slipknot live at Ozzfest in 2001. Photo Nikki George

and Godflesh guitarist Justin Broadrick. "I'm walking around the local village I live in, with little, tiny kids walking around with baggy pants and Slipknot tops, throwing me an evil stare. And I'm looking at them thinking, 'You fuckwits wouldn't even be here if it wasn't for some of the shit I did.' I don't wanna be so egotistical or self-celebratory, but that's the fact."

"I would have thought some of those kids were listening to Napalm," seconds former Napalm drummer Mick Harris. "Certainly, the Americans are more into the hip-hop thing than the British side. And the whole nü metal thing, it's an amalgamation of everything—your Godflesh is there, your Napalm, your Carcass. They're just doing their new friendly pop version, which is musically very sad, I'm sorry to say. It does absolutely nothing for me. I look for extreme. I look for something that's pushing. They're pushing nothing. The only thing they're pushing is big bank accounts from making very, very dross music."

"Out of all the nü metal movement, we are by fucking far the most extreme band there is," says Jordison. "There is nothing whatsoever friendly about Slipknot. Corey may have a singing voice, but it's always been done with so much passion that it's always been brutal."

Despite detractors, there are clearly even more death metal and grindcore musicians—past and present—firmly in Slipknot's camp.

"Slipknot's totally a death metal band—all the elements are there," says former Morbid Angel bassist/vocalist David Vincent. "They don't call themselves death metal, but I'm very impressed with them."

"To me," says Vincent's former Morbid Angel bandmate, Erik Rutan, "the natural transition from death metal to the mainstream are Slipknot. A commercial metal band like that—it's a lot heavier than Nirvana or the alternative movement."

"If you listen to their music, there are many elements of death metal in there," explains Immolation frontman Ross Dolan. "There's the blast. There's the down-tuned guitars. There's the vocals. And I think little by little, with bands like Slipknot mentioning bands like us, I think the little things like that will help. It may not boost any of us to that level, but it's definitely gonna turn some heads and maybe get some kids interested in this type of music. I think a lot of kids that are into Slipknot would be into this type of music. A lot of kids just don't know this exists."

But when it comes to backing their words with action, Slipknot have often been thwarted. To date, Swedish post-death metallers In Flames are the only group in any way affiliated with death metal that Slipknot have taken on the road as a supporting act, while the multiplatinum thrash act Pantera took Morbid Angel on a pair of 10,000-seat-arena tours in the spring and summer of 2001.

"That's all thanks to [former Pantera vocalist] Phil Anselmo," enthuses Morbid

Angel guitarist Trey Azagthoth. "No doubt, it's all him. I mean, of course, the other guys in Pantera were very cool and they weren't rebuking us, but Phil, he really likes Morbid Angel and really wanted to have us be on a tour with them, and it was just wonderful that we were able to do it. He did everything he could to get us on there when everything was against him, because that's not the way things work at that level—bands can't say, 'I just wanna bring my friends or this cool underground band on this huge tour who's not gonna buy their way on.' So he was really an absolute paradigm shifter."

"We had problems for a couple of years, but now we're under different management," says Jordison of Slipknot's inability to showcase more extreme talent. "Now we have a little bit more control over the bands that we're gonna be able to take out. So we'll try to do even more bands like that."

Perhaps more apparent is the clear influence Slipknot have exerted on extreme metal bands, such as the aforementioned In Flames and fellow Swedish death metallers Hypocrisy.

"[Hypocrisy founder] Peter Tägtgren told me how much of an influence Slip-knot played on [Hypocrisy's 2002 record] *Catch 22*—that freaked me out," states Jordison. "Nothing is better than giving something back to the music community that meant so much to me when I was growing up. Fuck any of the money, and any of that, what it really comes down to is giving something back. Those are my fucking heroes. It's so awesome, man. And I think the reason these death metal musicians are fans of Slipknot is because they can tell directly listening to our shit how much death metal's influenced our music."

While bands such as Slipknot are crucial to death metal's survival and evolution, groups that further push the genre's perceived boundaries of extremity, such as Hate Eternal and Nile, are just as essential.

"The musical form has developed, and people have been taking it seriously for long enough that there is a fair standard of musicianship nowadays, whereas back in the early days, bands could barely play," says Nile founder Karl Sanders of death metal's technical progression. "They were experimenting with music forms they couldn't quite get yet. Listen to a death metal record made in 1988 compared to one made now, not only have they figured out how to make death metal records, but the people playing it have figured out how to genuinely play that kinda music."

"I know I'm helping the movement," says Hate Eternal founder and guitarist/vocalist Erik Rutan. "Us and newer bands like Nile are pushing the envelope and making awareness with new death metal. But we're also waking people up to the

Hate Eternal circa 2003. Photo: Mark Coatsworth

(bottom right) Nasum circa 1993. (left) Nasum live 2001

fact that death metal is just con-
stantly getting more brutal. And that, to me, is fucking exciting. I
mean, I love when I listen to new bands just pushing the envelope to a whole new
level. And to me, it sparks people's interest when you've got newer bands creating
styles of music that are totally rooted in traditional death metal, but yet so elaborate and expanded; to me, that's exciting, that's what keeps me going too.

"By now," he continues, "most people would have retired, for sure. But I
haven't reached a peak. I'm not even close to my peak yet. Not until I do ten Hate
Eternal records, man. That's the goal. And then after that, I can reassess what the
fuck I'm doing, but until that point, I'm on a mission. You can't get rid of me.
You'd have to kill me, because I love death metal, and I'm gonna be playing this
music for a long time, until I just can't play it anymore."

Though its players rarely discuss it, there is indeed a limit to how long they
can physically withstand the rigors of writing and performing extreme music. In
2000, Nile's original drummer Pete Hammoura was forced into early retirement
due to a severe shoulder injury he sustained playing Nile's outrageously fast beats.
According to Sanders, such physical side effects are fairly common in death metal
and grindcore musicians.

"I try to practice out on tour with warm-ups every day, but there are some
days when I'm playing in pain," admits the guitarist, who in his early 40s is one
of the genre's oldest musicians. "There are some days that even if I'm not playing
guitar, all of a sudden I have these horrible pains in my wrists for absolutely no

reason. It's like a knife going through my wrists, and then it goes away. So I don't know that I'm any more invulnerable to the wear and tear that it takes to play death metal. I think most people my age playing death metal have already retired from active touring. Certainly there is some toll extracted by the metal gods for those who wish to follow in their steps. People kinda take it for granted that you can go out on tour and play music like this forever. You can't. There's a cost. The cost is physical."

Though still operating well below even death metal's commercial radar, the grindcore movement continues to exist in small pockets throughout the world. Fiercely political and deeply personal, no band embodies the genre's original ethos better than Sweden's Nasum.

"You can hardly make a living out of playing grindcore, like you can by playing death metal," says Nasum drummer and founding member Anders Jakobson. "Grindcore is not popular in comparison. But on the other hand, I think that the grindcore bands that are around are really cool and healthy in their own way."

With essential new bands like Pig Destroyer and Soilent Green blasting through the underground, that may well be true. But ultimately, grindcore's stringent musical formula has denied the genre even the slight creative evolution that death metal has enjoyed.

"There are drums, there are guitars, there is bass, there are vocals," Jakobson points out, "and as soon as you expand that formula with keyboards or strange instruments, you are drifting away from grindcore. Drum machines are *not* grindcore. I hope that we will see the return of true grindcore bands in the future, but I don't want to sound like an extreme, one-vision grindcore freak, because I really like some of the more experimental stuff as well."

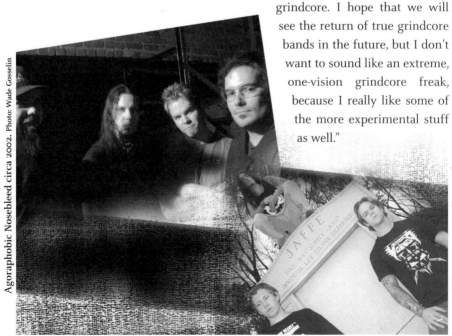

Agoraphobic Nosebleed circa 2002. Photo: Wade Gosselin

Pig Destroyer circa 2001. Photo: Jon Canady

Pig Destroyer's Scott Hull live. Photo: Scott Kinkade

From that end of the spectrum, there's Scott Hull, guitarist of the drum machine-propelled Agoraphobic Nosebleed and the more traditional grinding outfit Pig Destroyer.

"The big grind bands that are out there are more hybridizations of grind and metal, or grind and hardcore," says Hull, who formed Agoraphobic in 1994 and then Pig Destroyer in 1997. "My bands are not excluded from this. Both Pig Destroyer and, to a lesser extent, Agoraphobic Nosebleed are both moving towards the metal end of the spectrum. I imagine in the future, grindcore will eventually become a mostly inactive nostalgia genre, much like the crossover thrash shit from the mid-'80s. People will seek out polished reissues on big labels and original pressings, which will command a pretty penny on eBay.

"To the issue of experimentation," Hull continues, "on one hand, there's plenty of room for experimentation, but most of that experimentation ends up being metal-like, rather than *truly* experimental. Then again, the limitations grindcore has on it really doesn't allow for much experimentation if you're a purist."

Those genre restrictions certainly don't apply to the San Diego, California quartet The Locust, whose expeditious, keyboard-filled eruptions attract nearly as much attention as the lurid tight green hot pants and mesh masks they sport during live performances. But even though the act's image—and their song titles, which include numbers such as "Anything Jesus Does, I Can Do Better" and "The Half-Eaten Sausage Would Like to See You in His Office"—may intimate otherwise, the Locust are a very serious band in the grindcore tradition.

"Sure, we have tongue-in-cheek song titles, but I think if you read the lyrics, there's definitely a message behind everything," Locust bassist/vocalist Justin Pearson contends. "It's got a lot of political undertones dealing with social issues. But it all blurs together. It's kinda like life itself. There are the funny aspects to life, and then there's the serious shit.

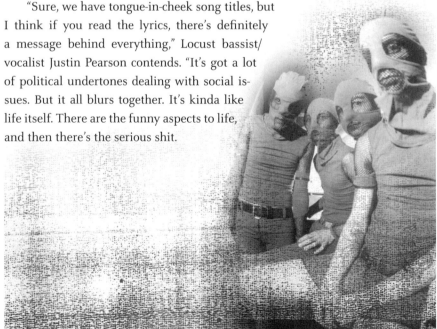

The Locust. Photo: Scott Smallin

Soilent Green's Benjamin Falgoust. Courtesy Relapse Records

"I'd rather abide by these rules than some of these other bands that are overtly political or overtly boring," he continues. "It's rehashed bullshit. There are already 150 bands that act the same and sound like that, and do we want everyone to be the same? No. So we're challenging ourselves or trying to challenge people. Sure we love Napalm Death, but they already wrote *Scum* so we don't need to do it again."

"There's always gonna be that traditional sound that everybody's gonna go back to," says Soilent Green vocalist Benjamin Falgoust. "But there's also gonna be the bands that advance things, which have taken a grindcore element and made it even more drastic—like even The Locust. In the future, when they don't even exist anymore, they'll be the people that created this new angle. They won't be making a million dollars ten years from now, but they're paving a new direction for bands to drive into, and that's the important thing. It will never die, and a lot of people still go back to the roots of it, but it kinda evolves and changes. It's the same thing with death metal. Some people say, 'Cannibal Corpse and Morbid Angel were the originators, so screw all the new death metal bands.' But without new bands like Hate Eternal and Nile changing things, the shit just dies. It just gets stale and it disappears completely."

But perhaps that's part of the problem. In their original context, the initial impact of death and metal and grindcore can never really be recaptured after two decades of desensitization to extreme music.

"I tend to disagree with that," says Earache Records head of A&R, Dan Tobin. "Okay, you could never recapture the time when you were 15 and you first heard Napalm Death or Morbid Angel. I don't know, maybe in a way I'm still hankering after what I had when I was 15. But I still think you can root out the great stuff that is still out there. I mean, Nile are really carrying things forward for death metal, Decapitated, Hate Eternal—they are all great bands and they're not copycats of what's gone before. They take the best elements of the old stuff and they take it further. I'm sure you could have had a conversation ten years ago and someone would be saying, 'Well, Napalm just sounds like Celtic Frost mixed with Discharge.' And you would have had to agree with them but, they were doing something exciting and different, and taking the extremity forward. I really fight against this whole argument that it was better back then, because I'm not sure it was as exciting as it is now."

"Now a fan has a choice," offers Cryptopsy drummer Flo Mounier, "whereas before there was maybe one type of thing that you could listen to, now he can say, 'I'm gonna relax to Cryptopsy, and then I'm gonna work out to Nile.' It's just really good, because it gives the scene a lot more credibility because it's not just one thing. It's good to have the old stuff like Cannibal Corpse with their bloody pictures, because that's their trademark and it worked for them. It's just like rock 'n' roll—the rock 'n' roll formula hasn't changed over the past 50 years. Death metal has worked in the same way."

So while much of the genre clearly continues to evolve and expand, a new gerneartion of artists led by Exhumed, Dying Fetus and Krisun draw their inspiration almost exclusively from death metal and grindcore's past. Additionally, some of the movements' oldest artists refuse to progress out of the genre or, in some cases, even travel far beyond their band's original stylistic approach.

"We decided that even if the scene disappeared, we'd keep on playing death metal," explains Dismember frontman Matti Kärki. "All of us felt that if we were going to change the music, we might as well change the name of the band as well. As for the other bands [who've left death metal behind], well, we never thought of them—their band, their problem. But in the end, staying faithful has served us well."

"I'm gonna tell it to you like this," says fellow Swede and Unleashed frontman Johnny Hedlund. "If I were finding myself in a situation one day where I didn't like death metal as a music form—maybe wake up some morning and say, 'This is too aggressive. I don't like this anymore—I'm just too darn old.' I would not play it anymore. I would not record another record, but that doesn't seem to happen. It's pretty strange, because my entire society here in Sweden has been telling me ever since I was 14 years old that this is gonna stop. Now I'm 35 years old, and I'm working on the next record. It doesn't stop. So I'm pretty excited about that, because especially back in '96 to '97, when interest was really low for death metal, I was thinking, 'Maybe this is the end. Is it really that tragic?' So I don't see where it would suddenly just die, because it can't die more than in '97. So from that I think we take quality steps upwards. I don't think we would tour like crazy for six months in a row, like we could back in the early '90s, but we can still do quality shows now.

"And I wouldn't go so far to say that death metal has to be an extreme underground movement for eternity," he continues. "Times can change. AC/DC started up back in the '70s, and they still play to full houses in Stockholm with 16,000 people watching. I think that can happen to death metal as well, but there is no doubt that it will not happen to 10 or 15 bands. Maybe one or two bands that could stand out and make something serious for a number of years, it's not gonna be enough with ten years. I think maybe in another, five, six or seven years, we will know."

"Me and a few of the other guys in some of the bands, we'll talk about the state of death metal a lot, actually, when we're on tour together," says Cannibal Corpse bassist and co-founder Alex Webster, "and I don't think most people feel these songs that we write. They hear it, but they don't feel it. They don't get the emotion out of it that we do. They don't feel the brutality. It just goes over their heads. There's only a certain kind of person that death metal reaches. I don't think it could ever be true death metal if it's for everybody. I would love it if it was—I would love to play music this brutal and be a millionaire. Anybody that says they don't wanna make money playing something they absolutely love is a liar. But it's not gonna happen if you're into death metal. You gotta be into it because you love it, if not you're gonna end up giving up on it when it's not cool anymore. A lot of that happens. A lot of bands that were into death metal just because it was getting a little more popular in the early '90s, what are they doing now? A lot of them are gone or changed their style drastically."

"I think death metal was meant to stay underground," offers Incantation founder and frontman John McEntee. "Death metal is only death metal if it's extreme, and I can't see the mainstream ever accepting death metal in all its savage purity. I feel that if it's compromised it's not death metal. It needs to be in the underground, where there are no limits to how extreme it can be. If someone is concerned with being mainstream, then start a boy band."

Still, the motivations driving these bands to persevere are often unclear to the artists themselves. For some, it's a way of avoiding a typical adulthood, while for others, it's a necessary, therapeutic part of their everyday lives.

"The reason why I play angry music is because I'm an angry person," Hate Eternal's Rutan explains. "Some people play death metal because they just appreciate heavier music, but for me, it's more deep-seated. From childhood, it's a very deep-seated rage that exists within me, and playing death metal is my outlet. Playing death metal gives me the opportunity to live like a normal person. Before I played guitar, I got in trouble with the law. I got in fights. I was a fucking wise-ass. And once I started playing guitar, I was able to focus my negative energy into a positive attribute, and that's what totally changed my life."

"We are like kids—like old kids," says Immolation's Dolan, a nearly two-decade veteran of the scene. "Of course, we have full-time jobs and a lot of responsibility. But there's that balance. We still have that passion. And we do everything in our power to make it work. I couldn't envision life without this. But believe me, it's not a lucrative business. We really don't make any money. If we come home with a few hundred dollars after being out on the road for a month, it's a lot. But I love it—traveling and going to Europe. My mother has never been to Europe in her life. She's 70, and she's so excited for me, because she's never seen Europe and I have a chance. It's priceless. It doesn't matter if we go out and we don't make a dime, it's not about that. And I still have that 15-year-old in me when it comes to this band."

Other artists, such as Deicide's Glen Benton, offer more succinct reasoning.

"It's hard, man, very hard to keep doing this," he says. "I thought many, many times of letting it go. But what else am I gonna do, go work at Checkers?"

Napalm Death's Shane Embury circa 2003. Photo: Aaron Pepelis

But for genre progenitors Napalm Death and Morbid Angel, the constant desire to innovate and expand are key reasons they have managed to persevere—in one form or another—for over 20 years. And it's a similar progressive and uncompromising nature that still propels them, despite a clearly limited audience for such extreme music.

"It's still about the feeling of the music," says Morbid Angel guitarist Trey Azagthoth. "I feel there's definitely some more exploring I need to do, but I can't really force it. It's not like going to work at some mundane job. For me, it's creating something from nothing. I keep going back to the original concept of even making a band and why do I wanna do it. I wanted to make a glorious impact on this universe. I really wanted to do something big. I know that we haven't sold millions of records and all that, but I would never take away from the extremity of the music to do that.

"It's about the paradigm shift," he continues, "the breaking the rules to do things our own way. We've been the first in death metal. We've paved the way, and even with getting our videos played on MTV. I'm so proud of that. I look back and think we've done some really cool things. I wanna continue doing it, and that's why I get so much fun out of it. And people getting inspired by our stuff and maybe paving the way for other bands as we've done, I think it's wonderful. That's when I go back to being the instrument—making things work in a good way."

For Napalm Death, their position as grindcore forefathers remains intact. In early 2003, the band even began repairing the publicly acrimonious relationship with former longtime label Earache Records, ultimately burying the hatchet with a best-of compilation called *Noise for Music's Sake* that Earache released in mid-2003 with Napalm's full cooperation. But more importantly, the band's relevance and the influence they exert on extreme music continues to be as strong as it was nearly two decades ago.

"I feel part of the furniture, almost," says Napalm Death vocalist Barney Greenway. "And I'm very proud of the name and the ethos. It's very difficult to get away from this. The day you did, you know you'd miss it so terribly.

"But I'll be brutally honest," he continues, "at different times I've felt that I'd really like to quit. I've felt that being on tour, because I find it a very lonely environment. When I'm out on the road I miss my family very much because I'm on my own. I don't have a girlfriend or a wife, and because of the situation it just makes me feel really supremely fucking lonely at times, and that's got to me. That's made me question the validity of what I'm doing, but when it comes to the crunch, the dawning of the realization of why you're doing it comes to your head. And I think about all the good things that we've achieved, the awareness that we've raised, the benefit stuff that we've done, and that makes me swell with

Deicide's Glen Benton circa 2003. Photo: Frank White

Morbid Angel circa 2003. Photo: Alex Solca

Napalm Death's Barney Greenway circa 2003. Photo: Aaron Pepelis

pride. We've just always had this sense of pride. We would never let anyone grind us down. There's been so many people that have hated the very existence of Napalm Death, and the point is, we thought, 'Go and fuck yourself. We'll just carry on and do it until it irritates you so much you can't deal with it anymore.' I've always taken on board a Motörhead song called 'Don't Let 'em Grind Ya Down.' And I always took that phrase to heart, and I just thought, 'Fuck it, let's just keep on doing it.' And there never seems to come an end point. From time to time, I think everyone in the band, we all question what we're doing and should we not do it anymore. And we still will—in the near future and the distant future. But we keep on finding that extra impetus to carry on."

"There are times when it can get pretty low," offers Shane Embury, the longest tenured member of Napalm Death. "Without jumping on a soapbox, I don't exactly make the greatest living from what I do, and that doesn't really bother me. I'm not one of these people that runs around screaming that the music industry owes me a living. Besides, I just meet people along the way that vibe me up, really. I could be at the bottom and think, 'Fuck this. I'm going nowhere. I'm getting a real job,' And then two minutes later I'm with a friend doing a project in his 8-track studio in Birmingham, and there's no monetary value or anything to that, I'm just doing it for fun. That keeps me happy."

Life After Death

Irving Azoff: Folded Giant Records in the late '90s, but is still one of the most powerful figures in the music industry. Manager of Jewel, Van Halen, and the Eagles.

Jeff Becerra: In 1988, Possessed split. A year later, Becerra was shot during an attempted robbery and left paralyzed from the waist down. Currently works in the health care industry and resides in California.

Justin Broadrick: After Godflesh disbanded in 2002, formed new band Jesu. Also a member of a number of electronic and indie hip-hop projects, such as Final and Techno Animal.

Mike Browning: Provides drums and vocals for extreme metal act After Death. Still resides in Florida.

Richard Brunelle: Currently guitarist of death metal band Paths of Possession. Still resides in Florida.

Karl Buechner: After the demise of Earth Crisis in 2001, formed metallic hardcore band Freya.

Nick Bullen: Formed Scorn with Mick Harris in 1991. Was dismissed from the group in April 1995 after assaulting a bar patron with broken glass (he was sentenced to six months in prison for the attack). Currently designs online learning tools and spearheads the dark electronic project Black Galaxy.

Scott Burns: Retired producer now works full-time as IT Consultant/Application Developer. Still resides in Florida.

Scott Carlson: Reformed Repulsion for a few live dates in 2003. Currently plays guitar in garage rock band The Superbees.

Max Cavalera: Split from Sepultura in 1996. Immediately formed marginally successful nü metal band Soulfly.

Steve Charlesworth: Continues to play drums in a number of punk and hardcore bands after the breakup of Heresy. Currently works with post-punk act Wolves of Greece.

Mitch Dickinson: Currently works in the IT field. Plans to record a new Unseen Terror album soon with Shane Embury. Also recently started an underground record label called Purist Records.

Oscar Garcia: After the demise of the original Terrorizer in 1988, formed grindcore band Nausea. Still resides in Los Angeles.

Lou Giordano: Now a high-profile rock producer who has recorded albums for Goo Goo Dolls, Belly, Sugar and Sunny Day Real Estate.

Mick Harris: Continues to record ambient electronic music as Scorn as well as Lull. Currently employed as a music technician at Hallesowen Technical College in England.

Dave Hewson: Although Slaughter officially broke up in 1990, Nuclear Blast Records remixed and remastered their *Strappado* LP and *Not Dead Yet/Paranormal* LP in 2001.

Pete Hurley: Left Extreme Noise Terror in 1995. Currently resides in England.

David Kahne: After leaving Columbia Records in 1995, returned to work as a producer. Has since produced albums by and performed with Paul McCartney, Sugar Ray, Tony Bennett and Stevie Nicks.

Erich Keller: After a 15-year silence, reformed Fear of God in late 2002. However, the band disbanded once again in January 2004.

Borivoj Krgin: Currently operates heavy metal news website www.blabbermouth.net. Resides in New York City.

Kam Lee: Fronted a number of underground Florida punk and metal bands before moving in 2002 and leaving no forwarding address.

Danny Lilker: After the breakup of Brutal Truth, reformed S.O.D. in 1999 and then reformed Nuclear Assault in 2002. Also plays bass in death metal project The Ravenous. Currently resides in Rochester, NY.

Tomas Lindberg: Immediately formed Hide, later to become The Great Deceiver, after the breakup of At the Gates in 1996. Has since also sung for The Crown, Disfear, Lock Up, and Nightrage.

J Mascis: Guitarist/vocalist disbanded successful rock band Dinosaur Jr in 1997 and formed similar new act J Mascis + the Fog.

James Murphy: In August 2001 Murphy was diagnosed with a brain tumor and underwent an immediate lifesaving operation. He is currently recovering with his family in Florida, receiving follow-up treatments and has begun work on a new Disincarnate album.

Martin Nesbitt: Head of Point Blank Management, whose current roster includes Echoboy, among other acts.

Eva Nue: No longer works on *Headbanger's Ball*, but still produces and develops many shows at MTV.

Matt Olivo: Moved from Flint, Michigan to Los Angeles, where he composes music for independent films. Plans to release material from new band Dejecta in 2004. Reformed Repulsion for a few live dates in 2003.

Ken Owen: Formed metal/rock band Blackstar with former Carcass members Jeff Walker and Carlos Regadas immediately after Carcass' breakup. Suffered a near-fatal brain hemorrhage in February 1999 and spent the next several months in a coma, followed by a long and difficult rehabilitation. Since then, he has made a significant recovery and has actually begun walking and even playing drums again.

Trevor Peres: Formed death metal band Catastrophic in 1999 after the demise of Obituary. Released *The Cleansing* through Metal Blade Records in 2001. Surprsingly reformed Obituary with founding members John and Donald Tardy in early 2004.

Riki Rachtman: Former *Headbanger's Ball* host now hosts a weekly metal radio show in Los Angeles known as "The Ball." *Headbanger's Ball* has since reappeared as a weekly program on MTV2.

Colin Richardson: Last produced a death metal album in 1999 (Cannibal Corpse's *Bloodthirst*). Currently produces and mixes music from bands such as Anathema, Machine Head and Slipknot.

Calvin Robertshaw: Works as a prepress supervisor at a printing press in Bradford, England.

Daz Russell: Still promotes punk and hardcore shows, including the annual European punk rock festival Holidays in the Sun.

Josh Sarubin: Left Columbia Records in 1999. Currently A&R director at Arista Records. Signed multiplatinum recording artist Avril Lavigne.

Kevin Sharp: After the demise of Brutal Truth in 1998, Sharp began promoting concerts in the Chicago area. Recently formed grind punk band Venomous Concept with Napalm Death bassist Shane Embury and Melvins bassist Buzz Osborne.

Tomas Skogsberg: Still owns and operates Sunlight Studio. Now produces mainstream Swedish rock bands, such as The Hellacopters and The Backyard Babies.

Bill Steer: After the demise of Carcass, Steer formed Firebird, a new band inspired by the '70s sounds of Cream, Free and Humble Pie. Currently resides in Paris.

John Tardy: Employed as a computer network administrator. Reformed Obituary with founding members brother Donald and Trevor Peres in early 2004.

Nick Terry: Left *Terrorizer* magazine in 2000 to complete his PhD in History. Currently a Visiting Research Fellow at the United States Holocaust Memorial Museum in Washington, DC.

David Vincent: Changed stage name to Evil D and joined Florida shock rockers the Genitorturers as bassist in late 1996.

Jeff Walker: Although Brazilian MTV reported he died during a surgical operation in the late 1990s, Walker is alive and well in Liverpool, England. Now, according to the man himself, he "splits his time between waiting for the phone to ring with offers he can't refuse and hoping for a nü metal band to do a Carcass cover before the bubble bursts."

Jim Welch: After leaving Columbia Records, Welch moved to Atlantic Records A&R from 1997 to 2000, then to Epic Records/Sony as Vice President of A&R from 2000 to 2003. He's currently Vice President of A&R at Arista Records.

Jim Whiteley: Relocated from Birmingham to Cheltenham in 1990. Currently employed there as a postal worker.

Robert Williams: Released three records with the dirge rock combo Nightstick. Also co-founded improvisational free-jazz-meets-grindcore band The Death's Head Quartet. Williams' former band Siege will re-release their original recordings via Deranged Records in 2004.

Choosing Death
Essential Discography

1987:
Death – *Scream Bloody Gore* – Combat
Heresy/Concrete Sox – *Split* – Earache
Napalm Death – *Scum* – Earache
S.O.B. – *Don't Be Swindle* – Selfish
Various Artists – *Raging Death* – Godly

1988:
Carcass – *Reek of Putrefaction* – Earache
Death – *Leprosy* – Combat
Fear of God – *Fear of God* 7-inch EP – Temple of Love
Napalm Death – *From Enslavement to Obliteration* – Earache

1989:
Autopsy – *Severed Survival* – Peaceville
Carcass – *Symphonies of Sickness* – Earache
Doom – *Total Doom* – Peaceville
Extreme Noise Terror – *Holocaust in Your Head* – High Speed
Morbid Angel – *Altars of Madness* – Earache
Napalm Death – *The Peel Sessions* – Strange Fruit
Napalm Death – *Mentally Murdered* EP – Earache
Obituary – *Slowly We Rot* – Roadrunner
Repulsion – *Horrified* – Necrosis (Reissued by Relapse 2003)
Terrorizer – *World Downfall* – Earache
Various Artists – *Grindcrusher* – Earache

1990:
Death – *Spiritual Healing* – Combat
Deicide – *Deicide* – Roadrunner
Entombed – *Left Hand Path* – Earache
Extreme Noise Terror – *The Peel Sessions* – Strange Fruit
Napalm Death – *Harmony Corruption* – Earache
Obituary – *Cause of Death* – Roadrunner
Various Artists – *At Death's Door: A Collection of Brutal Death Metal* – Roadrunner
Various Artists – *Death is Just the Beginning...* – Nuclear Blast

1991:
Atheist – *Unquestionable Presence* – Metal Blade
Autopsy – *Retribution for the Dead* – Peaceville
Autopsy – *Mental Funeral* – Peaceville
Bolt Thrower – *Warmaster* – Earache
Carcass – *Necroticism: Descanting the Insalubrious* – Earache
Death – *Human* – Relativity
Dismember – *Like an Ever Flowing Stream* – Nuclear Blast
Entombed – *Clandestine* – Earache
Grave – *Into the Grave* – Century Media
Immolation – *Dawn of Possession* – Roadrunner

Malevolent Creation – *The Ten Commandments* – Roadrunner
Morbid Angel – *Abominations of Desolation* – Earache (Reissue of scrapped 1986 LP)
Morbid Angel – *Blessed Are the Sick* – Earache
Napalm Death – *Mass Appeal Madness* EP – Earache
Pungent Stench – *Been Caught Buttering* – Nuclear Blast
Suffocation – *Human Waste* EP – Relapse
Suffocation – *Effigy of the Forgotten* – Roadrunner
Various Artists – *Projections of a Stained Mind* – CBR

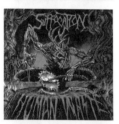

1992:
At the Gates – *The Red in the Sky Is Ours* – Deaf/Peaceville
Carcass – *Tools of the Trade* EP – Earache
Brutal Truth – *Extreme Conditions Demand Extreme Responses* – Earache
Deicide – *Legion* – Roadrunner
Malevolent Creation – *Retribution* – Roadrunner
Obituary – *The End Complete* - Roadrunner

1993:
Carcass – *Heartwork* – Earache
Cynic – *Focus* – Roadrunner
Morbid Angel – *Covenant* – Earache
Entombed – *Wolverine Blues* – Earache

1994:

Brutal Truth – *Need to Control* – Earache
Cannibal Corpse – *The Bleeding* – Metal Blade
Siege – *Drop Dead* – Relapse (Reissue of 1984 cassette)

1995:

At the Gates – *Slaughter of the Soul* – Earache
Bolt Thrower – *For Victory* – Earache
Dark Tranquillity – *The Gallery* – Osmose
Morbid Angel – *Domination* – Earache
Opeth – *Orchid* – Candlelight

1996:

Arch Enemy – *Black Earth* – W.A.R. (Reissued by Century
  Media 2002)
Cryptopsy – *None So Vile* – W.A.R. (Reissued by Century
  Media 2001)
Vader – *De Profundis* – Impact (Reissued by The End 2003)

1997:

Brutal Truth – *Sounds of the Animal Kingdom* – Relapse
Deicide – *Serpents of the Light* – Roadrunner
Dismember – *Death Metal* – Nuclear Blast
Obituary – *Back From the Dead* – Roadrunner
Suffocation – *Despise the Sun* EP – Vulture (Reissued by
  Relapse 2002)
Vital Remains – *Forever Underground* – Osmose

1998:

Cryptopsy – *Whisper Supremacy* – Century Media
Incantation – *Diabolical Conquest* – Relapse
Morbid Angel – *Formulas Fatal to the Flesh* – Earache
Nasum – *Inhale/Exhale* – Relapse
Nile – *Amongst the Catacombs of Nephren-Ka* – Relapse
Opeth – *My Arms, Your Hearse* – Candlelight
Pig Destroyer – *Explosions in Ward 6* – Clean Plate
Soilent Green – *Sewn Mouth Secrets* – Relapse

1999:

Cannibal Corpse – *Bloodthirst* – Metal Blade
Hate Eternal – *Conquering the Throne* – Wicked World
In Flames – *Colony* – Nuclear Blast
Opeth – *Still Life* – Peaceville

2000:

The Crown – *Deathrace King* – Metal Blade
Cryptopsy –*And Then You'll Beg* – Century Media
Discordance Axis – *The Inalienable Dreamless* – Hydra Head
Dying Fetus – *Destroy the Opposition* – Relapse
Napalm Death – *Enemy of the Music Business* – Dream Catcher
Nasum – *Human 2.0* – Relapse
Nile – *Black Seeds of Vengeance* – Relapse
Vader – *Litany* – Metal Blade

2001:

Akercocke – *Goat of Mendes* – Peaceville
Arch Enemy – *Wages of Sin* – Century Media
Opeth – *Blackwater Park*– Music for Nations
Pig Destroyer – *Prowler in the Yard* – Relapse

2002:

Agoraphobic Nosebleed – *Frozen Corpse Stuffed With Dope* – Relapse
Decapitated – *Nihility* – Earache
Hate Eternal – *King of All Kings* – Earache
Napalm Death – *Order of the Leech* – FETO/Snapper
Nile – *In Their Darkened Shrines* – Relapse

2003:

Akercoke – *Choronzon* – Earache
Arch Enemy – *Anthems of Rebellion* – Century Media
Exhumed – *Anatomy Is Destiny* – Relapse
Master – *Unreleased 1985 Album* – From Beyond Productions
Napalm Death – *Noise for Music's Sake* – Earache
Nasum – *Helvete* – Relapse
Zyklon – *Aeon* – Candlelight

Note: *This discography includes proper full-length records and EP releases only. There are a number of artists whose demo and rehearsal recordings are equally essential listening, but they've never been granted a legitimate release.*

About the Author

Albert Mudrian was born in Wilkes-Barre, Pennsylvania in 1975. Since 1997, he has served as an editor of all Red Flag Media publications. He currently resides in Philadelphia where he waits in vain for a Philly team to bring home a sports championship of any kind.

You've Read the Book.
Now Own the Album.

FERAL HOUSE
www.feralhouse.com

"The most courageous and incendiary publisher in the U.S." – *Headpress*

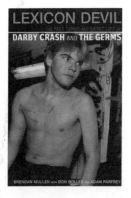

Lexicon Devil
The Short Life and Fast Times of Darby Crash and the Germs
Don Bolles, Brendan Mullen and Adam Parfrey

Lexicon Devil is more than a punk rock biography, it's a remarkable view of private lives in a surreal period of L.A. history, when est and Scientology cultists instructed a West Los Angeles public high school, and when underage prostitutes, drug dealers, chickenhawks, skateboarders, gay sadomasochists, and television stars tried to find their identities while hustling one another in apocalyptic scenarios. Darby Crash is to now what the Velvet Underground and the Stooges were to earlier rock generations; a legendary, but little understood icon, a brilliant and strangely charismatic Sun God, sacrificed on the altar of Rock and Roll.

6 x 9 · 294 pages · extensively illustrated · softcover · 0-922915-70-9 · $16.95

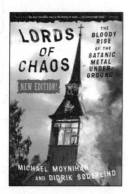

Lords of Chaos
The Bloody Rise of the Satanic Metal Underground
Michael Moynihan and Didrik Søderlind
Newly updated and expanded edition

"An unusual combination of true crime journalism, rock and roll reporting and underground obsessiveness, *Lords of Chaos* turns into one of the more fascinating reads in a long time . . ." — David Thomas, *Denver Post*.
"Gripping stuff, a book about scary rock that is really scary."
— Mike Tribby, *Booklist*

Lords of Chaos won the Firecracker Award for Best Music Book of 1998.

6 x 9 · 404 pages · illustrated · 0-922915-94-6 · $18.95

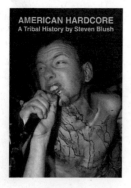

American Hardcore: A Tribal History
Steven Blush

This is the first history of "Hardcore," a genre of music begun as a response by alienated suburbanites to the angst and art of punk and new wave. Angrier, less pretentious and more stripped-down than its artsy, drug-addled predecessor, this harder-faster form of music was not very pretty—an angry and violent outlet to unfocused rage. Containing amazing oral histories interspersed with informed commentary and history, *American Hardcore* explains the gestation, whys and rationales of a scene that began in 1980 and fell apart in 1986. Steven Blush provides a complete national perspective on the genre, explaining all the regional scenes, complete with photos and discographies.

7 x 10 · 333 pages · extensively illustrated · 0-922915-71-7 · $19.95